CAN DO
(said Sue)

A rich life helping the poor

CAN DO
(said Sue)

A rich life helping the poor

Autobiography
By
Sue Sadow

Beaumont Books Inc.
Denver, Colorado

Library of Congress Cataloging-in-Publication Data

Sadow, Sue
    CAN DO (said Sue)
    ISBN 0-9616108-5-9

    1. Autobiography I. Title

90-83463
CIP

Cover design by Peter Masters

First Edition / First Printing

DEDICATION:
I dedicate this autobiography in honor of my parents,
Celia Hirshberg Sadow and Max Sadow.

ACKNOWLEDGMENTS:

I wish to thank the following people for helping me in the production of this book:

Peter Masters for his insights and professional expertise in helping me recall my work in service of the United States government; Luise Addiss, my dear and devoted friend and lifetime colleague, for her understanding, professional support, and encouragement to complete this autobiography; Gertrude Lotwin Rosenfield, loyal colleague, for her friendship; Janet Koch, who served as editor; Cathlene Gant, typist extraordinary; Margaret Malsam, publisher and friend; and Margaret Butler, who proofread the work and listened to me.

TABLE OF CONTENTS

Foreword by Dr. Carolyn Swift
Introduction by Peter Masters

PART I — Early Life in Plymouth, Massachusetts

Part II — School Days

Part III — Career Life

Part IV — Crusading in Later Life

Part V - Scrapbook of Memories   227
(Pictures, letters, and documents)

FOREWORD

> Shall the home be our world . . . or the world our home?
> *Charlotte Perkins Gilman*

Sue Sadow's story can be read on at least three levels: The first is a straightforward account of the critical events and periods in a most distinguished and productive life. Taken at this level, the story is engrossing. The daughter of immigrants rises to the top of the helping professions and, through her competence and commitment, directs the development of national and international programs to empower poor people and promote children's development in countries around the world. In her leadership positions at the United Nations Relief and Rehabilitation Administration, Project Head Start, and the Peace Corps, Sue Sadow has shaped policy and field practice in dealing with populations in need.

On the second level Sue's life is a stereotype-breaking model of what can be accomplished if one's capacity to act—one's "agency," as it is now called—is strong enough to create new patterns of action. Sue is a change agent extraordinaire. On this level her story is a running account of changes advanced ahead of her time, brought about by her commitment to empowering the poor. From the experimental kitchen she set up during the depression years in New York City, to the food delivery and health maintenance programs she organized for World War II refugee camps in Italy and North Africa, to the nutrition program she created and implemented for Project Head Start, Sue Sadow has led her profession in developing innovative, effective strategies for helping impoverished people deal with their basic needs.

Successful change agents defy analysis. Each blazes an idiosyncratic trail through the conventions and traditions of their time. While Sue's life reflects this complexity, it is her passionate valuing of others coupled with professional competence that is critical to her success. She is sensitive to the needs of others for dignity and respect, as well as for food, clothes, and shelter. Her empathy accounts for the almost immediate bonding that takes place between her and those with whom she works.

During the depression years in New York City, as Director of Home Economics and Nutrition for the Department of Welfare,

Sue was responsible for providing food and clothing to millions of destitute families. Sensitive to the cruel labelling that can stigmatize children, she insisted on varying the styles and materials for government-issue clothing to ensure that children could not be identified as poor from their appearance. In the World War II refugee camps in North Africa and Italy she designed a special diet to promote children's development. Initally she was puzzled by parental objections. She learned that they didn't want even brief family separations, since many of them were survivors of Nazi concentration camps and feared that any separation from children would turn out to be permanent. Sue arranged for parents to be with their children in the camp dining rooms to ensure family security. Her shock, as a child, at the unthinking cruelty of her peers toward foreigners was an early realization of the destructive effects of prejudice. Her work reflects her life-long attempts to respond to need where she finds it—whether in Appalachia, Africa, or the slums of New York City.

On the third level Sue's story can be read as a tale of women's freedom to move beyond the responsibilities of home and hearth, to define the parameters of the world and work to change it. On this level Sue Sadow is a woman for the twenty-first century. Across Sue's 95-year odyssey her personal goals have been inextricably bound with the goal of improving life opportunities for others. Although women have always been committed to others, to relationships and connection, this commitment has customarily been fulfilled within the circle of family and friends. Through her professional life Sue extends this commitment to those whose lives have been affected by poverty, racism, and other misfortunes. Sue Sadow embodies the power of connection at all levels—individual, family, neighborhood, community, nation, and world.

One of Sue Sadow's most treasured projects has been the organization of women Peace Corps volunteers to work actively to bring about world peace. In passing this dream forward to younger generations, she realizes her status as torch bearer. On this level, the promotion of empowerment and peace that comes from women's increasing involvement in the world of public affairs is demonstrated in Sue's life. As she approaches her own centenary, it is fitting that she publish her life story in the twilight of this century, for the evolution of women over the last hundred years and the development of Sue's life have run parallel courses.

Sue's love affair with life is a constant theme that runs through all the levels of the book. She jumps into adventure and rejoices in overcoming adversity. Her rebellions against outmoded traditions and bureaucratic procedures—refusing to be chaperoned in Europe in the "roaring twenties," standing up to Mayor LaGuardia, defying the military bureaucracy in North Africa, confronting ageism in the Peace Corps—all reflect her extraordinary courage and her strong sense of self. From her zest in childhood friendships through her fairy-tale romance with an "Egyptian prince" through the dramas connected with her professional achievements, she passionately describes her interactions with the world and its affairs.

Sue's most powerful resource is the "agency" she commands, both in herself and others, to trigger change. This skill has guided her through this century's multiple mine fields of war, poverty, race, gender, and class. Repeated in her personal as well as professional life, interwoven with the major events of this century, this capacity to bring about positive change is the gestalt that has shaped Sue's life and continues to dictate her priorities in this, the ninth decade in both her life and this century.

The enormous gift Sue Sadow gives to each reader is not the work she is accomplishing in her blessedly long life—although this work is certainly a gift to those whose lives she's touched. It's not the experiences she shares here, not even the monumental energy, compassion, and resolve with which she lives her life. Her gift to each of us is the continuous and joyous pursuit of vision that occupies her every waking moment, a pursuit that sings of life's joys and of its inevitable losses. Sue Sadow's song makes life's rainbow, whatever shape it takes for each of us, an accessible vision for all who come to know her.

Can do, said Sue.

And you can, too.

It is my honor and pleasure to invite you to come to know Sue Sadow.

Carolyn Swift
Director (1984-89)
The Stone Center for Developmental Services and Studies
Wellesley College, Wellesley, Massachusetts

INTRODUCTION

"Here she comes again," my assistants would groan, "with crash-bang deadlines no doubt, wanting us to jump through flaming hoops!"

This was in the poverty program of the '60s. We had met Sue Sadow only recently, but she had immediately become the most demanding client of my design and publications department. She differed from all the rest of our customers—from Job Corps, VISTA, Community Action, and the rest of the Office of Economic Opportunity's programs—in that she wanted more work, quantitatively and qualitatively. But, more important, we soon realized that, when Sue arrived on the scene, there always was a product involved.

Others were occasionally indecisive, or they came to our pleasant studio just for rest and recreation—for these were turbulent times, times of frantic, stressful activity in the many difficult battles in the War on Poverty. So people liked to drop by to mull over some hypothetical projects, or just to chat.

Not so Sue—she knew she wanted a Head Start nutrition publication; she knew what it was that she wanted to communicate and to whom; she knew how many she needed; and she knew she wanted them tomorrow, or at any rate in record time.

One thing was certain: here was a dedicated, serious woman who cared about poor people—a totally unreasonable woman but a grimly determined one.

A decision had to be made about how to deal with her, and I made it: "Until and unless our leader (Sargent Shriver) tells us that we must not cater to this lady, we shall do our utmost to fulfill her impossible requests with our best work."

It was the beginning of a beautiful friendship that has lasted for nearly thirty years.

She was one of the older poverty warriors, but probably the most vigorous. When she retired, her activities did not diminish.

She continued to travel, to paint, to write, and to participate in many altruistic projects.

There are some important lessons to be learned from Sue Sadow's mode of operation. Apart from her unwavering decisiveness, she has a secret weapon: A great many of us, as we get older, handicap ourselves by being too proud to accept—let alone to ask for—help in reaching our goals. Sue fervently believes this to be foolishness. "Come here, young man!" she may be heard to call. "Hold that umbrella over me and help me walk up the steps to this Japanese temple!"

I am proud to have had the privilege of being able to help this extraordinary woman, once in a while with a step or two, to reach her always worthwhile targets.

Peter Masters,
Former Art Director of the U.S.
Office of Economic Opportunity

PART I

EARLY
LIFE
IN
PLYMOUTH,
MASSACHUSETTS

Chapter 1
CHANGING OF SEASONS

The changing of the seasons was what I loved best. In the spring, all the trees and bushes burst into leaf. Soon the hedges with their stiff green leaves would be trimmed by the gardeners into smooth, box-like shapes, and later little red berries would appear. As I walked by gardens of nearby homes, I saw crocuses blooming, acknowledging the coming of spring. I constantly visited my favorite rose bush in our backyard, waiting for the buds to produce beautiful pink roses that exuded such a delicate perfume.

Everything was coming to life. Dandelions and buttercups grew in wildest profusion on the lawn of the local Poor House, where old people sat out on wooden benches. I looked at them from afar, a little scared to come very close as they were not pretty to look at. Violets grew in profusion on the grounds edging the Poor House Pond. I managed to pick as large a bunch of dandelions, buttercups, and violets as my small hands could hold. I squeezed the flowers into a tumbler of water to surprise my mother when she got home from the store in time to make supper.

Mama, who must have been terribly tired from standing on her feet all afternoon waiting on customers, admired my bouquet with enthusiasm and praised me for my thoughtfulness. She put the glass in the center of the large kitchen table for everyone to enjoy during supper. After six o'clock, Papa came home and all of us sat around that big table, including the baby in a highchair, while Mama dished out the evening meal.

My brother Abraham (who changed his name to Alvin when he went off to college to avoid being called names that used to anger and hurt him) was just five years my junior. He used to watch over his little pet white mice, for which he built a cage with a runway so they could get exercise. He had placed the cage under my favorite rose bush, where he thought it was safe. One day, after feeding the mice, he forgot to close the door. Since they were unguarded, our cat had a good feast. I was sent out to investigate when he did not answer our mother's call. I found him crying his heart out. He was not easily consoled, and he did not want any supper that night.

As the grass on the front lawn and in the back yard of our 150-year-old house grew longer and thicker, Papa mowed it with our lawn mower, which he bought at Bradbury's Hardware Store. We kids used to follow him and rake up the cut grass to help him. How sweet it smelled!

I loved summer, too, because it meant vacation from school and lots of time to play and sew. I made tiny dolls' clothes from scraps of material left from things Mama made for the store as well as from remnants of cloth she was always buying to make our clothes. Elizabeth Morton, my playmate who lived next door, and I used to wander through Moore's Department Store just to look at the pretty things displayed on the counters.

We had to go down a flight of squeaky stairs to reach the toy department in the basement. My heart thumped as we stopped to look at the various displays of toys. I paused, overwhelmed with wonder at the variety of things that children could have. We stopped at the counter where small dolls were piled up. I had no money, of course; allowances were unknown to immigrant parents.

I wanted a small dolly so much and dreamed of making clothes for her. I cried and cried until Mama had time to visit Moore's Department Store. Finally her excuse for taking time off from our store was because she needed to purchase a veil for herself anyhow. She always wanted me to be present whenever she made a purchase, as she was never able to pronounce the letter "V" since it was not in her native tongue.

Her English at that time was hardly understandable. She and my father spoke Yiddish together at home, and I came to realize that it was easier for them after struggling with English in the store all day. There were no classes or schools they could attend.

I got my doll at last. She had real hair, eyes that opened and closed, and arms and legs that moved so she could sit or stand. She was about three inches tall, and she cost ten cents. My friend Elizabeth, whom we all called Tibbie, already had hers. What joy we had creating clothes for our dolls! We were absorbed for hours over tiny bits of rags and the time-consuming challenge of threading needles!

Then came autumn. "Put on your dresses of red and gold, for summer is gone and the days are cold" we sang at the tops of our lungs under the guidance of the singing teacher who came to each class once a week. Our teacher would take our class for a walk to the woods right after school to pick up the most beautiful leaves, which we used in our watercolor painting class when the painting teacher came. We could also press the leaves and paste them on oblongs of plain white paper in any designs we cared to pursue.

Today it would be known as creativity. We were allowed to take them home to adorn the walls of our modest houses. To go for a walk to collect these leaves in Morton's Park, we had to bring a note giving us permission and signed by our mama or papa. What painful embarrassments this caused for many parents! Oh! the agonies of inferiority and humiliation endured by intelligent minds unable to communicate in the language of this strange land, now their permanent homeland!

Tibbie's mama visited my mama often as they were nearly the same age. When any notes to school had to be sent, she always wrote them for Mrs. Sadow to sign her name. When the quinces were ripe, Mrs. Morton showed my mama how to make jelly because the children loved it on bread when they came home from school.

As I grew older, my papa and mama, who could not write English, used to dictate letters to me to send off. They signed their names when it was a business letter. It took many years before they improved their broken English. They copied what the customers in the store spoke, many of whom were trying to learn English themselves. The result was often uniquely personal, colorful expressions, which could not be found in literature anywhere. These expressions told in a few words what was needed to explain their thoughts. I myself never learned to be so concise.

Both of my parents arrived in Boston on ships that left from Hamburg, Germany, or Liverpool, England. There are no records of any sort, so I am dependent upon memory of the stories they related to me during the course of a lifetime. They talked about their background when they read Yiddish newspapers that used to arrive in Plymouth from Boston, describing what was happening among the Jewish population in other countries. They told about the terrible pogroms, when Jews were slaughtered by drunken

Russian Cossacks who came to the towns to kill, rape, burn, and steal. The year of my father's and mother's arrival in Boston was probably about 1870. My mother was 15 years old, and my father was about 16. They did not know one another. They were born in different countries. My father was born in Doag, Russia. My mother was born in Kovno, Lithuania.

Ships leaving Hamburg and Liverpool carried thousands of immigrants to America to settle new places in the huge former English colony and to supply greatly needed manpower for the fast- developing industries. Generally these immigrants traveled steerage class under very uncomfortable, crowded, and unsanitary conditions. The fares for steerage class were approximately $25.00 per passenger and were usually paid in advance by relatives who had worked and saved every penny with one thought in mind: to bring over their dear ones, reunite families, and re-establish homes. It is almost impossible to imagine those meetings as the ships docked and relatives who had waited for hours met and welcomed their dear ones. Sometimes the separations had been so long that they did not recognize one another.

My mother, a healthy, robust, well-developed teenager of 15, was in charge of her sister, Rosie, age 12, who was frail, delicate, and small of stature. Their three brothers had arrived some years before when the sisters were little children.

The three brothers worked and saved every penny and made the usual sacrifices to save up the money needed for the steerage passage of their sisters in Kovno, Lithuania. Within a few years, they all saved up enough money to send for all the family members until the entire family was reunited in Boston before the end of the nineteenth century.

My mama's mother died when they were living in Kovno, when Rosie was one year old. That would have been my grandmother. My grandfather remarried as soon as he could find another wife to manage his household. It was the custom of the times. The new mother was generally depicted as a cruel stepmother favoring her own children. This was not the case when my grandfather remarried. His wife was young and had only one little daughter. Her young husband had died, and she was only too glad to take on the extra burdens of serving my grandfather and his children. It was a happy household for all the family.

Chapter 2

MAN'S INHUMANITY TO MAN

During my early childhood years, we lived in a big 150-year-old house at 29 Summer Street, known as Captain Doten's House after its original owner. Papa took great pride in this house, as it was the first property he owned. Captain Doten's ancestors came to Plymouth on the Mayflower. Their names were embossed in gold on the Pilgrim National Monument, which stood on a hill overlooking the town.

The rooms were large and airy, with high ceilings. The parlor, which faced the street, had tall windows from ceiling to wainscotting. They were covered with wooden shutters to keep out the cold in winter and the hot sunshine in the summer. Mama washed the long lace curtains and dried them in the sunshine on a stretcher so they looked like new. The pure woolen carpet that Papa had bought for their first house in Plymouth fitted perfectly from wall to wall. The parlor had furniture Papa had bought in Boston for his bride. The upholstered pieces were of green, gold, and red silk damask. In the center of the room a frosted colored glass lamp hung above the mahogany table, which held our family album. Our parlor looked every bit as lovely as pictures I saw of homes in the magazines at the public library.

Since the neighbors, the Mortons, had a piano and their three girls took lessons from Miss Bowditch, my parents decided to buy one for me. When my mahogany upright arrived, it was exactly like theirs.

Papa took great pride in showing our house to visitors, especially our Boston relatives who came on the train on Sundays. He took everyone down the steep wooden stairs leading to the dark, musty-smelling cellar to point out the hand-hewn beams supporting the house. We used to hear him say with admiration, over and over, "It is as solid as a rock. They knew how to build in those days!"

The only light came from small windows that could be opened only from the inside. The foundation of huge blocks of granite came from Plymouth and left spaces for the windows. Still, it was dark and musty; the floor was of hardened dirt and very uneven. Stored down there were barrels of sauerkraut made by Mama along with bright red cranberries from the nearby bogs and barrels of potatoes for our large family.

There was always a big bowl of apples on the kitchen table, which stood in the center of our big kitchen. My brothers usually were sent down to the cellar for supplies. Once I showed them how brave I was by leading the way with a lamp taken from one of the downstairs bedrooms. These kerosene lamps had to be filled and their glass chimneys polished every day. This was Cousin Ida's job. She came to live with us when she was little and stayed until she got married.

When the gas line was extended to Summer Street, my father was the first to modernize our house by installing gas. They used gas mantles, which were made of fragile material. When kids ran about very suddenly, the mantles in the kitchen would shatter into bits. Then the gas had to be turned off, oil lamps substituted, and new mantles installed the next day.

Off the kitchen was a large bathroom with a flush toilet and chiffonier. Each of us had a drawer in that dresser, where Mama put our clean clothes. It stood against the wall with a mirror on the top. If I dragged one of the kitchen chairs into the bathroom and stood on it, I could see myself in the mirror. We were not allowed to do this and were spanked if we were caught.

The highly polished black coal stove heated the bright copper boiler, which furnished us with hot water most of the time, especially on bath night. The adults usually bathed on Friday afternoon to be ready for the Sabbath. We had hot and cold running water for the bath and sink when the kitchen stove was baking the Sabbath bread and cooking the chicken soup. In winter, we used to warm our fleece-lined undergarments in front of the stove before dressing for school.

Leading off the kitchen was the buttery or pantry. This held the ice chest, with a huge pan underneath for collecting the water as the ice melted. There were several cupboards for the kosher dishes and pots and pans, and drawers for the silver. There was a counter that ran the length of the buttery. On this were fastened a number of *pushkes*. These were tin boxes with slots for coins; each repre- sented a charity. We used to put our contribution in each one. If there was not enough, Mama used to put coins from her handbag into them. The "collectors" came several times a year. They were religious Jewish men, dressed in long black coats and round black hats trimmed with fur. If they came to collect in summer when it was hot, they wore black straw hats and long black coats of shiny material. They drank tea in glasses that Mama offered them.

In the buttery there was always a jug of molasses and a big tin bread box with dark rye bread, which came by train from Boston with the kosher food order Mama wrote in Yiddish. After school our friends used come over to snack on rye bread covered with molasses. Mama always cut slices of the bread before she went to the store because we were all forbidden to use the sharp bread knife.

The window always had a screen in it for fresh air. Once our cat pushed the screen onto the counter. What a mess! That was the only time I ever saw Mama get mad!

Behind the house we had a big yard on three levels. On the top level were plum and peach trees. The big area was our play area, which had apple and pear trees. I was called a tomboy because I climbed the trees fearlessly and shook down the ripened fruit. Mama's rose and peony bushes lined the fences on both sides of the yard.

The front lawn faced the street. We were all very happy with our big house, and we all had playmates nearby.

Papa was a peddler three days a week, selling merchandise to nearby towns or villages where there were no clothing stores. He kept his horse and wagon in a stable and drove it early to his new store way up on Court Street. Mama worked in the store when Papa was away peddling, and Cousin Ida took care of the children. Our cousin, Sam Levine, my mother's nephew, who was an orphan, came to live with us and learned to be a salesman in the new store.

Papa had a big sign made in Boston for his store, "The Blue Store Clothing Company," which carried men's and boys' clothing. It was painted cobalt blue. By pressing a button inside the entrance it lit up and went out automatically. It was something new in the town, and people out for an evening walk used to watch the sign come on and go off. The store was open several evenings a week, and the sign attracted customers.

Papa and Mama worked very hard to support their children.

Prayers had been answered! My father, Max Sadow, was doing well as a merchant. All five of us were born within eight years. Phil was the oldest (born January 21, 1894). I was the next child (born July 28, 1896). After Mama recovered from a serious bout with phlebitis, another girl, Helen, arrived. She was about one year old and just learning to walk when we had to move out of our lovely Summer Street home.

One Friday morning Papa came running home from the new store on Court Street. He was breathless and as pale as a ghost when he burst into the kitchen. He flung himself into a chair at the table and started sobbing. Hysterically he pounded on the table with both fists. At first Mama could not get him to speak. All he would mumble was, "We are ruined. We are ruined."

Mama shook him and cried out in a loud voice, "Is it the children? Are they hurt?" He only shook his head. "Then tell me what is the trouble" she demanded.

"We are ruined" he said, still sobbing, "We have to move the store out of the building at once. Cohen came into the store when I opened up and told me I had to move out."

"Why? Is it the rent?" she asked.

"No. Cohen said Sam Medved wants the store building, and, after talking it over, I told him he could have it."

My father continued, "At first I thought he was joking. Then I found out he was serious. I thought I was on good terms with them. I pleaded with him not to ruin us, but he would not budge. I explained we had only been in the store a few months, and I did not know where I could put all my stock as there was not an empty building in town. I told him I had just bought a house, but he just looked at me, not saying a word." Finally he said, "You have to be out of the building in two weeks so Medved can move in."

Mama was flabbergasted and started to cry. "Why do they want to ruin us? They know how hard we work."

Then Cousin Ida started crying, and the baby began screaming. Papa continued to moan, "We are ruined . . . ruined."

When Mama stopped crying, she dried her eyes on the corner of her apron. It was Friday, time for Shabbos. The ritual white bread for the kiddush for the Sabbath services was baking in the oven. She said, "Max, go back to the store. We will pray for help when it is Shabbos. We will find a way with God's help."

Papa stopped crying. He washed himself with the hot water from the copper boiler. Papa walked slowly and calmly out the door and into Cohen's store. Facing Cohen he said in a firm voice, "You and Medved are out to ruin me. You know your purpose. My wife and I do not know why. My wife told me to go back to the store and close the store early. It is Shabbos. We will pray, and God will help us." Then he turned his back and walked out.

That is the story. There was not another empty building in town. But when Medved moved into our store, his old building was empty. Mary Jack owned that building. She came from Italy and worked day and night, saving every penny. Papa appealed to her. Medved lived in the tenement above the store. The main entrance to the tenement was in the alley. The other entrance was a door between the two stores, which led up to the parlor of the tenement and a room off the second flight of stairs.

Papa tried to bargain with her to rent only the store. She was adamant, "You must rent the whole space, Medved is moving out, and he had it all for five years on a lease." Papa knew he was licked. Mama and he prayed, and he signed a five-year lease.

My piano could not fit between the narrow windows of the upstairs tenement, so Papa found an old, out-of-tune square piano with two notes missing. Fortunately a Jewish baker moved to Plymouth and rented our house. He promised to take good care of our parlor and my piano.

I wept and wept after we moved to the Court Street tenement, where I had no playmates. At school, we were not allowed to speak to the Cohen and the Medved children. We truly believed these families were our enemies. I was seven years old and in the third grade when I had my first encounter with injustice . . . man's inhumanity to man.

Sue Sadow at five years of age with cousin Stella Hirshberg. Her dress, made by her mother, is of blue silk with white polka dots. Gold lockets worn by both girls were sent by an uncle.

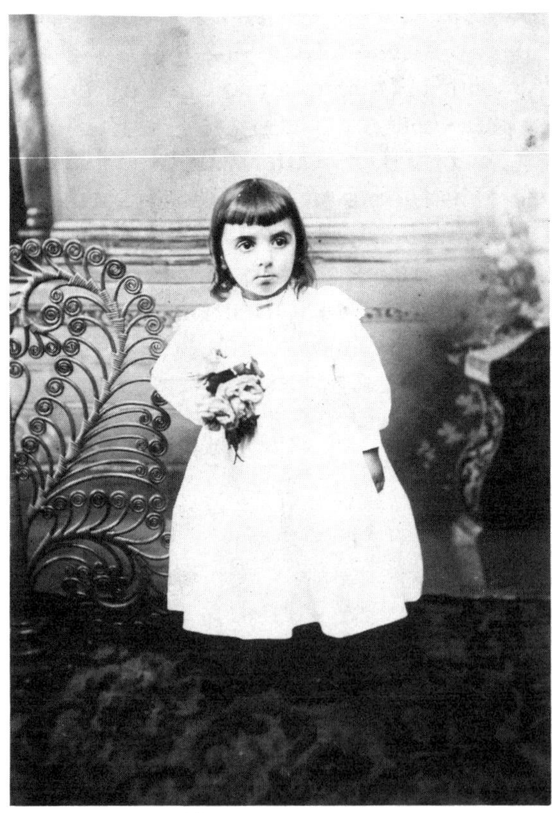

Sue Sadow
at four
years
of age.

Chapter 3
MOVING TO MARY JACK'S BUILDING

Mary Jack was known for her fruit and vegetable stand in front of the building she owned, a building that would be our home for five years. She was a small, shrewd, energetic lady who spoke broken English with an Italian accent. She always dressed the same way: a dark cotton dress with numerous petticoats and a dark blue denim apron with several pockets. These pockets, which served as an informal cash register, were filled with pennies, nickels, dimes, and quarters. Everyone in town knew about her stand, especially children wanting a penny's worth of candy and the "summer people," who arrived in a pony cart and were known as the "swells" of Plymouth.

Mary had arrived in Boston on a ship from Italy. She was one of those unemployed, poverty-stricken European youngsters who had been enticed by a steamship agent to purchase a steerage class ticket ($25) to come to the land where fortunes could be made.

Mary was young, strong, and frugal and had endured hardship all her life. Her brothers, Gino and Amadeo, begged to come along with her to America, but she preferred to go it alone and test the promises of the agents. For several years, she struggled as a poorly paid servant girl with no education to earn enough money for the ticket.

When she arrived in Boston Harbor, she spoke only Neapolitan Italian and soon found her way to the slums of Boston that were inhabited by Italians. Soon she was employed as a servant by an aristocratic Boston family on Beacon Hill, who taught her the ways of American life. Soon she found herself going on little excursions. One of these trips was to Plymouth, Massachusetts. Here she became acquainted with the newly arrived Italian people employed in the mills. She decided to move to Plymouth and go into business selling fruit and vegetables.

She opened her store at 7 a.m., and although her brothers later came to Plymouth, they didn't help her very often. Every morning she rolled out the heavy barrels and crates of vegetables and fine fruits in front of the opened windows, arranging them on stands.

All her customers depended upon Mary Jack to wait on them. She never sat down. Gino only helped her when there were crowds at the stand waiting to be served. She was small and moved about quickly and cheerfully. Only once did I hear her scolding Gino in a threatening manner in Italian. The younger brother went to school and only helped on Saturdays and Sundays.

Mary Jack owned the building at 40 Court Street. One half of it consisted of a store with a flat upstairs, which assured her of income from two sources in addition to her own store in the other half. Some years before, Mr. Boyd of the Plymouth National Bank, who admired her for her ambition, had encouraged her to buy the building as soon as she had sufficient funds.

When Papa approached her about renting the building after learning he had to move out of his building, she was angry and surprised to learn that her present tenant was leaving. She went into the store and lashed him with her Italian temper. (She was from Naples, where people were reputed to have hot tempers.) She felt she had worked hard for years and that now she commanded respect as a landlord. In a shrill voice in front of a store full of customers, she ordered her tenant to vacate the store and the flat within 24 hours.

Only then was she willing to talk with Papa about renting the building. When she heard how Cohen and Medved had tried to ruin him, she was outraged, but she insisted that the flat had to go with the store. She was shrewd. She demanded a five-year lease! She asked Mr. Boyd to draw up the lease in her favor. Papa talked to Mr. Boyd, and he tried to help him, but she would not change her demand for a five-year lease.

She knew Papa was trapped. After supper, Papa had to tell us that we would be moving to Mary Jack's flat. We all cried, thinking of the loss of our playmates and the change of schools and teachers.

"It is only for five years, and then we will come back," consoled Mama.

"How about my piano?" I cried. I knew my complaints, added to the others, tried Papa's patience.

"We are fortunate," Papa said calmly. "The Miller family has rented our house. They just moved to Plymouth from Boston.

They are in business baking Jewish bread. Mrs. Miller said she would take good care of your piano. I just heard about what is called a *square piano,* and you can take piano lessons and practice on one of those."

Thus we were forced to leave our beautiful home at 29 Summer Street (known as Captain Doten's place) and move to Mary Jack's flat above Papa's store for five years.

Sue Sadow's parents, Celia (Hirshberg) and Max Sadow

Chapter 4

OUR BELOVED LIZZIE

The approach to our flat in Mary Jack's building was a long, narrow alley, separated by a fence from our neighbor's alley. Papa's famous electric store sign, which said "The Blue Store Clothing Company," now lay lifeless in a corner. All its wires were hanging down, and there was no place to hang it.

The big white house next door to Mary Jack's building was occupied by the Dinsmores, a young couple with a small girl the same age as my little sister Helen. Mr. Dinsmore was a minister, and the house belonged to their church. Mrs. Dinsmore came to call on Mama and offered to help her get settled and to take care of our little sister, saying the children could play together every day except Sunday.

The door at the top of our long flight of stairs opened on to a covered entry, which housed our ice chest. The walls were covered with hooks to hang coats and hats, and there was plenty of room for our rubbers and rubber boots in winter. The other door opened onto the yard where we children played and where our Italian wash woman hung fresh-washed clothes every Monday morning. The only entrance to the kitchen was the door off the entry.

The kitchen was rather large and served as a family room and the center of our activities. A door led into the ladies' department of the store, and, when there was a customer, our bookkeeper, Lizzie, opened the door to warn us to be quiet. The upstairs rooms were reached by the stairs off the kitchen, and the sink room opened right off the kitchen.

Cheerful patterned linoleum was the floor covering. This was practical in case anything spilled. The kitchen was a light cheerful room with curtains that Mama had made. The square table of oak could be pulled out to seat the whole family. Usually we did not all sit down together. An oil cloth covering was used for the table except on the Sabbath, when my mother's white linen tablecloth was used.

On Sundays, our beloved Lizzie, who was Papa's bookkeeper,

often came to give Mama and baby Nell a ride in our two-seated carriage. Lizzie was from Canada. She had come to Plymouth through Mrs. Howland, one of our customers, who lived on a street leading down to the ocean near Mary Jack's building. Mrs. Howland, a lady whose ancestors came over on the Mayflower, had read one of the ads in our local newspaper, *The Old Colony Memorial*, about the availability of young Canadian girls who wanted employment as servants in the States. (The newspaper was owned and published by the Bittinger family, our former neighbors when we lived in Captain Doten's house on Summer Street.)

Mrs. Howland sent for one of them, and a young girl named Lizzie arrived. Mrs. Howland taught her how she ran her household, and she was pleased with Lizzie. She invited her to sit down to meals with the family so she would feel at home instead of like a stranger. She wanted Lizzie to have a good education so she could earn her living, and she enrolled her in the Commercial School, which had only recently been established in a building on Court Street.

Lizzie learned bookkeeping and typewriting. She came from "down East" in Canada from a large family of brothers and sisters. Her father was usually unemployed, and they had a hard time supporting the family. Lizzie sent almost all her wages home every week and kept little for herself. At first she was very lonesome because she was far from home and family for the first time, but she was very grateful to Mrs. Howland for sending her to the Commercial School.

When Papa advertised in the *The Old Colony Memorial* for a bookkeeper, Lizzie applied for the position. The portable office, brought over from the other store, was now put in the ladies' department next to our kitchen. All sales from the men's and boys' department downstairs were accompanied by a slip that Lizzie used in her bookkeeping. Change was always made from the nearby cash drawer. When Lizzie was not there, either Papa or Cousin Sam, who worked in the store and lived with us, would run upstairs and make change from the cash drawer.

All of us kids loved Lizzie. She was like a big sister. When we were absent from school, she wrote the notes to our teachers for our parents to sign. She even ran to the railroad station to pick up the kosher food order that came from my grandfather in Boston twice a week.

Mama invited Lizzie to eat with us on rainy or snowy days, and she always washed the dishes. She taught us table manners, which she had learned herself at the Howland house. She was so loved by all of us that she knew how to stop our fighting, especially when there were customers in the store. She was very tall and carried herself with head held high and shoulders back. When I was growing very fast and getting round shouldered because I simply would not stand up straight, she demonstrated how I would look unless I walked with my head held high and my shoulders back. I assumed this straight posture for the rest of my life and was often called a "snob" as a result.

Lizzie wore old-fashioned pince-nez glasses, and her lovely dark hair was combed in pompadour style because she felt servants should look older. Her skirts were ankle length for the same reason, and she wore low-heeled Canadian shoes that looked as if they would never wear out. Mama taught her to dress like a stylish young woman and not like a "Down Eastern Servant Girl." With the help of Mrs. Howland and my mother, Lizzie soon dressed like an American student attending the Commercial School.

Later Lizzie, who had such an influence over our lives all during those five years of exile at Mary Jack's, moved back to Canada to be with her family when we returned to our big house at 29 Summer Street. But we never forgot our beloved Lizzie.

Chapter 5
THE LARKIN DOLL

Every Sunday when we lived in Mary Jack's building, we had the newspaper delivered to our door. It had many sections, and we each were allowed the one of our choice. Mine was the brown Rotogravure section, because it was full of pictures and I could only read the few words we had learned at school.

One Sunday there was a picture of a big French doll with arms outstretched in the middle of the front page. She looked as if she wanted me to take her and hold her. Her outstretched arms seemed to beckon me. She had big blue eyes with eyelashes and looked as if she had real brown hair. She was wearing only a one-piece cotton garment, white leather shoes, and white socks. I could not take my eyes off this picture even though I could not read what it said.

Since it was Sunday, our beloved Lizzie was also in the kitchen, all dressed up in her Sunday best, waiting for Mama to finish dressing herself and the baby and for Papa to return from the stable with Nellie, our spirited young horse with beautiful brown and white markings. Lizzie came every Sunday afternoon to take Mama for a ride. She loved to drive Nellie. Papa would hitch Nellie to the "democrat," our two-seated buggy with rubber tires, for the Sunday ride.

Papa had two more vehicles besides the democrat in the stable. One was his covered wagon, which he piled high with men's and boys' clothing to peddle during the week in small nearby villages. The other was the two-seated carriage with a cover with a "fringe on top." He used to take all the family for rides during the summer to Billington Sea, which was a park a few miles from our house when we lived in Captain Doten's house. Here we used to pick blueberries, which Mama would put up in jars so we could have blueberry pie at Thanksgiving.

He was always glad when Lizzie came to take Mama and the baby for a ride, saying it was good for Nellie to have the exercise. Nellie liked to trot at a brisk pace. At the sound of an electric car, her ears went up and she would take off, galloping so fast that people would think she was running away. Then Lizzie would "show off" and control Nellie. The baby, who was scared, would hold on to Mama and bury her face in her shoulder. Mama always said she felt young again after the Sunday ride!

While Lizzie was waiting for Papa to return with the horse and carriage, I grabbed my newspaper section and ran to Lizzie and begged her to explain the writing under the big doll in the center of the page. Lizzie took the chair beside me and said the doll was being given away as a prize. She explained that all you had to do to win this prize was to sell a box full of Larkin products, which were bottles of flavoring for cakes. The flavors were vanilla, lemon, and orange. You had to sell them for 25 cents each. When you sent them the money for the Larkin products, the company would send you the doll.

It was quite a large doll and had joints like a real little girl. The doll could sit, bend her elbows, close her eyes, and bend her knees. I looked at Lizzie and told her, "I must win this prize. I will give it to my baby sister. She only has a doll with a china head and a cloth body. I'm going to win the prize, and Mama can make clothes for the doll from leftover remnants."

I could hardly wait for Papa to come to the kitchen so Lizzie could explain to him how I would win the prize for my little sister. I was eight years old, and I assumed, of course, that Larkin products would be easy to sell.

Lizzie looked at me and smiled: I was so positive! I took the scissors from Mama's machine drawer and cut all around the doll—my prize.

I planned to sell Larkin flavoring after school every day. Mama thought it was a good idea. Lizzie and Mama smiled at each other. Now it was only Papa, who needed to send the money. Lizzie said she would figure up what a box of Larkin products would cost and tell Papa tomorrow. I could hardly wait to come home from school. I ran into the store, where Papa was waiting on a customer. I ran upstairs to ask Mama what Papa had decided.

Mama and Lizzie looked at each other. I knew that they had talked it over. Sensing that Papa had not agreed to send for Larkin products so I could win the prize, I cried, "It was not for me, but for the baby."

I took the picture of the doll that I had cut from the Sunday paper and held it up for Mama and Lizzie to see. I started to cry. "Now I **know** that Papa will not let me win the doll."

Mama said, "Wait until Papa explains it himself."

When there were no customers in the store and Cousin Sam was there to wait on any who came in, Papa came up to the kitchen and looked at his tearful little girl. "Why can't you let me win the prize?" I sobbed, holding out the picture I had cut out of the Sunday paper.

My father explained, "It will cost a lot to have Larkin products send you a big supply of Larkin bottles for 25 cents each. Do you know how long it will take to sell all the bottles so we can send them the money and they can send you the prize? How many weeks will it take you?"

"I have already told Jenny Dale about the doll, and she said she would help me after school."

"Do her parents know what she has promised you?" asked Papa. Her parents both worked at the Plymouth Cordage Company and were good, respectable customers. They lived in a wooden house next to the railroad depot. They had told their daughter that she must first go right home from school and do chores that they had left for her. Her most important chore was to pick up the loose coals dropped off the train and dump them into the box next to the kitchen stove until she had collected several pails full.

My father finally said, "All right. Lizzie has figured out what I'll have to pay now. You are sure you and Jenny will sell all the bottles?" he asked. He gave Lizzie instructions to order the products, and I was very happy.

Every afternoon when I came from school, I asked Mama if the box had arrived. One afternoon she smilingly pointed at the sink room off the kitchen.

"Your box is here," she said in her beautiful calm voice.

I dashed into the sink room, and there stood the box. I knew I did not know how to open it, and there was an envelope stuck onto it. I called Lizzie, who was making change from the cash drawer in the office next to the kitchen. Lizzie knew how to open the box, and she saved the envelope with the bill inside and put it back into the cash drawer so it would not get mixed up with other store bills.

We opened the box and carefully counted the bottles. There were three flavors: vanilla, lemon, and orange.

"Now," said Lizzie, "you are in business." You must keep track of how many you sell each day. They are 25 cents a bottle. Where do you want to put the quarters ?"

I looked around the sink room full of dishes on the shelves. "How about that cup on the top shelf so the quarters won't get mixed up with the store money?"

"A good idea," she said.

I met my classmate Jenny Dale the next morning at school and told her enthusiastically about the bottles of Larkin flavors. After school that day, we ran up the stairs to our kitchen, where Mama gave us each a cup of hot cocoa. We put four bottles in a bag and we were off.

We knocked on the door of the Hedge house, the yellow brick house on the corner.

Mrs. Hedge said, "Oh, you are Mr. Sadow's daughter."

"Yes," I said shyly, as I was very shy around strangers.

"You want me to buy a bottle of Larkin products?"

Jenny and I got the giggles. I replied, "I'm selling Larkin products so I can win the prize of a doll for my baby sister."

"That's a very nice thing to do. What flavors shall I buy?"

I got up my courage. "Mama thinks the vanilla is the best."

"How much are they?"

At this point, I had forgotten the price. Jenny spoke up. She was not shy like me. "They are 25 cents a bottle and come in three flavors."

She said "I'll take three bottles, one flavor each, please. I hope you win the prize since the doll is for your baby sister. Do you have change for a dollar?"

Jenny and I looked at each other. "I'll run over to the store and get the dollar changed," said Jenny.

Mrs. Hedge was amused by us and talked to me until Jenny returned. I explained that Jenny had chores to do after school but that she had promised to help me sell the Larkin products so I would win the doll for my baby sister.

Jenny returned with four quarters. Mrs. Hedge purchased the three bottles, and we gave her a quarter in change.

We both ran to our house and put the three quarters in the cup. Our first sale, and at the first house we tried!

The next day at recess, Jenny told me she could not help me any more. Her mother scolded her for not getting her chores done. At first, I was frightened because I didn't have another friend to help me. Then I had an idea: it would be easy. I would take my baby sister in her carriage and tie the bottles to the carriage.

I could hardly wait to get home from school. Mama was only glad that I would take my baby sister for a ride in her carriage. I was prepared to make sales. I carried change in a little pocketbook that Lizzie had loaned me.

We didn't make any sales at four houses. Finally one woman asked, "Haven't I seen you playing at the Dinsmores?"

"Yes," I said, adding that Mrs. Dinsmore had promised to buy all three flavors."

"Then I will also. Wait a minute until I get my pocketbook," she said, and she bought all three flavors.

This was my beginner's luck. No matter how I tried knocking on people's doors after that, I could not sell any bottles. I got discouraged, and I already knew I would not win the prize. Mama and Papa tried to encourage me, but I was not happy ringing door bells after school each day until supper time.

I had tried to win the prize and failed. I asked Lizzie what I should do. She told me my father was worried about me as the days were getting shorter and it was nearly dark when I was ringing door bells on streets farther away. My parents also stopped letting me wheel the baby on streets where we did not know anyone. But I still wanted to win the prize more than anything.

When it really got dark early, Papa told me I would have to stop until the days got lighter again. He told me I had not failed and not to get discouraged. He suggested that I ask Mrs. Dinsmore, our neighbor, to buy the three bottles that she had promised to purchase earlier.

When I asked her, Mrs. Dinsmore said, "I promised you I would buy three bottles and I'll not go back on my promise. I will buy them today, and what's more you're invited for supper. Ask your mama if it's all right." I was happy again.

One day when I got home from school, Mama was smiling. Papa came into the kitchen. Lizzie was there too, as mother had invited her to stay for lunch because the weather was bad.

Mama said, "There's a big package for you that the mailman delivered this afternoon while you were at school."

"A big package for me?" I shouted so loud that they must have heard me down the street. "Where is it? Where is it?"

"In the sink room," said Lizzie. "I'll open it for you."

I was jumping up and down with excitement. I had never received a package before. Everyone was standing around me. Lizzie was excited too. Her hands were trembling. Mama was smiling as if it were the happiest day in her life.

Lizzie pulled out the prize from the box. She held up a doll, just like the one in the Sunday paper!

Papa was so happy. I ran over to him and hugged and kissed him. Lizzie told me that Papa had instructed her to pay the remaining amount on the Larkin products so that I could get the prize.

My baby sister looked at the doll and screamed, wanting to hold her. I gave the doll to her and she started kissing it. "Mine," she said over and over.

Papa had done the right thing. "It was on account of Lizzie," he said.

For all the years we lived in Mary Jack's flat, Mama put the Larkin bottles between the china tea cups and saucers to decorate the sink room at holiday time. Mama made the Larkin doll many outfits from leftover remnants. Uncle Simon came to see us on the train one Sunday. He had a furniture store, and he brought along one of the samples from his store for his sister's youngest child. It was an English doll carriage, and it was just the right size for the doll. We wheeled the Larkin doll around in the English carriage for many years. There was just enough room for it in the entry outside of the kitchen.

For many years—even after we were all grown up and they had moved to Boston—Mama kept the doll in a big shoe box. One time after I had taken a job in New York and had come back to visit, Mama took the shoe box down and showed me what had happened to the Larkin doll. All the rubber bands that kept her body together were stretched out.

"Can't you get a doll factory in New York to have her restored?" she asked me. "As you know, that baby that you won the prize for is now married and has a small daughter. I was thinking if you had the doll restored, I would dress her the way I used to and you could take her the doll for a surprise when you visit them in Milwaukee."

I did this, and my sister was surprised. She kept the Larkin doll for many years after her daughter was grown. When my sister and her husband were living in Florida, she visited a doll museum one day. She decided to dress the doll in a beautiful handmade baby's outfit. She took it to an exhibit at the museum, and the doll won first prize. The expert at the museum said the doll was worth several hundred dollars even though one finger was missing.

Many years later my sister (who gave the doll to one of our cousins who had a baby girl) told me the story behind the missing finger. It happened when we were living in Mary Jack's building and my mother was doing the alterations for the women's department. Her sewing machine was placed at the window where she could watch the two youngest children playing in the yard. My sister and youngest brother (who was 14 months older) had a fight. The Larkin doll was in the English carriage. In a sudden fit of childish temper, he broke the doll's index finger to get even with my sister because he knew she valued the doll so much.

Despite her missing finger, the doll was loved and treasured for three generations.

Chapter 6
ANY RAGS, ANY BOTTLES?

Among the population of Jews were a few families, like my family, whose businesses were located in the center of Plymouth. They chose to have their homes as close to their businesses as possible for convenience's sake. The homes were scattered in a variety of neighborhoods among the Christian population. The neighbors, exposed to Orthodox Jews for the first time, were greatly interested in their customs and traditions and especially the strict observance of the Sabbath and the religious holidays. Friendships developed among these close neighbors as their children played together and attended the same schools. They shared their troubles and joys as good neighbors do.

There was another Jewish community of about 20 families in Plymouth that was a tight, self-contained group. Many were related to each other. They had all arrived in Boston after the great exodus from Eastern European countries during the last decades of the nineteenth century, when many Jews left their "shtetls" forever.

These poverty-stricken people had endured the most devastating religious persecution. Before coming to America, they had been prevented from engaging in other than the most menial occupations, and they had been barred from educational institutions.

In America, they were enjoying their new independence and freedom. Following the advice of Jewish agencies (which met them on arrival and took responsibility for them in the days of adjustment), they did not settle permanently in the already over- crowded slums of the city but rather explored the possibilities for settling in nearby towns. These families established their own small community on the outskirts of Plymouth, and generally were too timid to appear often in the center of the town. Their children attended schools provided in their area, which was known as "over South."

The men folk sought work to earn an honest living to provide for their large families. They had no skills and were ignorant of the ways and manners of their surroundings. They could only speak a few words of broken English to make themselves understood. Usually they appeared unkempt in their strange-looking clothes, which they brought with them as immigrants.

It was obvious that they could not meet even the simplest of job requirements. They turned to rag picking and became rag peddlers as it required only a few words in English. As rag peddlers, they could be independent. With the help of their wives and children, they could sort out items from the day's collection, which they could sell for cash.

Their only capital investments were scrawny old horses. These people's unattractive, unkempt appearance made them even more conspicuous as unwanted foreigners. To increase their income, they drove up and down the streets of the residential areas, bargaining for items no longer used. I remember the loud sing-song of our local peddler. From the high front seat above his team of horses, he would chant, "Any rags, any bones, any bottles today for the rag man?" This brought the housewife to the door, offering odd items she had assembled in anticipation of his arrival. The bargaining started and ended when they mutually agreed on a price, which ranged from a penny up.

The visits of the rag peddler aroused joking among the neighbors, who discussed their "profits." Often children ran after the peddler, teasing him by mocking his sing-song until, in exasperation, he would wave his horse whip threateningly.

He had to endure much ridicule, name calling, and jibes for his day's collection of the "penny stock," which he hoped to turn into cash to feed and clothe his brood. Interestingly, in later years this rag peddler's son graduated from a prestigious law school as a distinguished student and opened his law office in Boston—much to his father's pride.

This Jewish community enjoyed the new freedom of observing their strict Orthodox religious customs without interference, a luxury unknown in the countries from which they came. They observed the Sabbath as a day of rest and religious observance. They observed the dietary laws with all the inconveniences and prohibitions, the Passover season, and especially the High Holidays of Rosh-Ha-Sha-Na (the Jewish New Year) and Yom Kippur (the Day of Atonement).

These rag peddlers were a trial and tribulation to my father, as they were always getting into trouble with the town authorities for not paying the license tax of $2.00 for peddling. They could not understand the justification of this expense to them. They reasoned that the town was unjustified in imposing this tax as they were no trouble or expense to the town. Town authorities asked my father (the leading merchant in the town who could communicate with the rag peddlers in Yiddish) to plead with them to pay the taxes so that they would not have to go to jail. But "those stubborn, ignorant blockheads," as my father called them in exasperation, brought criticism to the entire Jewish community. My gentle mother had more patience with them and tried to keep them out of trouble even if it meant paying the fee for them.

Twice a year all the Jews in the town met and worshiped together on the special days of Rosh-Ha-Sha-Na and Yom Kippur. On these days, stores were closed, all business transactions were postponed, absences from jobs were respected, and children were excused from school.

All the Jewish community observed the personal hygiene rituals, and everyone was attired in his best out of consideration and respect for the seriousness of the meaning of these days. Unusual attention was devoted to the strict observance of every ritual connected with these holy days of the Jewish calendar.

It was, of course, known that wherever there were Jews in any part of the world, from the biggest cities to the remotest villages and hamlets, these holy days were similarly being observed by everyone. Traditions were followed no matter where they were and under any circumstances. In spite of all the anti-Semitism, the Christian population respected the feelings of the Jews on these particular holy days. They realized the significance of these days to these people as well as the sacrifices that were made by shutting down businesses for these religious observances.

There were no synagogues yet in Plymouth for the observance of these holidays, so each year the large meeting room of the town hall was rented and used as an improvised place of worship. A rabbi and cantor from Boston were engaged to conduct the services. A dealer loaned the necessaries for setting up the altar with the ark with sliding doors where the Holy Scrolls were ensconced complete with a velvet cover and gold fringe trimming, a sculpture of the ten commandments, and the eternal light to be placed above the ark.

Two wooden stands were also provided for holding the Siddurs (bibles used for these occasions), one for the rabbi and one for the cantor. Prayers for these occasions were read from these bibles. A cloth drapery extended the full width of the hall to divide the space into the improvised sanctuary, in which the men and the boys worshiped facing the altar and behind which the women and girls sat.

This separation is observed only among the strict Orthodox Jewry. In synagogues, the women sit upstairs in the balcony, where they are able to observe the sanctuary and follow the prayers. In this improvised space, the drapery was drawn at specific places during the services so that women could participate when the ark was opened and the Holy Scrolls removed. Services were conducted in Hebrew, and those who were able to read the Hebrew followed the service. Participants included men and boys who had received training for their bar mitzvah. Women who had been trained at home could also follow the services from their Siddurs. On Yom Kippur (Day of Atonement) everyone remained in their seats praying all day long. It was a day of fasting for 24 hours. Sometimes women fainted, and others brought their smelling salts with them. Sometimes the services were interrupted by the cries of a baby brought by a member of the family to the worshiping mother to be nursed.

Shortly after Sue's mother, Celia, arrived in the United States, she posed for a picture before attending her first ball in Rochester, New York.

Chapter 7
IS CHINESE EXCLUSION JUSTIFIABLE?

We were now living in Mary Jack's building. I was about eight years old and had no playmates in that part of town. One day I was invited by one of my classmates to join them on an escapade after school.

They told me "It's lots of fun—we go every day." Hungry for companionship, I readily agreed as my curiosity was aroused, although it was a rule at our house for us to come right home from school so Mama would know where we were. This after-school adventure was only for school mates who were invited.

These youngsters had discovered a secret place to gather on the way home from school and organized themselves into a kind of secret society. They made it clear that it was an honor to be invited to join them, and of course I was flattered.

One day we walked as a group to a secluded street where I had never been before. It was lined with tall beautiful trees with branches in full leaf stretching across the paved road. I had never known of the existence of this street. Looking around at the beauty, I decided only the Plymouth "swells" (what we used to call people who lived in luxury) could live here and made it a point to remember to ask my father if any of our customers lived on this street.

There was one very small store with a bay window piled high with neatly tied bundles. Each bundle had a paper slip on which was written a language I could not understand. It was for customers who had their laundry done by the laundry man, a lone Chinaman trying to eke out a living by doing washing and starching for the elite members of the Christian community.

Suddenly the group of children burst out in unison at the top of their lungs in a sing-song voice, "Chinky, Chinaman, Chinky, Chinky Chinaman" until it was such an annoyance that a very small man appeared shouting "Go 'way."

I had never seen such a strange-looking man in my whole life. I was frightened. I later learned he was Chinese and always dressed

in the same way. He came from a country that was very far away.
Perhaps his wife lived in the back of the store, but we didn't know. His
skin was yellowish and he wore a long pigtail down his back—so long
that he could sit on it. He wore felt slippers and very loose baggy pants
and a loose jacket to match. He was very thin, and my companions
told me he ate only rice.

The children kept chanting mockingly, and again he came out of
the small door of the store shouting "Go 'way." The children only
sang louder and came nearer to the door.

Finally, after what seemed a long time to me, the Chinaman came
through the door carrying a hot iron from which steam was escaping.
He waved the iron at them threateningly. He shouted "Go 'way," but
the children only kept laughing and shouting. I felt like crying.

Suddenly Mr. Boyd, the president of the local bank, appeared on
his way home to pick up his bundle of laundry from among the many
in the store window. He shouted at the children who knew him as a
neighbor. In fact, his own little boy was among the school group who
was "daring" the little Chinaman.

"Stop," shouted Mr. Boyd. "I'll tell your parents where you go
after school," he said angrily. The frightened children ran home, and
I ran to our store, nervously hoping that Mr. Boyd would not tell my
father.   My parents would surely ask me if I had stayed after school
helping the teacher. I knew I did not have to tell my parents where I
had been. It was my secret, and I never told Papa or Mama or Lizzie.

Years later I went to Simmons College in Boston, where I took a
course in social economics in my junior year under the professor, Dr.
Stites, whom we all loved. We had to select a research topic from a
long list on the blackboard. I chose "Is Chinese Exclusion Justifi-
able?" When I saw it, my thoughts went back to my childhood secret,
I was the only one of the class who chose that subject, and I never told
why I chose that subject. I spent many hours researching this subject
and got a well-deserved "A" on my paper.

This childhood incident of the unjust treatment of helpless people
troubled me. It would be the basis for my choice of helping people
who were poor to get out of poverty. It was the basis of my devotion
to the subject of nutrition and social welfare.My interest in working
for justice for all people (which was later my life's work) must have
stemmed in part from my childhood experience of "Chinky, Chinky,
Chinaman."

Chapter 8
VOTE "NO" FOR MY SAKE

It was a beautiful spring day, and at recess time the school playground was crowded with children from several grades. I noticed that several, by no means all, were wearing round celluloid pins in the shape of a big button. I knew two little girls who were wearing their pins attached to their dresses, and I ran up to them. One had a picture of a little girl with a serious expression. The other girl had a bigger pin with a picture of a girl and a boy who looked like brother and sister. I said that I admired those pins and wished I had one.

"Anyone can get them for free. They do not cost anything. You have to go to the town hall, and they give them out," ventured one child.

"Did you go?" I asked.

"No, my mother came home with a big handful. She pinned them on all the kids on our street."

"Can my father get some for my brother and me?" I inquired, sensing a problem.

"Sure he can. I can even get a whole bunch for free." "There is writing on it. What does it say?" I inquired.

"I dunno. Just writin'."

As soon as school was over I ran to the store to tell Papa of this great find for free.

"Were all the children wearing them?" he asked.

"Not everyone. I only asked the kids I know, but a lot of kids were wearing them. They are free and I want one. I want a brother and sister with writing on it. I like that the best." "What does it say on it?" he asked.

"I couldn't read all the words. Only 'my'."

My father smiled and promised to stop at the town hall to pick one up on his way home for supper. I was so excited I could hardly wait.

When supper was over my father called my brother and me over to him. He was sitting down, and we stood in front of him. He was not smiling any more, and I was afraid that he was going to scold me. He held up a pin with a picture of a brother and sister on it—just what I wanted.

"This pin is not for you to wear," he said with a serious expression on his face.

"Why not? Other kids are wearing them. Why can't I?" I asked, bursting into tears.

"Because you can't read what it says and you can't understand what it means anyhow." I could tell that he was upset.

He read very slowly, "Vote 'No' for My Sake" as he pointed to each word. Then he explained why the only children who should wear them were those whose fathers stopped on pay day at the saloons and drank with their friends until all the money in their pay envelopes from the mill was gone. "When they go home smelling of liquor and hand their wives the empty envelopes, there's no money left for food for their children," he tried to explain.

I was puzzled. Papa explained the word "vote" and said he hoped the saloons would be closed down if enough people voted "no." This was my next lesson in social justice. I was nine years old.

Chapter 9
FREEDOM TO WORSHIP GOD

The population of Plymouth, Massachusetts, was largely made up of the descendants of people who came from Plymouth, England. Since they did not follow the same Christian beliefs as the others, they were being persecuted. It was in 1620 that the Mayflower carried 101 passengers over the turbulent Atlantic Ocean where they could be free to worship God according to their beliefs. Years later, there was a monument erected to them on a hill overlooking the town. The residents who were descendants of the original colony were very proud of their heritage.

The population of this little town grew in size as the years rolled by. Drastic changes took place in every respect, including religious beliefs. Industries invaded the town, and there was need for workers. These people established homes and schools for their children and built churches of various denominations so they could remain free. The Plymouth Cordage Company remains to this day in a location a short distance away from the center of the town. A variety of woolen mills sprang up in various parts of the town and employed most of the men and women residents. These woolen mills became noted for the fine quality of their woven goods in various parts of the fast-developing country. The garment industry of New York City was among those that used the woolen cloth woven in Plymouth.

The mill owners built houses for their employees within walking distance to accommodate the fast-growing families. Since the wages were low and the families large, the children were unsupervised for the most part, and they grew up like "Topsy" (a term used to describe these undisciplined children).

Although we lived in a different part of town, we children attended the same schools. Our fathers usually had stores in the center of the town, and the mill people were our customers. Usually both parents worked in the mills to support the large families. When the whistle blew at 7 o'clock in the morning, parents were on their way, walking hurriedly in order not to be late.

The town thrived with the increase in population, and by the time our family grew up, my father and mother were both working at our store. In order to increase the family income, Papa continued to peddle men's and boys' clothes for three days a week in small towns where there were no stores. We always had a relative who worked in the store and lived with us. Papa had a horse and a covered wagon piled high with clothing, which he sold in the small towns. He always came home on Thursdays to be home for Friday and the Sabbath, which was strictly observed by Jewish people.

The population was divided according to the denominations of the various churches, which had been built not only for their beliefs but also for their social position. The families who worked in the mills were usually Catholic. They worshiped in one Catholic church, which was a wooden structure a good distance from where they lived.

There was no more religious persecution as there had been at the time when the Mayflower sailed from England into Plymouth Harbor. The early settlers seeking religious freedom prospered, and their descendants mostly supported the town over the years.

It was the custom to have the noon meal as the main meal of the day, and school children went home for "dinner" and then returned for the afternoon session. Papa always came home for dinner. Mama set out the nourishing soup at each child's place to cool.

One day, as it was spring and the trees were sprouting little leaves, I walked slowly to enjoy the trees and the robins that were hopping about on the grass. Tommy Collins, who was known to be a mischief maker, started throwing stones at me. He was Catholic and his church was farthest away from the center of the town. Both of his parents were gone from home when the 7 a.m. whistle blew to summon the workers. They never came home to dinner. Tommy's sisters, who went to different schools, put on the table the food for the children their mother had prepared before leaving.

Tommy kept calling me names and the other kids kept laughing, and he kept saying loudly, "You killed my little Lord Jesus and you will be punished."

I yelled back, "Even when the other kids stepped on the ants to watch them die, I did not step on them." My brother Philip, who was 1-1/2 years older than I, taught me also to say to teasing kids like this, "Sticks and stones may break my bones but names will never hurt me."

He kept screaming at me, "You killed my little Lord Jesus because you are a Jew." He added, "We learned this in Sunday school, so there."

I burst out crying and yelling "I never killed anything" and ran home screaming all the way. Mama and Papa and my brother Philip were finishing dinner. My brother said, "After school, I'll fight Tommy."

Papa looked sternly at Philly and pointed to his belt. "If you ever get into fights, this strap will lick you so hard you will never get into a fight again, remember." My mother held me close in the long apron she always wore and dried my eyes and quieted my sobs. My soup was getting cold. My father and mother spoke Yiddish, which I did not understand.

Then my father spoke severely to us, "The Collins family are customers in our store. Don't get into fights. Run right home after school. I will explain everything after supper when the store is closed." He left the house in a hurry so Cousin Sam, who worked in the store, could come home for his dinner.

After supper that same evening, Papa told us to sit around the kitchen table while Mama washed the dishes. He told us we were Jews and did not kill anybody. We worshiped our own God. We were proud people. He said only ignorant people called other people bad names, and no matter what happened we must never do this. He told us we must always be proud and hold our heads high, for we never had anything to be ashamed of.

"Other people have their religion. That is why we have so many churches," he said. "Some day we will have our own synagogue. We have the Ten Commandments, which God gave us. We had the first Bible, which others have copied. Even if the Jews were driven out of every country in the world, God watches over them."

Chapter 10
UNCLE JULIUS TRAVELS TO GERMANY

My father's mother and her unmarried sister were the only ones remaining in the shtetl of Doag in what was either Lithuania or Russia at the time, as place names were changing in that area. All five sons and three daughters had emigrated to Boston. All but the youngest, a son, had married and had children. They were living in Boston or in nearby towns. All pleas in letters to their mother and aunt to come to America went unheeded. The only communication between them over what added up to 25 years was by exchange of letters and photographs. This was the means of acquainting them with all the daughters-in-law, sons-in-law, and grandchildren. They knew them all by name and appearance and through stories about them written in the letters. This must have offered much solace to the two elderly women during hours of loneliness. All attempts to persuade them to join the family in America, where they could be cared for and cherished, met with failure. Those who had served in the Russian army and those who had escaped without serving (as in the case of my father, who at age 13 joined a group in his shtetl of Doag that had left secretly) feared to return lest the officials prevent them from leaving and ever returning to America. Their mother was aware of this danger. She argued that, as these were the declining years of life for both her sister and herself, it was best for them to remain where they were, where they had their little synagogue for worship and neighbors who were friends. To take up a new life in a strange country seemed impossible.

Hearing about the pogroms and the massacring of Jews in the region, and fearing for the safety of these two elderly relatives, it was decided that another attempt should be made to save them. They would send the youngest son, Julius, over to meet them in Germany, which the women could enter safely and without suspicion, and bring them back. Julius, unmarried and in his late twenties, employed as a cigarmaker (and living with his sister Annie in the west end of Boston in a crowded tenement district with her four children and their tubercular father), was chosen as the one person who was able to leave his work and make the trip in 1901. Whatever risks there were and fears that had to be overcome were resolved, and the happiness of the reunion dominated the visit, so that worries and tears were set aside as the two old ladies absorbed news for days about every member of the family until they felt really reacquainted with each one.

They had arrived in Germany with huge bundles they could hardly carry. Julius was overjoyed, thinking they had brought their possessions and were ready to accompany him back to America. The days of visiting and learning about each member of the family drew to a close. Then the sisters announced their decision to remain in Doag, where they were comfortable and now too old to travel and make a new life in a strange country. All the huge bundles contained gifts for every member of the family down to the last grandchild, and they were sending them back with Julius. For him there was a very special gift since he was not yet married. This was the pair of Russian silver candlesticks to be used on the Sabbath by the wife in saying the prayers to welcome Queen Sabbath every Friday at sundown, observing the arrival of the day of rest. They parted, the two old ladies having accomplished their mission. Uncle Julius arrived at our house in Plymouth laden with gifts for all of us. For me there was a little double purse of pink crocheted cotton laced with tiny blue beads to hold the tiniest of coins; as a decoration hung over my belt, it was treasured for years. It is now in the possession of my sister Helen Michel, who appropriated it for her collection of family "heirlooms." For my mother were a number of pillows of softest goose down and two huge featherbeds of the same type of goose down that were used mostly for extra beds for unexpected guests who decided to spend the night. Today these would be considered in the category of sleeping bags. Then they were used as bed coverings in winter and on the floor when extra beds were needed, which was considered a great privilege by the children. At my parents' 25th wedding anniversary, Uncle Julius presented them with the silver candlesticks, as he considered it the appropriate occasion for this particular gift, knowing that they would be used for the purpose his mother intended them. He never married. They now grace the home of my mother's namesake, Carolyn Sadow Leshin, who uses them for the purpose they were meant for. Uncle Julius was looked upon as a kind of Santa Claus, as he distributed to each member of the family the gifts so thoughtfully assembled by the grandmother we never knew. Her picture, rescued from our family album, is beautifully framed and is prominently displayed in the home of her great grandson, Leon Sadow, in New Bedford, Massachusetts.

Was it a premonition? Shortly after the return of Uncle Julius, word arrived of the death of this brave woman, who gave up the opportunity to be re-united with her children, whom she had not seen since their departure as young adolescents.

A sadness settled over our household. Never before had we encountered death. Our neighbor, Mrs. Conners, who had experienced death several times in the loss of her babies, knew how to console us. She assured us that my grandmother was now safely in heaven and that no harm could ever come to her. My father was very quiet and did not scold any of us. Cousin Ida, who still lived with us, helped to keep us all quiet. My father stayed home from the store for a whole week, which meant my mother had to go there all day long. He was sitting "shiva" at home, which is the prescribed period of mourning by Jewish law as observed by Orthodox Jews. He had to cut the lapel of his jacket, as it is said in the Bible . . ." ye shall rend thy garments . . ." for those who mourn. He sat on a low stool, was in his stocking feet, prayed all day, and looked sad. Each morning when it was still dark at six o'clock my mother awakened us and put the house in order. Nine Jewish men arrived in their working clothes. They were the men who lived "over South" and whom we saw only on the holidays at the improvised synagogue in the Town Hall. It was cold outside.

They came to say the prayer for the deceased before going to work. It was called "kaddish," and every son in the family is expected to say this prayer at the death of a parent. The ceremony requires that there be ten men present to form a "minyan" to participate in the prayer. Our kitchen was crowded with these big men, who had walked all the way from where they lived to form this "minyan." My mother prepared glasses of tea to serve them before they left, knowing that it was a requirement that those who participated in this ceremony had to come without having eaten any food. The same group arrived at sundown every day for the week of "shiva" to say the required evening prayer. If there had been a synagogue in Plymouth, they all would have met there for this ceremony according to Jewish Orthodox belief. Instead, they came to our house, meeting their responsibilities as Orthodox Jews to help my father during the week of mourning.

Sue Sadow's Grandmother Sadow, who remained in Doag, Russia.

Chapter 11
UNCLE JACOB COMES TO AMERICA

Shortly after this period of mourning, another family event occurred in 1906. One day, when we returned home from school, we found a lot of excitement going on. Suddenly there seemed to be a crowd of people in our kitchen. We were surprised to see my mother home early from the store. Cousin Ida was hunting around trying to find chairs so everybody could sit down. Uncle Jacob, my father's older brother, his wife, and their five sons had arrived from Manchester, England. We did not know anything about these relatives, as there were no pictures of them in the family album, and my father never spoke about them. They had been on a big boat for many days sailing from Liverpool, the embarkation port to Boston. One of my uncles who lived in Boston, having emigrated from Doag shortly after my father left the shtetl, met the boat on their arrival, and, since there was no room at any of the relatives' flats in Boston, decided that it was best for them to take the train directly to the country, to Plymouth, where there was plenty of room. My father met the train and brought them to our house and then hurried right back to the store so my mother could go home, as there would be plenty to do to welcome them so they would not feel so strange and to get them settled and make a plan for this large foreign family. They spoke English, but it was so different that hardly anybody understood what they were saying. You had to get used to it.

The smell in our kitchen was overwhelming. They had all been on the boat for many days, travelling in steerage, and had probably slept in their clothes the whole time, as steerage accommodations were very crowded and uncomfortable. So many little boys! We had never known about these cousins. We all just stood and stared at each other. The two biggest boys spoke to us. Although they were small of stature, they were quite grown up, older than we were. We giggled, as we could hardly understand their Cockney English. Then we asked them all to come out to our yard to play so we could become friends.

My aunt, a small lady with blue eyes and light hair, was crying as she told my mother over and over what had happened and why they had all left England. My mother was crying, too. The story was that their little girl, only three years of age, was standing in front of the open fireplace and her dress caught on fire. She was screaming, but my aunt just stood and watched, so horrified that all she could do was scream also. The neighbors heard the screaming and rushed in to see what was happening, but it was too late. The little girl had burned to death. Since that moment my aunt had nearly gone out of her mind, and nothing anyone could do was of any help. She cried and wailed day and night. It was decided that the best thing to do for her was to get her away from the scene of this terrible tragedy, hoping she would be able to overcome it. That is when the decision to come to America, where my uncle had many relatives, was arrived at, and now they were here with us. My mother embraced her and tried to comfort her and assured her that now that she was here, everything possible would be done for them, that she would help her to get settled, that she would help her recover from this terrible tragedy. I could not understand what it was all about and why they were all crying. My mother shooed us all out of the kitchen and told us to play in the back yard until they called us. None of our other playmates had come from school to play, for which we were very glad. Mother and Cousin Ida were busy getting lots of hot water ready for baths for all of them. They all had such strange-looking clothes in the big bundles they brought with them. Everything was different from ours.

It was really a full house, and, as there was not enough room at the table, we ate in two shifts. Since now we were acquainted, we fought about who should sit next to which new cousin at the table. This amused them very much and made them feel welcome. It was a very busy time for everyone, and our neighbors, so near us that they could see everything that was going on, were curious about these new relatives. Practically all of them had to sleep on the floor on the featherbeds that my grandmother had sent over with Uncle Julius.

Uncle Jacob was very religious, much more so than my father, who was always too busy to say all the prayers that were expected of the Orthodox Jew. Every morning my Uncle Jacob rose very early and said all the prayers, which meant putting on his tefillin (phylacteries) and talith (prayer shawl) and reading his prayers out of a small bible. It was understood that no one could speak to him to interrupt him while he was praying. Of course he had his hat on all the time, as it was the custom of all Orthodox Jews to keep their heads covered while in the house. My father followed this practice but not while he was in the store or any other business building or the home of Christians. He discontinued this practice later in life. Even at breakfast my aunt wept all the time, and we children did everything we knew of to make her laugh and help her get over her sorrow.

Soon all the boys of school age were put in school. The two older boys got jobs in the woolen mills. A house was found for the family right on our street at the corner of the road leading down to the Poor House Pond. It was near the school and convenient for the small boys. My mother went every day to show my aunt how to keep house and arrange her day to get all her chores done. She also sewed a couple of cotton dresses for her so she would be comfortable and neat and would be respected by her Christian neighbors. They all felt sorry for her when they knew about her tragedy, which she spoke about incessantly. The happiest day for my aunt was when she gave birth to a little girl, whom she named Anna. The rooms got furnished little by little, the kitchen first and the bedrooms. My aunt was so confused that it was hard for her to remember what to do. She was always so happy to see my mother and me, as my mother thought I could be of help to her. She had a problem making her boys obey. At first they came often to our back yard to play, but soon they made their own friends at school and did not come so often.

My Uncle Jacob, a small, frail man (who was so religious he wore a beard), observed the Sabbath, the other Jewish holidays, and all the other religious rites followed by the strictly Orthodox Jews. He became a peddler and carried all his stock on his back. Today, accustomed as we are to backpacking, it would not be so conspicuous, but at that time, meeting him on the street all bent over under his heavy load that reached from his shoulders to his ankles, I was both sympathetic and ashamed, and hoped the kids would not make fun of him. He spent a lot of time at our house evenings and Sundays when he was not peddling. He loved my mother and appreciated all she did for his family to help them get settled. He was a devoted friend and tried to do as many errands and small favors as he could to show his gratitude. He did not understand his wife's problems well and was not very patient or as sympathetic as he might have been. After a long, hard day of peddling, he had other problems on his mind and got angry when he had to listen to her crying and wailing, and for relief used to come to our house down the street in the evening. He admitted to my mother that his wife had been a beautiful young girl with white skin, pink cheeks, blue eyes, and lovely curly light hair. This was unusual among Jewish girls and greatly favored in contrast to his dark complexion. He worked hard and long hours as did my parents but remained in very modest financial circumstances, trying his best, with no skills at his disposal to earn a good living to provide for his large family. His greatest ambition from the day of his arrival in Plymouth was to see that there was a synagogue, and he did not at all approve of renting the Town Hall for an improvised place of worship where the Sabbath could be respected and where there could be a Jewish religious school where the boys could be prepared for their Bar Mitzvah, the day they reached manhood and accepted the responsibilities that accompanied this important event, of participation in all religious functions. He himself had taught his older boys and was concerned about his younger ones. He toiled for this project for years. My father used to lose patience with him for spending so much time trying to convince the Jews in the town of their responsibility to help him with his project, which meant that he visited them often to persuade them to contribute to his fund. He even begged his Christian customers to make contributions during their own holidays; some did because they were impressed by his conscientious desire for a place of religious worship. The prayers that were prescribed for the Orthodox Jew for every morning and every evening were strictly adhered to, and he let nothing interfere with this observance. He used every "ruse" he could think of to "collect" money for his project. He never tired of telling my impatient father about it, to whom the impracticality was foremost and who, as a business man, could not foresee how this would ever be possible.

One evening my Uncle Jacob arrived when he knew my father would be at home. He was all enthusiasm. He had found an unoccupied old colonial house, of historical origin, which could be purchased. It was in the perfect neighborhood, easily accessible on foot, no matter where the Jews had their homes. Riding on the Sabbath was one of the prohibitions in the Orthodox Jewish rules of restrictions. He persuaded my father to go with him to look at it, and this time my father could not resist his earnestness. "How is it going to be paid for?" asked my practical father. To his amazement he learned that his brother had banked all the "collections" over the years. He was very persuasive in insisting that all the Christians would be impressed if the Jews had their own synagogue for worship just as they had their churches. Worshipping in the Town Hall was so distasteful to him, he even considered it a sin, as he used to say. His persistence finally won out, and my father dealt with the bank and guaranteed what payments were necessary to purchase the old gray clapboard house, much to the elation of his impractical religious brother. Alterations had to be made inside to convert it into a sanctuary for the men and boys on the street level and a staircase leading to a balcony for the women and girls, to make it possible for them to participate in the services. He came to my mother, after the alterations were made and the synagogue was ready for the first observances, with a Holy Scroll purchased in Boston and yards of a lovely shade of blue velvet and yards of gold fringe for her to make the "mantel," the covering for the Scroll. Uncle Jacob lived to see the realization of his dream.

The old gray clapboard house remains just as it was at the time Uncle Jacob discovered it and set his heart on having it for the Plymouth synagogue. The Jewish population has grown a great deal since the original 25 Jewish families of rag peddlers and store keepers, and many of them are not only merchants but professional people like doctors, dentists, lawyers, and teachers.

During the bicentennial celebration in 1976, on a nostalgic visit to the scene of my childhood, I visited the site of the synagogue. There were visible changes since the date of purchase of the little old gray house. It was locked, and there was no possibility of seeing the interior. As this remained the only synagogue in the town, I spoke with one of the Jewish businessmen and expressed surprise that, now that the Jewish population had increased in size and affluence, they had not seen fit to build a synagogue more in keeping with their financial situation.

"What do you mean?" an indignant voice came over the phone. "We love our little synagogue. It is historical, and we want to keep it that way. Of course we've made a great many alterations on the inside, which are more in keeping with what you have in mind, if that is what you mean."

In addition to the plaque on the outside of the building, giving the date of origin and a few other historical facts, there should be a plaque dedicated to Uncle Jacob for his efforts as the original founder.

PART II

SCHOOL
DAYS

Chapter 12
BABY SCHOOL

The Baby School in Plymouth, Massachusetts, stood on a piece of sandy land. It was a wooden building with two entrances facing the street and two outhouses in the playground, both with wooden signs marking one for the boys and one for the girls.

On July 28, 1901, I turned five years old, just in time for entrance into the first grade in the Baby School, which was a hop, skip, and a jump from our house at 29 Summer Street. Tibbie Morton lived next door. Her birthday was July 24, and we remained close friends all our lives.

All schools in Plymouth began the day after Labor Day. My brother, Philip, who was 1-1/2 years older than I, was in the second grade. We were dressed in new outfits Mama had made.

Walking toward the school, my right hand was firmly squeezed in Papa's hand. I was trembling as if I were going to my doom. Just ahead of us, I saw Tibbie clutching her mama's hand.

"Now that you are a big girl going to school you will not cry, will you?" Papa asked. Frightened as I was, I managed to gulp "No, Papa" in a quavering voice. When we approached the street where the school was, we heard boys and girls screaming and crying as if someone were whipping them with a strap. Little girls were hanging onto their older sisters and screaming to be taken home. But no one was home because their parents had been working in the mills since 7 a.m. It was the responsibility of the older sisters to take the younger ones to school the first day.

Papa was walking toward the teacher, who was trying to console the children. She was surrounded by the older sisters who held the screaming little ones.

The teacher said to one of the older girls, "We have this happen all the time the first day of school. Take your sister home now. Come back tomorrow and tell your mama the teacher said it was all right."

Papa was smiling. He knew the teacher as she was a customer at his store on Market Street next to Mr. Caviechi's fruit store, where Mama sent me to buy oranges. Our store was painted blue, and the sign above the entrance read "The Blue Store Clothing Co."

The teacher greeted Papa, "Good morning, Mr. Sadow. Philly is in back playing with the boys. Your brave little girl does not cry like those you saw. We have that every year. The older sisters bring them to school because the parents work in the mills. They have to bring them two and sometimes three times before they get used to it and learn to walk home."

Papa said, "Teacher, please I want to tell you something about my little girl." He spoke in broken English, as if he were confiding something painful or disgraceful. "She does everything with her left hand since she was a baby. We don't know what to do. She used to cry when we took the spoon away and put it in her right hand. Please, teacher, make her use her right hand." He seemed relieved as if he had disclosed the problem very much on his mind. I know Mama made him promise to tell the teacher about my left handedness.

I was frightened and on the verge of tears. "Don't worry, Mr. Sadow. We will help her," said the teacher, gently patting me on the head.

The teacher carried a big brass bell, which she rang vigorously to summon the children to the front entrance. All the children playing gathered in front of the entrance and formed into two long lines, one for the girls and one for the boys. The boys scuffled in the sandy entrance with their new shoes, making noise and raising dust. The teacher tried to quiet them; then she said, "Forward march!" The boys pushed each other through the entrance. The girls marched in more slowly. We entered the cloak room first and then the school room. There were rows and rows of wooden desks, and the seats were mounted on movable iron stands, which the janitor adjusted to fit each of us after the teacher decided upon our permanent seating.

The teacher stood behind her desk at the front of the room, which was next to a big round pot-bellied stove. She rang the bell to silence the boys who were making a great deal of noise scuffing their shoes.

At noon, she rang the bell again. "Please, children. Quiet! It is time to go home for dinner. When you come back you will play in the playground until I ring the bell for you to line up. Then we will have the afternoon session. On this first day of school, you will be assigned to a seat. Tomorrow we will begin school, and I know you will be happy here."

Tibbie was waiting for me. We ran home for dinner. Philly had already run ahead of us and was gobbling his soup. Papa was home from the store. Mama had a plate of soup waiting on the table for me. I put the spoon in my left hand. Papa and Mama spoke in Yiddish, which I could not understand.

After eating, I ran over to Tibbie's house, and we ran back to school hand-in-hand to keep from being late. My first day of school was over, and Tibbie and I changed into our play clothes.

Dr. Brown's little girl, Rachel, lived farther away than Tibbie and I, and we let her walk with us. We loved Dr. Brown. He always came to the house when anyone was sick. He had a horse and buggy, and he used a round iron weight attached to a rope, which he put on the ground so the horse couldn't run away. When I saw that buggy in front of our house, I was always frightened and I ran as fast as I could to see if it were Mama who was sick.

At age 7, I was in the third grade and was at the Cornish School, which was farther away. We passed the Baby School and ran through the cemetery where the Pilgrims and their descendants were buried.

Four school buildings were situated on one plot. The third, fourth, and fifth grades were in one building, and the sixth, seventh, and eighth grades were in another. Children from all over Plymouth attended these schools. Most of us walked to school. Some children who lived farther away took the streetcar, which ran along Main and Court Streets. Then they walked up the hill to the school building. In the winter, the streetcar was sometimes late due to heavy snows. The children had to climb the hill in their clumsy rubber boots, and they were excused for being late.

Chapter 13
THE CHEAT

It was a beautiful spring morning. The sky was blue, and there was not a cloud to be seen. Robins hopped around on the green lawn leading up to the court house. The Atlantic Ocean remained calm as the tide was going out. I used to stand at the foot of the street that led from the court house to Water Street, where we kids, during the summer vacation, used to watch the angry waves roll over on their way to shore. I hated living in Mary Jack's building where we were so crowded, and I had no playmates except the girls in my class at school whose parents worked in the mills and were customers in our store, and they had lots of chores at home after school. I loved the fresh air; we were told by our teachers to take deep breaths to build strong bodies and be healthy.

Everyone at home got up early to have breakfast and open the store, which was connected to our flat at Mary Jack's. Mama always said we had to make the best of it, and the five years would pass and we could move back to our big house at 29 Summer Street with our big yard and all our playmates. I was in the seventh grade and was eleven years old. I was very tall for my age and had thick brown hair that Mama had to comb every morning. It was parted in the middle with four braids. The bottom braids had narrow red ribbons braided into the hair so I would not lose them. My petticoat never showed like the "mill" kids'.

Our teacher, Kitty O'Brien, was very strict. Most of the kids were scared of her. She never smiled. Behind her back we called her names like "old maid." She wore pince-nez glasses. I was not scared of her. I sat in the next to last seat in the A class because I was tall for my age. Rows began with the smallest pupils; Chrissie Rogan sat behind me as she was bigger. Her family worked in the mills and were customers in our store.

Our teacher had told us the day before that this morning we would have an arithmetic test for both classes A and B. I was not scared because I loved arithmetic. I was really smart in everything and always brought home papers marked "A" with gold stars. My parents were very proud and praised me.

My brother, Phil, was in the lower seventh grade although he was older than I and very smart. He was held back because he played "hooky" frequently despite lickings with the strap by my father. His teacher always smiled at me and said "Good morning."

The room was very quiet on account of the arithmetic test. The tall windows on each side of the room were open, and I heard the birds chirping. The test was written on the blackboard.

The usual "pets" selected by the teacher passed out the test papers. The teacher said, "You may start now. I'll tell you when the time is up."

You could hear sighs from kids who were scared. It was easy, and I finished quickly but kept my eyes glued to the paper to be sure I had made no mistakes. I felt Chrissie poke me in the back with a sharp pencil and pass me a note, which I received with my outstretched hand so no one would see it.

She wanted to know the answer to a question. I wrote the answer on a small piece of paper and was trying to pass it behind to Chrissie when I suddenly heard the teacher's sharp voice, "All pupils put down your pencils and face me." Standing at her desk facing the students, she said in a loud voice, "We have a cheat in this room! Sit quietly in your seats while I deal with this terrible problem."

Then again in a loud voice she called my name. I started to tremble. "Get out of your seat and stand beside your desk so everyone will see who the **cheat** is," she declared in a piercing voice. The mean kids started to titter.

"Clean out your desk and move to this front seat where I can watch you. You can't be trusted," she said, pointing.

To a scared, very small-sized girl sitting in the front seat of the class she said, "Empty your desk so the CHEAT can move into your desk."

The boys especially were enjoying the performance and were not only tittering but laughing. The teacher was furious and promised to punish them.

Crying and sobbing, I obeyed the teacher's instructions. My playmate and best friend from 29 Summer Street, Tibbie Morton, started to cry and sob at the injustice. Neither of us had handkerchiefs. Obediently, I carried the contents of my desk to my new quarters and sat cramped in my new seat, which was much too low for my long legs.

The noon bell rang for dismissal of all four classes. We were supposed to stand beside our desks until the teacher dismissed us, march quietly out of the room, run home for dinner, and return for the afternoon session. As soon as I reached the door I darted toward home. I burst into the kitchen screaming as if my heart would break. My mother had soup waiting at my place at the table.

"I'll never go back to school," I repeated over and over. My temper was rising, "No one will ever make me either."

Papa finished his dinner and spoke in Yiddish with Mama. Cousin Sam came up from the store to have his dinner. Lizzie, our bookkeeper in the portable office, came into the kitchen to find out what the trouble was. They could not understand what was going on because I was exploding with temper "just like her father," said my sweet-tempered mother.

Lizzie, who was only a teenager, took me in her arms protectively. She wiped away my tears as she listened to the whole story. "That teacher ought to be fired," she said. "She is not a teacher but a bully. She has hurt this child. I know what it's like to be bullied and hurt. Listen to me, Mr. Sadow. Don't make her go back to school yet. That teacher is mean. Your child is not a cheat; she was only trying to help her friend. Besides, the family are good customers."

Mama heated my soup. She told me to go to the bathroom and wash up. She promised not to send me back to school. "We'll talk it over with our neighbors; they'll know what to do," she said. "He is a minister and has a good education." I calmed down after I realized everybody was on my side.

I missed school terribly that afternoon. I tried to help Mama with the dishes as she was very busy doing alterations at her sewing machine. She also had the youngest children to put to bed for their naps. I kept wondering what Tibbie would tell her mother.

That evening Papa sat down at the kitchen table after supper. He thought it over. In his broken English, he tried to explain. My father taught me my first lesson about encountering injustice. He said everybody knew I was not a cheat, only trying to help a friend.

"That got you into trouble and you will have to pay the consequences," he said. "You should always hold your head up high when you know you are right. Don't blame others for your mistakes."

Earlier I had suggested I would go back to school only if I could be placed in the low seventh grade with my brother Phil, who had a kind teacher. But Papa decided I should go back to school in Kitty O'Brien's class. "She will discover that she was wrong. Be honest with yourself and have others respect you. Respect is more important than love," he emphasized. "It's only a few months before vacation, and I'm sure she won't hold you back. Don't you think this is the best plan?"

"But Papa, the seat is too low for my long legs, and I sit all doubled over," I insisted.

"Don't ask to change your seat. Be proud and show others that immigrants can endure with dignity what is not comfortable."

For the rest of the year I ignored my teacher as much as possible, seldom looking up from my desk. She was always polite and displayed my paintings and my compositions as "the best" many times. She tried without success to win my attention. Without any further ado, she passed me into eighth grade.

Chapter 14
HIGH SCHOOL DAYS

In an experiment, the Board of Education of my home town selected ten above-average children to skip one grade and finish high school more quickly. They wanted to determine if it were really necessary to have all eight grades of grammar school and four years of high school. If the children could graduate from high school faster, then it would save the town a lot of money.

It was 1909 when the idea was implemented. I was one of the ten (five boys and five girls). Each student followed the program they wanted to follow. Practically all chose the commercial course, which was the most popular because it assured a job right out of high school. This, however, was not my selection.

I knew that if I took the commercial course, my father would expect me to work in the store as his qualified and trustworthy bookkeeper, and I would be doomed to a life in Plymouth. At age 12—just before entering high school—I was already determined to "get out of Plymouth." I was critical of the "two-faced gossipers," as I termed many of the customers talking to my mother in our store. My mother was always a good listener, never saying a word.

Because of my natural outspokenness, my parents constantly admonished me to keep my ideas to myself. If it ever got out that I was critical of any customers, they would surely go somewhere else to make their purchases. "Once you get customers, do everything possible to keep them," cautioned my father as he attempted to instill in us the best business practices. "So keep your ideas to yourself" was their constant advice.

At this early age, I had other ideas for my future. I wanted to take the classical course to prepare for further education. Both my parents appreciated higher education, but it was not considered important for Jewish girls (especially immigrants of the early 1900s) to go past high school. It was expected that they would marry soon and establish their own families, and thus education and the expense would be wasted. It also was felt that further education would "give girls ideas" of becoming too independent.

My father wanted me to take the commercial course, but I begged tearfully to enroll in the classical course. Stomping my foot, I promised to help out in the store at any time I was needed and to help with the younger children. "I'll do anything you ask of me," I pleaded. I won the argument and was permitted to matriculate in the classical course that would prepare me for college—my dream.

I had never had any contact with anyone who went to college, nor did I have the remotest notion what it would be like. I only knew about college from the books in the public library, which I devoured in spare moments. These stories made college life sound like a dream world of parties, pranks, and lasting friendships. I wanted it—this was the life for me!

Of course I could not expect my parents to begin to understand what was in my mind. I shared my secret thoughts only with my playmate, Tibbie Morton, who lived next door. She approved of my ideas and promised not to tell anyone. I told her when I finished college, I would get a job helping people, because I thought I would be good at that. I had gotten this idea from stories my parents told about all the miseries in this world.

My four years of high school passed, and I was scheduled to graduate in June 1913 even though I was not yet 17 years of age. Once I overheard my father telling a Boston salesman that I was mature for my years. I took advantage of this unexpected piece of information and fancied myself all grown up. I had more than passed all my courses those four years, never even having to take a final test or exam because my grades were high enough for a diploma.

I was the first in my family to complete high school. My older brother Phil, much to my parents' chagrin, preferred to work in the store rather than finish school. He hated the confinement and discipline of school and therefore was always in trouble there. He liked working in the store and preferred to be a businessman rather than a doctor or a lawyer, which was my parents' dream for him.

Weeks before graduation my major concern was choosing material and a pattern for my graduation dress. I looked at pattern books and the many bolts of newly arrived white materials at Moore's Department Store. I collected innumerable small material cuttings to take home. The sales girls were always patient and advised me about what they thought would be appropriate.

Tibbie and I went to the store many times after school. We finally chose what we thought would be best. Before buying it, I told the sales girl that my mother would need to see it because she was going to sew my dress.

I was tall for my age and very skinny, and I wanted a pattern that would not make me look like a bean pole or a dressed-up scarecrow, which were the teasing remarks I got from my brother.

Finally my mother helped me decide on embroidered cotton voile; the dress was lavishly trimmed with rows of lace and included a cotton slip that had to be worn under the sheer voile. I chose white silk stockings to wear with medium-heeled white kid slippers (which were far from comfortable as there was no time to "break them in"). They were higher heeled than my other shoes and made me walk awkwardly. I practiced walking in them in the house so I would not turn my ankle walking across the platform on graduation night.

My mother was very busy at this time of year, and finishing my dress was not her highest priority. I worried that the carriage would be waiting while she sewed on the last hook and eye. Indeed, this turned out to be the fact! I was on "pins and needles," which was the descriptive expression of the times. Everything for us was last minute because of the work pressure at the store; our personal needs had to come after that. I have often wondered how my mother could divide herself to meet so many situations!

At last I was ready. I waited impatiently for the arrival of the horse and carriage my father had hired for the occasion. I was dressed in white from head to toe. My thick, dark chestnut brown hair was combed up into an adult style bun on the nape of my neck. It was so uncomfortable that I was in constant fear it would loosen and drop below my waistline. I wore long white kid gloves (a school requirement) up to my elbow. When the carriage arrived, my family peered out of the parlor window. Tibbie was already seated, as it had stopped first at her door. Hurrying out our front door, I carefully took our stone steps one at a time to the sidewalk. Mr. Watson, the owner and driver, helped me pull myself up on the black leather footstand into the seat beside Tibbie. I was careful not to scratch my white slippers. Mr. Watson, who had known us all our lives, constantly gave me compliments as we drove along, which embarrassed me.

My mother and the children stood at the window until we waved good-bye. The high school was not even a mile from home. How often we used to run all the way in order not to be late for school! The horse and carriage started off on this important journey. People we knew greeted us warmly and waved as if we were off on a honeymoon.

When we reached our destination, Mr. Watson alighted first. Carefully he placed a huge, heavy metal disc attached to a sturdy rope under the feet of the horse; it was to keep the horse from running away when left alone. He helped each of us onto the school steps at the girls' entrance and wished us luck.

As the graduates assembled, we entered the building. We were very silent, not even greeting each other. It was a solemn moment. We all marched quietly into the main hall, which had been specially arranged: all the desks had been removed, and the hall was now filled with wooden settees to accommodate the townspeople gathered together every June to witness this great occasion. High school graduation was considered the event of the year in Plymouth.

After a marching drill, the girls and boys went once again into our respective cloakrooms. There was no mingling of the sexes in those days! The crowded, stuffy dressing room was stifling. The temperature and humidity were merciless that day, and there was no air conditioning. My hands sweated inside the white kid gloves, and I could feel the moisture build up under my armpits.

We could hear the townspeople arriving and the scuffing of feet on the wooden stairs. I was in a panic, fearing my parents might be late. The store was closed that evening, and my father had promised to come with my mother, which rarely happened as both could not be away at the same time. I kept wondering where they would be seated. They had never been inside the high school before. Would they know how long it would take to walk there?

Finally, after what seemed an eternity of waiting, the teachers in charge of the graduation exercises gave us final instructions on marching in and taking our seats on the platform that the teachers and our principal, Mr. Williams, used each day to introduce the day's activities and make announcements.

This evening we sat in their places. As the orchestra struck up a familiar tune, we marched in: the girls from the left and the boys from the right. The boys were really sweating it out in their prescribed dark navy woolen suits. The audience applauded vigorously as we marched in and stood before our assigned seats. We waited for the signal to sit down in unison. I didn't look out at the audience because I feared that my parents were not there yet.

The guests in the audience and each of us received a small white cardboard card as the program. On one side was printed the order of the exercises and on the other was the list of graduates. I noticed a small star beside some names. By the star at the bottom of the program was written in tiny letters: "honor students." I looked for my name and was flabbergasted to find a star beside it. I could feel the blood rushing up to my cheeks; I was trembling all over. There had been no preparation for this surprise!

The exercises began. A number of prominent men in the town made speeches. Members of the Board of Education spoke about the experiment, mentioning that all ten were sitting on the platform as graduates. We were all asked to stand up. This also was unexpected, even to the teachers. We did not know what we ought to do until Mr. Williams said to us, smiling, "You may stand now. For you are the youngest graduates. All of you proved what the Board of Education hoped, and your parents can be proud of you."

We all stood up, and the audience clapped and clapped. Other graduates were not as pleased because they felt it was unfair to feature us. After all, we were graduates just like the rest. The orchestra played between speeches.

Mr. Williams, the principal, whom we all loved, made the final speech. He praised all of us for studying so diligently all four years. It was a proud moment in our lives. As diplomas were awarded, one teacher stood on his right holding a huge bunch of long-stemmed American Beauty roses for the girls, and another teacher stood at his left holding a basket of buttonhole red roses for the boys. As Mr. Williams called out each name (alternating between boys and girls), there was mighty applause. With one hand we girls accepted the diploma and with the other the long-stemmed rose. The boys only had to accept the diploma; the teacher pinned the rose in the buttonhole of their jackets.

As each of us honor students marched up to accept our diplomas, there was a pause as Mr. Williams made a short speech about us and told our class rank. I was third on the list. The applause seemed thunderous for us honor graduates. I felt my eyes filling up with tears and was determined not to make a spectacle of myself. I felt the blood rushing to my cheeks and was so angry that I never could control blushing. My brother remarked later, "You were as red as a beet."

After it was over, the audience was invited to stay for dancing. Portable benches were removed to make room for it. A boy who was home from college came up and asked me for the first dance. Previously I had had a "crush" on him, and I was so overwhelmed that I was tongue-tied. I sought out my proud parents and handed them my rose, kid gloves, and diploma. I was so clumsy and really did not know how to dance, even though I'd taken lessons some years before and my brother and I often practiced in our parlor when one of the girls played the piano.

Even though I was not a good dancer, it did not seem to matter to him. He was tolerant and talked while I was trying to control my feet so that my new white pumps would not get marked. He asked me if I were going to college. I said "Of course," as if it had already been decided. As yet my father had not given his permission, nor had I even applied to any college. When he asked where I'd be going, I had to admit I didn't know.

After the dance, my parents were waiting for me. They were surrounded by a small crowd of customers from the store, who all congratulated my parents as well as me. On the walk home, I could feel they were bursting with pride, not so much at my graduation, for that was expected, but at the star beside my name on the program. "Why didn't you tell us?" asked my father. They just did not believe that it was as much a surprise to me as to them.

It had now turned into a pleasant, balmy evening. Stumbling along in the uncomfortable pumps, I held onto my mother's arm for support. As my father walked beside us, he said "If that is the case, then I guess Mr. Williams is right—you'd better go to college." I stopped in the middle of the street and hugged and kissed them both, forgetting that this display of delight and emotion was ordinarily confined to the home.

"But," said he, "It won't be Sargent's College just because you are a good swimmer and ball player. If you are going to get a good education—which is what you say you want more than anything in the world—then Mr. Williams told me where to send you. That is Simmons College in Boston."

I knew all about Sargent's College in Cambridge as I had secretly sent for the catalog. I knew it was co-educational, which was very much in its favor, but I hadn't heard about Simmons. I decided, however, that Mr. Williams knew what was best for me.

"Anywhere. . . . anywhere was fine—just to get out of Plymouth," I thought to myself. I was so ecstatic I could hardly sleep that night. I could hardly wait until morning to tell my classmates, especially my best friend, Tibbie. I knew Mrs. Morton would be happy, for she knew how determined I was to go off to college.

But I had quite a summer ahead of me. Aunt Ida was going to try to persuade my parents not to send me to college, and I was going to defend myself most vehemently.

Sue Sadow stands in front of her home at 29 Russell St. in Plymouth, Massachusetts. Built by Max Sadow in 1912-13.

Sue Sadow, 16 years old, holds her high school graduation diploma.
She wears long white kidskin gloves.

Chapter 15
OVERCOMING AUNT IDA

On a lovely May afternoon in 1913, when I was a senior in high school, my Aunt Ida from Boston suddenly arrived at my parents' clothing store in Plymouth. Mother was very excited about her arrival, as we were a closely knit family who always greeted visiting relatives warmly. Mother arranged to leave our store early so she could have a good visit with Aunt Ida. She was instinctively worried by Aunt Ida's sudden appearance, hoping that she was not the bearer of bad news.

When I arrived home from school that day with my friend Tibbie, I was surprised to find Mother already at home entertaining Aunt Ida in the parlor. With much apprehension, I wondered why she had come all the way from Boston, 40 miles away, in the middle of the week. The trains did not run often during the week, and I wondered if she had come to stay for a few days because of some trouble in her family. My mother looked worried. Aunt Ida was smiling as I entered the room.

"Aren't you going to kiss your Aunt Ida and make her welcome?" my mother asked. I went over and embraced her halfheartedly, remembering Aunt Ida and her quirks and her "swoons" from times when I had visited in her home during vacations.

Aunt Ida's daughter, Helen, was my own age, and I had begged to spend the holidays with her one year, even though she gave me a good deal to envy with her petite frame, blonde hair, blue eyes, and clear skin. I was skinny and dark-haired and so tall that my older brother teasingly called me "bean pole."

My boy cousins in Aunt Ida's family also humiliated me further by calling me "farmerke" (the little farmer) because I came from the small country town of Plymouth. They probably weren't even sure what a farmer really was, but because Plymouth was much smaller than Boston, they liked to tease me.

It was during this visit that I discovered what my family meant when they laughingly said Aunt Ida "swooned" when she couldn't get her way. Aunt Ida, who loved to boast about her side of the family and their connections in Boston society, always wanted to look as regal as possible.

One day I caught her admiring herself in front of the full-length mirror in the bedroom. I stood still, entranced by her lovely dress and its long train. She turned around as she saw me in the mirror.

"Why are you looking at me, my little farmerke?" she asked, piercingly repeating that humiliating nickname. I became tongue-tied with fear at being caught. "Doesn't your mother look in a mirror?" she persisted.

"We don't have a looking glass like that," I answered truthfully. "We have a small mirror on the bedroom dresser. Mama looks in it when she combs her hair, and sometimes I stand on a chair and look in it."

At noon the same day, Uncle Simon (Aunt Ida's husband and my mother's brother) came up from the store downstairs for dinner, which was prepared by the maid. "The girl" (as my father called their maid, who also served as a nanny) had set the table and rung the bell to summon the children to dinner.

"Where's your auntie?" asked Uncle Simon.

"I don't know. I saw her earlier in your bedroom," I said.

"Here I am, " called out Aunt Ida cheerfully, wearing the regal dress with the train and standing close to a big chair in the parlor.

"Where in heaven's name did you get that dress?" he demanded angrily, his face turning red.

"Never mind where I got it. It's for the wedding in my family. Do you like it?" She smiled as she struck a pose beside the chair and then leaned toward Uncle Simon to show off her bosom in the low-cut dress. She did indeed look like a queen!

"It must have cost a fortune," thundered Uncle Simon. "Take if off before it gets ruined. It's for an heiress," he said, almost plaintively. "I can't afford anything like that."

"Oh . . . Simon, Simon." Her voice started growing weaker as she braced herself against the huge upholstered chair. She seemed to be swaying and losing her balance. We all ran to help her before she fell to the floor. I feared she might die, but my cousins and the maid were accustomed to her episodes, and they went to get her a glass of water and to wring out a napkin with cold water to place on her forehead.

Soon she opened her eyes, and looking up said feebly, "What happened?"

"It's all right, my love," said Uncle Simon, comforting her. "Take off the dress, and we'll have dinner."

Later that day I heard the maid laughingly tell the weekly wash woman, "She swooned again. That's how she gets what she wants."

All these memories of my extravagant Aunt Ida, her fashionable parties with fine food, her lovely dresses, her swooning, and—most of all—her way of humiliating me, suddenly loomed in front of me. As a result, I had trouble giving Aunt Ida a warm welcome because I kept wondering why she had arrived so unexpectedly in our home.

After we had exchanged brief greetings, my mother said to me "Wouldn't you like to set the table for supper? It must be getting late, and Papa will be coming home." I was about to leave the room when Aunt Ida stopped me. "Don't go. There's something I want to talk to you about."

I paused. "What is it?"

"Well," she said with a practiced smile and the sweetest possible tone of voice, "we're all so proud of you now that you will soon be graduating from high school."

"Yes," I answered positively, adding, "And then, best of all, I'm going off to college."

Her smile disappeared. "You are? Whatever for?"

"Because I want to get more education and see the world," I said with assurance, suddenly realizing Aunt Ida had come to Plymouth for something more than a family visit.

"A **girl** get more education? Why? Don't you want to get married and have children?"

"What has that to do with getting an education and doing some good in the world?" I argued.

"That is for **men** to do. A **girl** gets married and raises a family."

"But all girls aren't alike. Our high school principal even told my father to send me to college." I could feel the anger rising within me. I wondered what business it was of hers if I went to college and why she had come to make trouble.

"Listen, my dear," she said with a smile spreading across her face, "you must be reasonable and not put your father and mother to so much trouble and expense. Don't you realize how hard they work to bring you all up respectably? Don't you think they should be spared the worry and expense of a girl away from home? Don't you feel that now that you are getting through high school you should stay and help them and not run off for your own pleasure while your mother slaves to keep you in school? What will college get you? You may even get to be an old maid and never marry at all."

My mother sat quietly listening, not saying a word. I wondered if they had already discussed my going away to college before I came home. As this flashed through my head, Aunt Ida continued, "Why do you have to be different from all the others in the family? No other girls ever went off to college. If you go to college and get all those big ideas of being better than anybody else, you will make your mother feel that she is a nothing—a nobody while you set yourself up on a pedestal, thinking you are better than everyone else."

At that point, I could no longer control my temper. "Who are you to criticize someone else? You only came to make trouble, not to help me or my family. Does that mean everyone else's family has to follow the example you set? You always call me 'farmer' when I come to visit you. If you don't want your girls to go to school, that's your business. My father has the right to send me to college. We 'farmers' know what's good for us, and we don't need relatives coming down from Boston to tell us what to do," I finished angrily.

Mother was shocked, and Aunt Ida was too startled to move or respond, but I was just getting started. "You talk about my mother working hard, but what do **you** know? You never did a lick of work in your life. You are always making Uncle Simon slave to get you whatever you want and staging those silly 'swoons' if he disagrees. Our family is so different. We **like** to be educated. My principal told my father I was too smart just to be wasted in the store. He told my father to send me to college so I can get a **good** education and do some good in the world. My father knows what to do for us children, and if he thinks it is best for me to go to college, then he doesn't need any advice from the rest of the family!"

By that time I was truly hysterical and hardly able to control my trembling body or voice, but I continued while my dumbfounded aunt was still trying to find her voice to interrupt. "I've always helped with the younger children and also in the store," I said. "My mother will tell you how responsible I've always been. I'll keep helping out all my life even if I do go to college because I love my family and would never think I was better than any of them. Anyone with sense would know that! Only you don't know what's best for everyone, and now you're trying to keep me from going to college."

I was crying uncontrollably at that point. My poor mother tried in vain to calm me. Since her husband and her family were not there to help Aunt Ida, she didn't dramatize a swoon. All she did was to sit up stiffly in her chair, turning paler and paler. A relative had finally gathered up the courage to tell her off for the first time in her life.

Completely losing control, I kept screaming over and over, "Nobody is going to prevent me from leaving Plymouth. I will run away to Boston and make my own life. I **will** go to college!"

Mother had never seen me exhibit such a temper before. She tried to calm me down, and I went out to the yard behind our house. I sat under the peach trees where I could not easily be found and continued to cry and cry.

I pondered how long Aunt Ida had controlled the lives of the family, and if I would be doomed to a life in Plymouth working in the store and waiting for a husband. I feared I had disgraced the whole family, as they would hear how disrespectful I had been to a grownup—one of the worst disgraces in that day. I feared that my parents, too, would be disgraced for raising such a headstrong girl. I took some consolation in knowing that my father, who had always disliked Aunt Ida, would be on my side.

I decided to knock on our neighbors' door and ask for my friend Tibbie. Seeing my swollen eyes and tear-stained cheeks, Tibbie's mother asked me to come in. She took me into their parlor and gave me a clean handkerchief. She was so kind and gentle, and soon my sobs stopped and I felt much better. She invited me to stay for supper and to stay overnight with Tibbie. Then she sent Tibbie's little sister to fetch Tibbie and also to give my mother the message about my staying for supper and overnight at their house.

After supper, Tibbie and I took a long walk in the spring dusk, and I poured out all my troubles to her. We both decided that I was right in thinking Aunt Ida had no right to dictate my life. My father **did** know what was best for me, and the principal had even given him the name of a college in Boston where he thought I should go.

The next day I learned my father was openly delighted that someone had finally had the courage to tell Aunt Ida off. The next morning, knowing about the scene between her and me (which really proved to be a turning point in my life), he put her on the train and waved her off. Both were smiling and on good terms. Aunt Ida was convinced that she would have her way and prevent my going away to college.

At our house, though, my father teased my mother, "So it took my daughter to tell your sister-in-law that for once she couldn't have her way! Why didn't she swoon? Was it because there wasn't anyone to pick her up?"

All my mother would say was, "Stop it, Max. Enough is enough. Get to work."

Later, when I was actually in college, no relative could have been prouder of me and my academic accomplishments than Aunt Ida was. Whenever I spent weekends at their home, she would purr as she introduced me as "the daughter of my husband's sister, Celia, from Plymouth—the college girl in our family. **We're all so very proud of her.**"

I always suspected that she got a thrill out of presenting me to her friends because it gave her prestige to be the aunt of a college student. In a few short years, I had progressed from being referred to as "farmer" to being joyously introduced in Boston social circles as "our college girl."

Chapter 16
OFF TO COLLEGE

The Plymouth High School graduation was over. Both my parents attended, as it was in the evening and the store was closed. I learned later in life that it was not only household and business duties that kept them from attending various functions but also that they felt embarrassed—afraid they would not know how to act.

Their only social contact with "gentiles" was in business with the customers. Although my father was popular with the selectmen on the various boards of the town and attended many meetings, that was different from social functions. So concerned was my mother about conforming to all the behavior patterns of the gentiles that she was often referred to by our relatives as the "Yankee."

After graduation, Mr. Williams told my father of this wonderful college in Boston where students learned how to be a scientifically trained housewife besides getting a wonderful academic education for a profession. "If the time ever comes when she would have to earn her own living, then she'd have the training for it," he said.

This seemed to appeal to my father because it was practical, but he admitted he still had misgivings about sending me to college because we were Jews and Jews believed in marriage. He said he feared that, if I went to college, I would be a teacher and most of the teachers in Plymouth were old maids.

I had set my heart on Sargent's School, where I had heard one could get a good training in physiotherapy. It was also the nearest thing to training in medicine, and I wanted to be near a certain boy who was at medical school. It was my idea to spend the rest of my life helping people as well as keep up all my athletic interests. I was an excellent athlete, and I thought I could perfect myself there.

The decision had to be made soon because the application deadline was nearing. My father informed me of his conversations with Mr. Williams. He said I could go to college on one condition: that I chose Home Economics at Simmons College. It was that or nothing.

Well, I gave in, thinking once I got there I could transfer to any school I wanted and he'd never know the difference . . . so thought I! I felt very brave and secure and yet my heart was filled with fear and worry. I had won—I was going to college, but I had many fears, which I dared not mention to anyone. What would it be like in a huge college away from home? How would I know how to study? What if I should fail? How do college girls dress? How do you behave at college? How is it different from high school? How do you make friends?

The high school principal showed my father how to make all the arrangements for my entering Simmons. Because I was an honor student, I was excused from taking any entrance exams. Also since my grades were close to "A" all four years, I never had to take a single test or exam. The only exam Simmons required of every student was a routine arithmetic exam. Since I was good at math, I was sure I would pass and did not worry.

It was a great relief to know that my future was settled, most of all to know that I would "get out of Plymouth." My status suddenly zoomed in the town because very few youngsters from Plymouth went to college. It was regarded as an "honor."

My older brother must have boasted about his sister going off to college. He worked in the store, but the way he behaved anyone would have thought he was the proprietor (which he eventually became). He presented me with the most beautiful china tea set, six sterling silver teaspoons, all on a large white papiermaché tray, and also a beautiful pair of bookends. I suppose someone must have advised him that this was appropriate for a college girl. He himself never finished high school because he preferred entering the business. However, he had a great respect for higher education.

All summer long on the street, in the store, or on the beach, everyone greeted me approvingly . . . "So, you'll be going off to college!" Everyone was so proud of me; all the Boston relatives boasted about me, for I was the first to achieve such heights. I had always been the little country cousin. Suddenly they spoke to me with respect in their tones. I tried so hard to act nonchalantly as if it were an ordinary occurrence in my life, but the romance of "going off to college" really scared me because I didn't know what to expect.

Chapter 17
CHALLENGES AT COLLEGE

Simmons College, where I went from 1913 to 1917, was designed to prepare every young woman to earn a living in her chosen field upon graduation. There were schools that prepared students in their chosen field of work and also included courses in the liberal arts to guarantee a well-rounded education for students in Business Administration, Nursing, Science, Social Work, Library Science, and Home Economics.

I chose the School of Home Economics. The autumn I entered college, we were having Indian summer in Boston. It was so hot, and I tried to cover up how miserable, how strange, and how insecure I felt.

Registration was a special misery! How could anyone remember all those rooms? I had never been in such a large building before. All those laboratories and that odor: what was it? When I registered for chemistry, I had heard the word chemistry but had not the foggiest notion what it really was. I had never seen a lab before and wondered if I would have to work in those smelly places.

When I registered for physics, a required subject, I trembled. What was THAT? For me it had another meaning: medication! In English, a theme every night was the assignment, but this did not worry me too much because I used to love to write little stories. One hundred pages was assigned every night on the history of Western Europe. For the household management course . . . well, I had plenty of experience cleaning our big house, so I felt "at home."

Almost all the freshmen girls had somebody with them. Parents came to see that they were all right and to help them get settled. The girls were from all over the U.S.A. My parents could not afford the time to leave home because the store had to be tended. I was by myself and was really scared, and I remained scared all through my freshman year.

Everyone tried to be nice and kind to me. A junior "sister" and a senior "sister" were assigned to each freshman to guide us and help us get adjusted. This was wonderful, except I feared they would find that I was a little girl from the country who did not know how to behave. Therefore I resisted and refused all their invitations, giving all sorts of excuses why I could not attend any of the "teas" they gave for us to get acquainted. I had never been to a "tea" in my life. Even though I wanted to attend, not knowing what to do prevented me from going.

Those first months remain a nightmare to this very day, so deep was the emotion from which I suffered. I wandered about those long corridors, hunting for the rooms in which my classes were held. My whole freshman year was filled with dread of failing. I didn't know where I could go to hide if I failed, and furthermore I feared my father would never be able to hold his head up again in the town because of my "disgrace." I was so worried and filled with anguish that I wished I had never even tried to go to college. I was comfortable in Plymouth and felt perhaps I should have stayed there. At college I felt very insecure and didn't know what to do. Because I was afraid to take advantage of available means of help, I had to maintain a "front" by myself.

One thing I was good at was making friends with classmates. It was a consolation to find other girls as scared as I was. Mary Parker, the only Negro in the entire school, became my pal. Because of the spelling of our names, she was always seated next to me in all our courses. That was most reassuring, for in the labs she was so helpful. She was the most brilliant girl in our class, and she was generous and helpful. We often studied together; everything came easily to her. She was living in Roxbury with a white family, who brought her up from the South. The man had been principal of the school she attended and recognized this girl's brilliance, so he "put her through Simmons." There were no scholarships in our school in those days. We were both good athletes and were on the freshman teams for several sports.

Athletics, I think, is what saved me both physically and mentally. I adored the outdoors and never had to worry about excelling in athletics. Being on our college teams gave me prestige with my classmates and made me popular, which was what I desperately wanted.

I will always remember--with gratitude--our dear Professor Norris, in chemistry, who also taught at MIT. He was so kind. I must have looked like a scared rabbit all the time, for he never called upon me in class until he had explained things so simply that he was sure I knew the answers. I was not afraid of him. I had a terrible "crush" on him. He often helped me after class in his office, where we were invited to come if we had any questions and needed extra help.

I took advantage of every offer in each course for I wanted so much to understand and not fail. In the chemistry lab, Professor Norris never failed to come to my desk to encourage me. I think he must have been glad that the brilliant Mary Parker was also at my side. It seems everyone wanted me to succeed.

PHYSICS! I plowed through the assignments. I never understood one word! At the lab I was even more miserable than in chemistry. What saved me was the young instructor who came over from Harvard to teach the course. Mr. Schaeffer (I even remember his name and exactly how he looked) had the largest brown eyes and the most awful skin, marked by acne. I was sympathetic to him for I suffered from the same condition, which was embarrassing and made me very self-conscious.

He was fairly tall, skinny, shy, and blushed easily. There was a girl in our class who was far more sophisticated than the rest of us small-town girls. She boasted about how she knew how to make him blush, which she did very successfully. When she did this flirtatious act, he always turned his back to write on the blackboard, but we could still see how red his neck was above his collar due to the embarrassment caused by this young rich girl from the city. She always boasted that she would get married, but if she did not like it, then she would get a divorce! I'll never forget how shocked I was. Marriage, as far as I was concerned, was forever. Divorce! That was the most scandalous thing I'd ever heard. Nobody who had any self-respect did a thing like that!

I used to frequent the offices of all the teachers who offered help, and they were so kind and patient. I believe they all noticed my insecurity, which was my "cross to bear" that first year. The worst of it was that I had to put on a good front at home and give positive assurance to everyone who inquired about the "college girl." It was such a novelty in those days for relatives in Plymouth and Boston.

Another item that frightened me to death was the "blue card" system of informing students who were doing poorly in their studies. These were posted every six weeks on the main bulletin board where we ordinarily picked up our messages. I used to literally "haunt" this board, feeling sure I'd get one. It was such a terrible public announcement, and if I ever got one, I'd feel so disgraced! My junior year, I finally got one blue card notice in a millinery course, but it was at a time when I was a well-adjusted and secure student. We had to make hats from scratch, from the buckram frame, covering it with velvet and trimming. I got a D on the lab work. I'll never forget that brown velvet broad-brimmed hat with the feather ornament on the front of the tall crown! When I wore it home to Plymouth for a weekend, my brother Lawrence, who was the comedian of the family, stared smilingly at me and said, "Where did you get that hat? It looks just like John Alden!" And as a matter of fact, it did. However, it matched my lovely brown suit with the beaver collar that my father had chosen for me, one I wore with pride.

Then came mid-year exams! I had never heard of such a thing! I feared this would be my undoing. How could one ever cover all we had learned and remember it? Then, another thing that scared me was the HONOR SYSTEM. How would I ever be able to squeal on anyone cheating if I saw them? Best never to see, I decided. So I sat stiffly in the exam room, never once lifting my eyes from the exam book. With my New England conscience I knew I'd have to tell IF I saw, so I made certain I didn't see. Butterflies never left my insides the entire ten days of exams.

When exams were over, I usually took several girls home to Plymouth to celebrate and forget the agony. My brothers were on hand to join us in many outdoor activities.

At that time, there were about four Jewish girls in the college of about 1,100 students, which made us conspicuous as well as insecure. Few of the students had ever known or encountered a Jewish girl before, and there was much curiosity and prejudice.

Ever since I had known I was going to to college, clothes had been a great worry to me. The summer before I left for college, my father brought all kinds of beautiful blouse "samples" from his weekly store-buying trips in Boston. I had not yet worn skirts! I suspected he boasted about his "college daughter," and perhaps these salesmen advised him what would be appropriate for me. After all, the salesmen were city folk.

Anyhow, when I looked around and saw what the other girls wore at college, I was satisfied with mine. I got my first "Peter Thompson," a navy wool skirt and navy blouse to match, which was all authentically made out of the best serge. I wore this proudly and happily the whole four years.

The other girls in my dorm enjoyed borrowing from my wardrobe, which continued to be well-stocked from our store and from my father's buying trips. The clothes got worn, even if I did not wear them very much.

My horizons were broadening! The big city of Boston offered so many wonderful advantages. I used to go "downtown," and I got manicures for 50 cents. I was introduced to Schrafft's and Bailey's, where we devoured chocolate sundaes with nuts and whipped cream, challenging each other to order a second one! They were so good.

We went to matinees. I was introduced to the Boston Symphony Orchestra. We used to cut the Friday afternoon classes and dash for the streetcar to Boston Symphony Hall to get in line for the student tickets in the balcony for 25 cents. Then there was the Boston Art Museum, with the sculpture of the Indian on horseback. How I used to stand in front of this and recall the statue of the great Indian Chief Massasoit on Cole's Hill in Plymouth. My anger would assert itself all over again, for I felt the white man had been so unjust to the Indians who tried to help them even though the white men had taken their land. These early emotions cling to this very day, and throughout a lifetime I've been very vocal in defense of American Indians.

The next three years rolled away too quickly. I had "caught on" and began to understand what college was all about. Fear left me. I had one desire: to do well and get as much out of college as I could.

I was learning so much. Now I was enjoying lab work. I took all the courses allowed and was beginning to decide just what I'd do with my education. There were so many possibilities, I could hardly wait to get out in the world.

Should I be a bacteriologist? I took all the courses necessary for me to get a job. One thing I was certain about was I did not want to be a teacher. Was it my father's fear of "old maidhood" that got to me? What were the other possibilities? All my life I had worried about the poor, about the injustices that were heaped upon them. All my life I had thought about the necessity of helping people who needed help. Perhaps I could work in places where I could be of help . . . of service.

Then came graduation, when I was 20 years old. The long-awaited day, when a junior would turn my cap tassel over to the right, as I marched with all my senior classmates in the procession. That was the custom. That was the thrill. For the placement of that tassel meant that now I was a privileged graduate with a sheepskin and a degree!!!

Only my mother came to the graduation, as both she and father could not be spared from the store at the same time. I ran around in my cap and gown greeting all my friends and guests whom we had invited for the great occasion. I was full of pep, cheerful, and the center of attention wherever I went, as everyone usually wanted to hear the story of my most recent adventures.

My mother was just beaming with pride when I spied my physics instructor, now a Ph.D. "Mother, come with me!" I dragged her over to meet Dr. Schaeffer. "You must meet the professor who literally pushed me through physics. If it were not for him and all the help and encouragement he gave me that horrible freshman year, neither you nor I would be here today!"

As in bygone days, he blushed crimson and denied it. But I insisted, telling him I would always remember his help and encouragement—that it would be a lesson to me when I got out into the world and could help people.

I felt relieved that at last I had told him how I really felt about him. My mother beamed and thanked him for doing this for me. I have carried this gratitude in my heart all my life.

It is experiences like this that molded my thinking, emotions, and character and motivated me to go into social work. I seemed to be obsessed with the idea. I believe also that it had a lot to do with my unpopularity with men. I did not have many dates. I was painfully shy and tongue-tied in their presence. With a group I was so talkative and full of stories and always had a good listening audience. But alone with men, I was not comfortable.

My skin, constantly under treatment, was the horror of my life. My parents consulted every conceivable source to get help, but it just would not clear up for several years after college. I wonder if young people today with bad cases of acne suffer as much from inferiority as I did.

In my senior year, I was working out courses I wanted to take. I was told that there was one course in education that was compulsory. I had quite a battle with my advisor, and insisted that I did not need any points in education, for I knew I would never teach, but this course was a requirement for graduation.

What should I do? Then I was informed that field work was a part of the course, and that I had been requested for field work by Lincoln House, one of the worst slum settlements in the south end of Boston.

Miss Marjorie Foster, who was a Simmons graduate, was in charge of home economics activities at this house. She had observed me the past year when I was helping a senior teach a class of children of the "foreign born" (as they used to be labeled in those days). She thought it would be an excellent experience for me to teach a class of parents in the evenings. She thought I knew Yiddish, and these people had had no chance to learn anything about the American foods that their children needed if they were to grow up to be healthy Americans.

Would I be interested? WOULD I! Also I was flattered to think that I had been noticed and was requested! I signed up for the course. All the girls on my floor of the dormitory heard the news "straight from the horse's mouth" (as we used to say).

In those days we were not allowed out unchaperoned after 6 p.m., so arrangements were made for a graduate student (who lived in our dorm) to accompany me to the streetcar. She would tell the conductor exactly where to let me off and make sure that the person from Lincoln House was there to meet the car.

When it was time for me to return to Simmons, Miss Foster was there to walk through the long dark street (Fenway) with me. She would also telephone my dorm to tell them exactly when I was supposed to arrive at the stop. This graduate student was not many years my senior. The Fenway, even in those days, was not considered the safest place. We were admonished to travel in groups going back and forth to college during the day! Of course, living in Plymouth, where streets were dark, and having to pass so many alleys, I had no fear of anything. I often wondered how this young lady felt, waiting for my car to arrive, especially on rainy nights or when it was cold. This entire experience made me feel grown up and very important, since no such permission had ever been given in all the college's history.

As soon as I got to Lincoln House, the first thing I did was get into uniform. In all the courses in cookery (elementary and advanced), we had to wear a white uniform. It consisted of a stiffly starched white dress with long sleeves, white stockings, white shoes (I always wore high white buckskin shoes), an apron of special design with bib and a belt that fastened at the back. Our uniforms came almost to our ankles.

Fastened around our waistlines on a tape was a hand towel and white felt-like potholders, which we made. They were so practical because we could wash and starch these every week to maintain our pure white appearance.

There is something to be said for a uniform. It made you feel and look so professional that no one would ever think of arguing with you or disputing your expert knowledge. It made such an impression on me that when I'd be home in Plymouth for the summer, I would put on this uniform before doing any cooking. It gave me status! It also kept me at the ironing board during those terribly hot and humid days. But how could you cook a meal unless you were in uniform? The only one who had a sense of humor about this was my dear brother Lawrence, who would do "take-offs" on Simmons College cooking. I would get furious if anyone else dared to criticize the college, but Lawrence was so full of humor that all my anger was diffused in laughter.

At Lincoln House, I stood before my class in my uniform. Often the classes were attended by fathers as well as mothers. Later in life, I realized that this was the only recreation they ever had. Their little girls were so proud that their parents were learning to become Americanized by learning about American foods such as hot cocoa, one of the "American breakfast musts."

I demonstrated at least two or three food dishes and also emphasized hygiene in the kitchen . . . the type of pots to use, etc. I eagerly shared everything I had learned or was learning.

The problem was communication. They knew practically no English, and although Miss Foster thought I "knew" Yiddish, she didn't know that my vocabulary was restricted to the few words I had heard at home when my parents wanted to communicate with each other but did not want us to understand.

I made up words as I went along, putting what I thought was a Yiddish accent on English words. I often used words I had heard. Dressed in my professional-looking stiffly starched uniform, I was so serious about it that no one would venture to question my expertness.

One evening, while I was talking and holding up the demonstration dishes for all to see, I ventured upon a Yiddish word I had heard many times, but not at home, which seemed to me so impressive. The parents all looked at each other in surprise. Then one burst into laughter and kept laughing so loudly that Miss Foster came running into the room to find out what had happened.

They were rocking with laughter, with tears running down their cheeks. I learned later that I had used one of the most vulgar swear words in the Yiddish language—an expression suitable only for hoodlums on the street. But I thought I was speaking Yiddish! Hadn't Miss Foster told them I was Jewish and knew the language?

The parents adored me and never missed a class. I furnished them with sufficient amusing stories to relate to others. I told them firmly they could never hope to become good Americans unless they started the day with an American breakfast. I believed this from my Simmons classes. But later, when I taught evening classes on Americanization in New York, I modified my approach.

This evening field work so impressed my dorm floormates that they were all waiting to hear about my experiences in the slums.

Not one of them had ever seen a slum or been in contact with foreigners. The more they egged me on, the more elaborate my accounts became, as there was no one to verify my accuracy. Word spread about my unique field experience. By teaching so many subjects to the poor as a senior, I was already preparing for a career in social work.

Sue Sadow, Age 20, Class of 1917, Simmons College

PART III

CAREER

LIFE

Chapter 18
MY FIRST JOB—SUMMER OF 1917

At Simmons College I was graduated from the School of Home Economics, which prepared one for a wide variety of choices.

Before graduation, opportunities for jobs in various fields were posted on the bulletin boards, with dates and rooms where recruitment would be taking place. There would be a teacher in charge to be present at the explanation and interviews.

Our department invited those of us who were interested to report. Several of us showed up on the reviewing date.

Mrs. Gardner was introduced, a handsome gray-haired lady, exquisitely dressed in a lavender linen outfit, who smilingly welcomed us. She was obviously a "blue blood" of one of Boston's privileged families. She was recruiting girls for jobs at Health Home, located in Coney Island, New York. She explained it was a vacation home for underprivileged mothers and children from the slums of New York City that provided them with a two-week vacation at the seaside, where they could breathe clean, cool air and have a daily swim, while the children could play in the sand at the private beach. The first two weeks were devoted to the program for mothers and babies. Since the capacity was 400, the guests were referred to as the "400." She herself had been chosen by the Board of Directors of the Children's Aid Society of New York as this year's director.

The rest of the summer was devoted to two-week shifts for children age 6-14. It filled a great need for children to get away from the crowded conditions of their homes in the filthy slums of New York and the unbearable heat.

Mrs. Gardner appealed to the missionary spirit of all of us, helping the poor and underprivileged. Just what I had always dreamed of! With my fieldwork classes at the settlement houses of Boston, I felt I was qualified and fully prepared. Simmons had prepared me for my whole life's work. "Going out into the world and upholding the honor of Simmons" was what was emphasized on special occasions during our senior year. I felt I was ready. I was strong and full of energy. I had proved it by being a good athlete! Of course, I would not mind working day and night and having only one day off a month! There were several categories of jobs from which to choose, and Mrs. Gardner thought I would make a perfect "dormitory supervisor." Think of it: already I was a supervisor!

I could hardly wait for the weekend, when I could dash home to Plymouth and tell the folks <u>I already had a job</u>! At supper that evening the family hung on every word as I described how I had been selected for the job as "dormitory supervisor." I had no idea of the responsibilities or what it meant. My father was extremely quiet. I knew beforehand that he would not approve: too far away from home. He did not know anything about the place. Coney Island and New York had a bad reputation as far as Boston was concerned. I thought he should be proud and happy that already I had been chosen to be a "supervisor." Then came the bomb-shell—"And how much will you earn for being this supervisor?"

I was shocked. Who worries about "earning"? The principal thing was, I had a job. I was disturbed the whole weekend. Mrs. Gardner was due the following week for another interview, when definite arrangements would be made.

How could I ask her about "wages"? I had not yet learned about "salary." What did it matter? I had already said I would take the job. When Mrs. Gardner came to explain the details and make final arrangements, I meekly asked about our wages. She smiled and said, "Of course that is important." This was a charitable institution, and they operated on a very small budget. Health Home was only one of its many projects for helping the poor. Even she, the Director, was paid no salary. The pay for a dormitory supervisor was $16.00 a month and full expenses for board and room. Yes, we would have to pay our own fare to New York and the fare to Coney Island, which, after all, was only a nickel. We would have one day off a month.

The date was fixed when we were supposed to report for duty. We would prepare the premises in readiness to receive our guests, the mothers and babies.

I dashed home again for the weekend to inform my father of

the $16.00 a month with room and board, but assured him he could not prevent me from going as I had already accepted and would not go back on my word!

I'll never forget the expression on his face—it really was all tenderness, that smile under his moustache. All he said was, "$16.00 a month. Why, I believe that will pay for your ice cream sodas!"

It was decided that my mother would accompany me to see what kind of a place Health Home was.

Graduation over, Mother and I were on the train to New York. There had been an exchange of letters with her sister Rose in Newark, New Jersey. Aunt Rose (whom my mother had brought to America with her when they were still children) visited us every summer with at least two of her brood of five children, as Plymouth was considered a vacation resort for city dwellers. My mother had not been anywhere outside of Boston and Rochester, New York, where she became an expert button-hole maker in her cousin's men's tailor-made clothing factory soon after she arrived in Boston as a 15-year-old immigrant.

We were met at Grand Central Station in New York and immediately went to Newark by train. All my cousins were so proud of me and boasted to their friends—"a college graduate, so unaffected, not even stuck up" they impressed on all their neighbors.

Aunt Rose accompanied my mother and me to Coney Island, where she had never been herself, although she was always referred to in Boston as a "New Yorker." Both sisters were dressed alike in costumes my mother made during our visit—white cotton blouses and black taffeta skirts—to be appropriately dressed to meet Mrs. Gardner.

Mrs. Gardner, the epitome of a high-class Yankee, greeted them cordially and showed them around the premises. She assured my mother I would be well cared for and my room was next to her suite, which had been prepared for her and her two young daughters in one of the new buildings. My mother swelled with pride and went back to Boston satisfied.

Health Home consisted of a number of low buildings built around a large sandy sort of playground. It was right on the beach, but a very high wire fence, the full length of the property, with the sign, "PRIVATE PROPERTY," was designed to keep out anyone except our residents and staff. There was a tall door with a fixed lock to which only we, the staff, had the keys. The mothers could go in swimming at certain hours but were expected to remain on the premises all the time. Covered pavilions connected all the buildings, so that in case of rain everyone was protected. Also, there were places to sit all along these pavilions, and the mothers could wheel their baby carriages (which Health Home furnished for this purpose) the full length. Their dormitories were in a separate group of wooden buildings.

My job as Dormitory Supervisor was to assign the beds and space for the babies and the mothers and to make sure that the beds were dry and aired before making them up. The small children invariably were "bed wetters," and this entailed extra responsibilities. The mothers were supposed to wash their sheets when this was the case, and there was ample room to hang them out.

Those first two weeks were quite an eye-opener for me. The other staff members, composed of other Simmons girls and Barnard girls, had other assignments. I was "favored" by Mrs. Gardner; I suppose my being an "eager beaver" had something to do with it. I was so full of energy that nothing was too much. I was busy from the moment we got up at 6 a.m. until we put the guests to bed. I did manage after awhile to get in a swim. Coney Island boasted a beautiful beach.

From the Butterfield Pavilion, where my room was, I had a perfect view of what went on on the beach, when hordes of people of all nationalities, arriving on the subway from New York, took over. I'd never in my life seen such crowds. Everyone was enjoying the fresh air and picnics on the sand— with food of every imaginable smell. What fascinated me the most was the BEHAVIOR! The hugging and kissing that went on between young boys and girls was a shocker! I learned more about sex that summer than in all my life! How awful! How shocking! How unrefined! How tough! The more natural and abandoned and full of enjoyment they were, the TOUGHER I considered them. I had never seen young people abandoning themselves to happy enjoyment before and did not know how to evaluate it. Of course, we from Boston knew that New Yorkers were not the least bit refined; in fact they were considered vulgar. Their pronunciation of the English language puzzled us, and most of the time we did not even understand them. Our Barnard College junior, who was Mrs. G's secretary, was born in New York, and her accent was a little strange to me. We became bosom friends, and formed a beautiful friendship that has endured to this very day.

This was one of the most exciting summers of my whole life! I was independent and free! Everything was going just right for me. All the staff were my great friends; we did everything together. I worked myself to the bone. I took on additional duties and gladly did anything Mrs. G asked me to do. There was a problem about the formulas for the babies. I had so much knowledge about bacteriology and sanitation that, of course, I'd make up all the babies' formulas, refrigerate them, and pass them out all sterilized and heated when the mothers called for them at the little station that was set up for this purpose. Thus my hours were extended, and there were no rest periods for me. I'd never heard of a "rest period" in my whole life anyhow. Mrs. Gardner had her two young daughters with her for the summer. They were "different" and never socialized with us. We only came together for meals, as we all ate together in the staff dining room after the "guests" were fed.

But we DID EACH HAVE A DAY OFF! Wow! Where would we go? To New York, naturally! Three of us staff members together took that long subway ride in the intense heat. Our Barnard friend went with us the first time to "show us the ropes." How excited we were! How we thrilled to absolutely everything we saw. The people and how they were dressed fascinated us the most. Language? We could hardly understand their pronunciation, although we had learned a lot from the East Side foreign-born mothers, most of whom could hardly speak English.

I'll never forget my excitement over the FIFTH AVENUE BUSES OPEN ON TOP. We tried everything our meager wages permitted. One day, and I can't remember why, we miscalculated our finances. We had no intention of spending everything. It was already dark, and we were supposed to be back. We dashed into the subway: we had just enough for all of us except for a nickel. What to do? We all stuck together. OHO! it was I who had the big idea. I was wearing the gold ring my father had bought for my graduation. A ruby (my birthstone) in the center with diamonds on each side. They were all pretty good-sized stones. I'd ask the ticket seller at the booth if he'd take my ring for security and give us one ticket so that we could get home. I told him we could exchange names and addresses, which was the same as a "receipt" as far as I was concerned, and that the next time any of our staff went to New York, they would pay the nickel and he could give them the ring. I'll never forget the look on his face. He yelled, "Are you crazy? Do you want me to lose my job?" Needless to say, he let me crawl under the turnstile so that the fare would not be recorded, and that was how we got back to Coney Island.

All that summer, some of my relatives and their friends visited me every Sunday. Health Home furnished them with a place to spend Sundays away from the heat. My letters to everyone, and I was a prolific letter writer, were full of enthusiasm for this wonderful place. The following summer, I got jobs for a number of my Boston friends. All I had to do was recommend them to Mrs. Gardner.

Chapter 19
GO TO THE TOP

The live-in requirement of my job with the Federated Jewish Charities of Boston had its advantages. It was situated near the Boston Common, which bordered on the streets where the large department stores were. One of the stores was R.H. White and Company.

I had received my pay check. I needed new shoes for walking up the hills in the area and climbing iron steps and what always seemed endless flights to the top floors in the dark, smelly hallways to reach my clients. I needed comfortable low-heeled oxfords that I hoped would last me "forever." R.H. White's advertised in bold type a new shipment of English oxfords for $10.00. I cut the ad out of the paper, and I was merrily on my way to R.H.White's with enough cash in my handbag for the advertised shoes and to stop by Schrafft's for a yummy chocolate ice cream sundae and all the fixings of hot fudge, marshmallow or whipped cream, and a handful of walnuts. (I was introduced to this favorite delicacy in my freshman year at Simmons College. At that time we even gorged on two and skipped a proper lunch!)

They had my size in the advertised oxford. The shoes were stiff and would require a lot of "breaking in." The young salesman (he must have been a student from one of the colleges in which Boston abounded) was appreciative of the cash sale and smilingly wished me luck as he put the shoe box in an R.H. White paper bag.

It was a beautiful spring day. My desk was piled high with work, and I decided to go back to the office to tackle the load. After all, I didn't need any lunch.

I wore the shoes around the office to "break them in." I was glad to get into the old stretched-out shoes. I wore the new shoes once on a visit to clients in the tenement buildings I've described above. They were stiff and hurt me. I couldn't wait to get back to the office. I noticed that the leather had split near the lacing. Disappointedly, on the following Saturday I took them back to R.H. White's in the same box and with the credit slip. There was another student salesman. He offered to take the shoes back and have them repaired. This procedure went on for about four weeks, and I saw myself saddled with a practically new pair of shoes that the salesman graciously offered to have repaired so they would "look like new." After five Saturdays spent going and trying my best to wear the uncomfortable shoes, I decided it was a lost cause. No longer was I polite when I encountered the salesman. I took the shoes back to the department and demanded a refund. The salesman said he had no authority to give a refund and "if I would leave the shoes with the slip, he would arrange with the supervisor what satisfaction I was entitled to."

Angrily, I left the store, determined that I would never again trade at R.H. White's. They were deceptive as far as I was concerned.

A few days later, when I was in a calmer mood, I found out the name of the president of R.H. White's. After spending hours and filling the wastepaper basket in my attempt to compose a suitable letter, I was finally satisfied with what I had written. I addressed the envelope, put a stamp on it, and dashed out of the building to mail it before I could change my mind!

A week later, I found an official looking envelope among the pile of mail on my desk that greeted me upon my return from my morning's visit "in the field" and my food purchases for the evening lesson for parents on "meal preparation for an economical nutritional meal for a family of five." Neglecting the other mail, I tremblingly opened the letter from the R.H. White president's office, thinking the worst—that the president was offended by my recommendations of a change of policy in the treatment of customers. I believed that the appointment made with me was to discuss this matter. I was sure he would call my boss, Maurice Hexter, Director from Milwaukee, Wisconsin, of the Project of New Directions in Social Case Work, and that I would be fired from the job that had given me so much satisfaction.

Until the day of the appointment I was consumed with worry. I dressed carefully in what I thought made me look like a professional social worker, putting an extra polish on my old shoes. I regretted that I did not have new gloves. I took the elevator at R.H. White's to the 12th floor, where the bulletin board gave the names, titles, and locations of the officers.

Exactly on time, by the gold watch my parents had given me for a graduation present, I got out of the elevator at the 12th floor. I did not expect to see rows and rows of desks at which sat beautifully dressed young girls, each one groomed as if she had just come out of a beauty parlor, busily engaged in deciphering the notes she had taken in shorthand that morning in someone's office.

Suddenly, a pretty girl came out of an office and walked toward me. She looked as if she were going out on a date. She welcomed me and said the president was ready for me and my appointment. It was all so formal that I wished I had never written my letter of suggestions.

A tall, blue-eyed, gray-haired man walked toward me with both hands outstretched and greeted me as if I were a great friend. All the typewriters stopped while the girls stared. The president ushered me into his office, waved me to a very comfortable chair, and opened the conversation.

He was delighted to receive my letter. He was terribly sorry that I had had so much trouble, but the clerks were only following the "instructions" that they had received in training. He was impressed by my letter and the suggestions I had for the treatment of customers. We discussed these for a little less than an hour.

He wished more people would deal honestly with problems the way I had and call them to his attention so he could work out the necessary improvements.

I was very pleased and must have looked it. My box of shoes was on his desk. He said it was not a good purchase as they had had many returns and I had helped him make a right decision.

He wrote on official note paper to anyone who waited on me. They were to give me a pair of shoes from any shoes in stock, regardless of price, and, in addition, give me a pair of comfortable oxfords of my choice for all the time I had wasted on Saturdays. And he asked me if I thought that was a fair adjustment for me, the customer, for my time and aggravation. I was overwhelmed.

I described my experience over and over to friends and especially to my family. My young nephew learned after hearing the story that "Going to the Top" is saving not only your time but the time and energy of the busiest person in the organization and brings the matter to the attention of the right person without delay.

Chapter 20
ROARING TWENTIES

For those of us who were young then, this was the most important period of development of experience, personality, evaluation, learning, cultivation, social, educational concerns that New York City, rather than any other spot in the world, had to offer. Youth seemed to take advantage of everything. It was the style of living, and those of us who understood that this was a period that could never be repeated took advantage to the fullest. We became joiners. We knew the importance of being in good physical condition, and we learned to organize our time, day and night, so that every moment counted.

First, there were our jobs in social work. Much was taking place in development and modernization of various aspects of social work. A new language to express what was happening in the field sprang up, even though some among us taking courses at the New York School of Social Work did not understand what the experts were driving at. We took courses in Mental Hygiene, Psychiatry, Advances in Case Work, and Cash Relief. We tried out our new knowledge by participating in meetings. It seemed we were constantly attending meetings at which we learned to foist our new language on our "cases," when all the poor women as heads of households wanted was "the rent paid to prevent eviction when the landlord came." In exasperation they begged the case worker "today, please give me my rent and come next visit and I'll talk as much as you want."

Among the specialists that social agencies were now adding to their staffs were a new flock of experts, home economists. They banded together in determining what was the minimum cash relief needed by dependent families for their expenditures. It was called Family Budgeting. These experts devised methods for determining the minimum standards on which families could subsist.

When I was director of this service with the Department of Welfare of the City of New York, I recall arguing with the Director of the Budget about how many bags of coal per week a family in the walk-up tenements in the slums needed to keep from freezing to death during New York City's bitter winters.

Agencies from all over the country consulted the New York City group of Home Economists and learned about their methods. My office was besieged by the agencies' social case workers, who lined up for appointments seeking help for their cases on budgeting and management of their cash relief allowances. The "magic" of my conscientious study of the needs of Boston's immigrant poor was published in *The Family*, the social case work journal of November 1930. The sudden influx of inquiries as a result of this publication from agencies all over the country was overwhelming. It launched me on my career with self-confidence in my expertise.

This period of the "Roaring Twenties" had so much to offer the youth who broke away from traditional communities and participated in the advantages the Great City had to offer.

The job came first. To develop our expertise in our chosen profession, we sought out advanced courses in nutrition and large-scale food preparation at Teachers College, Columbia University, with Dr. Mary Swartz Rose, Dr. William Sherman, and Dr. Grace Macleod, among others. We took night courses. With the permission of our directors, we attended day courses at the New York School of Social Work. We attended all the conferences in our respective fields—local, state, and national.

We took advantage of every moment in order to learn! learn! learn! Many young people learned how to economize and to take advantage of sales in their attempt to shake all vestiges of conservative life in Boston. We even used to quote our little poem making fun of the New York accent in our attempt to understand how native New Yorkers spoke. Here is an example that was popular in my group of extended friendships in the circles I joined in my hunger to become a sophisticated New Yorker:

DOITY GOITY MOIPHY
SHE SOITONLY WAS A BOID
SHE LIVED ON TOITY SECOND STREET
RITE NEXT TO TOITY TOID
SHE READS DE NOIRK JOINAL
ALSO DE NOIRK WOILD
I SOITINLY LUV DOITY GOITY
WHEN GOITY'S HAIR IZ COILED!

My circle of friends increased in numbers and interests. The Atlantic Ocean in Plymouth had been my "swimming pool," and I joined swim clubs, modern dance clubs, poetry reading clubs. New York offered many cultural and intellectual opportunities, and I wanted to take advantage of everything I could.

We stood in line for hours to get cheap tickets for the Metropolitan Opera, and we learned how to get cheap tickets for every Saturday theater matinee. It was a great period for theater, and we were young and our hearing and eyesight were perfect. I remember, clothes crazy as I was, sketching on my program the dresses of the leading lady and dashing it off to my mother in Plymouth to copy and tell me how much material I needed! She was a designer par excellence!

We attended concerts in Carnegie Hall and found out where the acoustics were best and the tickets cheapest. We attended lectures in Town Hall and discussion groups afterwards.

We found out about the Algonquin Hotel, where the famous writers, actors, and actresses met, joining others milling around the lobby for just a glance at the famous, whom we had seen at performances. After seeing Scott Fitzgerald, famous for <u>The Great Gatsby</u>, we dashed to the bookstore and bought our copy.

It was the Roaring Twenties to be sure—we joined the Flapper Generation. Up came our skirts, from the ankle length in Boston to the knees. Instead of sturdy oxfords, we wore flat-heeled patent leather oxfords and black silk stockings, and, of course, accompanied by Ruby, one of my roommates, I went to the barber shop, where she encouraged the barber, who held my length of thick hair in his left hand and shears in right and shouted, "Are you sure you want me to cut it?" Ruby shouted back "That is what we came here for." I sent my mother a box of my locks, and she had it made into a switch she wore for years until her own hair turned gray. My father never forgave me, because he believed that long thick hair was the "crowning glory of a woman."

It was the period when young people recently out of college from all over the country swarmed into New York City and shared the excitement of living in the most sophisticated part of the country. It was exciting to leave home, live independently, get jobs, pursue one's own interests, and widen one's circle of friends, while learning what this biggest city had to offer intellectually and socially. I had had some experience when my eldest brother, Philip, was in the Army in World War I, and I returned to Plymouth to work in our store during his absence. He used to go to New York, the center of the ladies' garment industry, as a buyer for special customers, and this was my early experience. Of course, I stayed at the home of my aunt in Newark, New Jersey, and commuted to the New York offices. I had difficulty understanding the English everybody spoke, as the accent was quite different from the New England accent.

Two recent Wellesley graduates and I agreed to a plan to be a part of the Roaring Twenties and to live in New York, get jobs, have our own apartment, and live independently. There was music, theater, lectures, and all the cultural advantages one could imagine. One Wellesley girl, Carolyn, nicknamed Puck, came from far away Fargo, North Dakota, which I had never heard of; she was a pianist and persuaded her parents to let her study with Leginska, the rage of the period. Ruby Hilliman of Worcester, Massachusetts, the other Wellesley friend, had a married sister who lived in Brooklyn, where her husband was principal of a large school. She could visit them while she hunted for a job.

I had learned of a job in New York with the New York City Jewish Charities, which had a vacancy for a Home Economist! The salary was almost twice what I was earning in my job in Boston with the Federated Jewish Charities.

We had it made! There was no limit to our enthusiasm. I could surely stay with my aunt in Newark, New Jersey, as there was a wedding I could attend in place of my mother, who could not leave the store.

The appointment with Frances Taussig, the Director of the New York City Jewish Charities, was scheduled for eleven o'clock. I was so sure she would engage me that it never occurred to me there might be some question. I could only concentrate on the $2,400 annual salary, which we counted upon for household and living expenses. I was dressed conservatively in my navy suit with hemline reaching to my ankles, sturdy low-heeled oxfords, gloves and dark blue handbag to match, and black straw sailor hat fastened securely to my heavy dark brown bun so it would not blow off in case of a sudden wind. All told, a Boston-style professional outfit for social workers.

The position I applied for had been held by a mature woman who was a graduate Home Economist of Teachers College and could no longer stay on the job because home duties required her attention. Miss Taussig explained why they needed someone with good qualifications to fill the vacancy. She was in the process of reading my application.

"You have had good experience in Boston?" she asked, looking up at me.

"Yes, I organized my department, which included working as a consultant to social case workers on the staff."

"Why do you want to change? It is hard working in New York."

"I want the experience of working in a big city."

"But you are so young to be applying for this big position and seeking to assume so much responsibility. Did you consider that when you thought of applying?"

"Oh, please do not consider my age; everybody since my childhood has always said of me, I am most responsible for my age." I was almost 22. I had not consulted my parents.

Miss Taussig was startled by my eagerness. I wanted that job in order to live in New York. I needed that salary of $2,400. I was practically sitting on the edge of my chair in my earnestness, stressing my maturity for my age.

Miss Taussig threw back her head, convulsed with uncontrollable laughter. Recovering herself, she became quite serious. "I could take you on trial for six months," she said, "at a reduced salary."

My spirits rose. "I'd be willing to be on trial. I was told the salary was $2,400 a year. Why should the salary be less for me on trial? If I'm worth $2,400 a year, which is the salary I was told about, then I'm not worth less on trial."

Miss Taussig looked at me with a smile. "If we decide that the job will be on trial for six months at $2,400 a year, if you do not work out, you will resign as we agreed?"

"Yes. But I <u>know</u> I'll succeed." Miss Taussig looked at me with surprise; I was so positive. "When can you begin?" she asked. "Today!" I practically leaped to my feet.

It was an oldfashioned building; Miss Taussig led the way up the staircase. I was practically dancing. On the frosted-glass window was written Home Economist, Consultation Hours 9 a.m. to 5 p.m.

That very afternoon, now that my salary covered the rent, Ruby, Puck, and I picked out where we wanted to live. We decided it should be on the outskirts of Greenwich Village, at that time considered the most sophisticated area; we hoped that by living close by some of the sophistication would rub off on us. We had no experience in renting a furnished apartment. So expensive! We did not like the shabby-looking furnishings, but we moved in, and Puck rented a piano. We decided we would decorate the apartment to our taste. We agreed on shiny black paint and cheerful colored-cretonne curtains. The apartment was on the tenth floor, and bright sunlight warmed the atmosphere. There was a fraternity down the street, so we would not lack for male companionship. Our new apartment was a ten-minute walk from my office and not too far from the Fifth Avenue bus, which was our favorite means of transportation.

We entertained, and we invited out-of-town visitors to stay with us. The apartment was often crowded. A year passed quickly by, and we dreaded to go our separate ways.

Our one-year lease was up, and we made an appointment to complete our business arrangements with the woman who owned the apartment and had rented it to us through an agent; we had never seen her before. She expressed shock as she entered.

"Who gave you permission to paint the furniture?" she shouted at us. "I can never rent this apartment when you leave. Wherever did you get the idea of <u>black</u> <u>paint</u>?" She was practically in tears. We learned that she counted on the rent for her living.

"We improved the apartment. We made it look cheerful and homelike and modern. We did not think we did anything wrong." We all spoke quietly and with our best manners, not willing to upset her further.

After a while, over coffee and homemade cookies and offers to put on a concert especially for her, Puck outdid herself in the music she selected for our guest. We also offered cigarettes from cigarette cases given us by boyfriends, and at last our middle-aged, very conservative landlady was impressed with our hospitality.

"Excuse me, girls, and thank you. I suppose I never realized that this is what young people coming to New York are like." We settled our business amicably, and she gave us another week to move.

We three separated at the end of the year. Puck went home for a visit to Fargo, North Dakota, and Ruby Hilliman moved in with her sister. I moved to the home of one of their Wellesley classmates in an exclusive part of Brooklyn. Her nickname was "Huggit" after her last name of French origin, Huget. She had often visited us in Greenwich Village, and she and I became good friends. She invited me to stay in their brownstone home in Brooklyn until the fall, when I could decide what to do. Her family spent the summer at Shelter Island, so the house was unoccupied except for "guests" like myself. Her father, Philip Huget, was a famous minister, and people came from all over to hear his famous annual sermon on Abe Lincoln.

I learned a great deal that summer at the Huget home. It was never without guests, who came for brief stays. The ministers from different parts of the country who had daughters my own age were impressed by my independence and especially by my job working with poor immigrant families and attending the New York School of Social Work. We often spent evenings at home, where we shared our cooking. In spite of the heat, we spent pleasant evenings together exchanging views about New York City.

Chapter 21
ROMANCE

The war ended. My brother returned from military camps, never having gone out of the U.S.A., and I was free to return to Boston and my professional career. During the summer of 1922 my dearest friend (a Wellesley graduate) and I decided on one of our summer vacations in Plymouth that we would go to New York, get jobs, have our own apartment, and live our own lives.

This story is a chapter by itself. I lived in New York during the "Roaring Twenties" and "changed" considerably. I was "popular" and highly regarded by everyone I met. Most girls had only one idea . . . "to get married." I met so many young men. What bores! Even when I was "pursued," I did not want to let anything interfere with my plans, for by now, with the thrilling life I was living in New York, I was enjoying my freedom very much and could think only of a career in my profession; I would take many courses in the New York School of Social Work and Columbia University to improve myself, and I would get as much culture out of New York as possible.

I persuaded a social worker friend of mine, Dora, from Boston, to go to Europe for at least a year, to learn and to experience as much as possible. I was full of fun during all those years and enjoyed making heaps of friends.

It was August 1924 by now in our European adventure. We never had an itinerary and just travelled where fancy took us, or on information given us by fellow travellers. Dora and I agreed that if she would go to Egypt with me to see the Sphinx, which I had read about since my childhood in _Stoddard's Lectures_, then I would go with her to Palestine, at that time under British rule. All Palestine meant to me at that time was that my classmate, Adele, lived there, having married an Englishman. I knew vaguely about Hadassah but was never particularly interested. Dora, on the other hand, was an ardent Zionist and member of Hadassah. The pact made, we spoke with a Swiss travel agent in Geneva, where we were as I just had to see the Palace of the League of Nations. We gave the travel agent all our American Express checks and told him to plan our itinerary to Egypt and purchase all the necessary tickets, with a good stopover in Venice. Off we went to the League of Nations Palace to learn as much as possible in the couple of hours we had at our disposal.

At noon the kindly travel agent had everything arranged with a few hours to spare, when he took us shopping for the precious blue enamel ball-type Swiss watch on a beautiful enamel chain to match, which I had seen in shop windows and dared not buy. We had been "warned" that all European countries were out to "cheat" unsuspecting Americans. He gave us our tickets, a strict account of expenditures, and the balance of our traveller's checks. I'm sure everything was in order. We both hated accounts, pooled all our money, and divided everything in half without even bothering to do any checking. We were absolutely trusting. I'm embarrassed to admit that this pattern of behavior has followed me throughout life! "What is money for anyhow? Just for spending to get what you need or want, to help friends who need it more than you do, and for enjoyment." My attitude always was, when anything went wrong, "After all, it's only money."

We followed the itinerary. There was a serious problem of "lost luggage" in Venice, where Dora and I had our first big fight. It was her turn to take care of all matters pertaining to our combined luggage. Somewhere along the route, crossing borders, she overlooked the important and necessary need to check to make sure that the luggage followed us on the same train we were booked on. What a headache! What a loss of precious hours in Venice, when we had to spend most of the three days chasing around to the offices that were looking for our luggage. Worst of all, the ship we were booked on from Genoa to Alexandria, Egypt, was to leave on the established date, and I could see us stranded in Venice and the ship sailing without us. Luck was on our side, and the luggage was found only a few hours before our train was leaving for Genoa! What a relief! We were our carefree, happy selves once more and never referred to the situation again.

There was no limit to my enthusiasm, excitement, and sheer joy, and my feet hardly touched the deck! My head was in the clouds. This was complete romance, as one read about it in books, and it was real. I was in heaven. I recalled my childhood, when I devoured _Stoddard's Lectures_, which could actually be blamed for my intense desire to travel and see and get to know as much of the world as I could pack into a lifetime. It was joyous "infection," a "disease" from which I have never recovered to this very day!

No sooner were we settled in our cabin than I dashed out on deck to see what it was like, who the people were, and what the city looked like from the deck of the ship. Oh, there was no limit to my happiness! Dora, a quieter and less outgoing girl than I, could only be amused. She was a very good-natured soul, far less "peppy" than I and very quiet, just as I was talkative, perhaps even garrulous, for I could not contain my excitement or stop expressing myself.

At last we were on our way, to Egypt of all places! Neither of us had ever known anyone who had been to Egypt. Think of it: our parents had no idea of where we were. They would get our letters telling them when we were practically in Egypt. We were faithful and truthful in our daily letters to our folks, who were worried enough about our travelling alone "all over the world." In 1924 we were among the first young American women to venture out on our own. Of course there was no limit to my confidence in ourselves. After all, what could happen? I kept consoling my worrying parents with how foolish it was to worry about anything.

On this lovely little ship, the dining room had tables at which passengers sat where they wanted. It did not make any difference to either of us. Beside me sat a tall, handsome, dark-haired young man. My attention was on the delicious food, for I was always hungry (in those days the word "dieting" had not yet been invented), and as I was sure no one on the boat spoke English but Dora and me, I never bothered to pay attention to any of the other passengers.

Suddenly, a voice next to me, in perfect English, addressed me. This led to conversation and an invitation to go for a walk on the deck. I kept poking Dora in the ribs. I was all excited. I'd made a "hit." It was just like in the novels.

This was Maurice. From then on, every waking hour on that ship, for the three to four days it took to get to Alexandria, we were together. His father, who looked ferocious, did not approve, obviously, for it was his opinion that two young girls travelling alone as we were could not be of good families, nor could we be "good" girls. Romance! What could be a more ideal setting than the beautiful, calm blue sea, the perfect weather, sunshine by day when we lazed around in our deck chairs always in conversation, . . . and oh, the evenings! Those skies studded with huge bright stars that seemed near enough to pluck by hand. If ever there was "romance," this was it. Right away, Maurice expressed his feelings for me. It was the first time in my life I'd had such an experience: love at first sight, with an Egyptian "prince"! He said he would look out for both of us in Cairo, where he lived. It was a city where we would require looking after. When the boat docked, he would help us through customs, since we did not know the language. Above all, he was Jewish; his name was Levy. He and his father were just returning from Belgium, where his father had taken "the cure," as all Egyptians like him did every year. Maurice had been educated in Belgian schools, which explained why he spoke perfect French and English, as the British were in control of Egypt, and Arabic, as that was the language of the country. Can you imagine! Three languages . . . all perfect. I began to recall my struggles with languages in high school and college.

For three days we were constantly together, and I was learning all about Egypt and all the activities Maurice was planning for us. How lucky we were! I could not tell if I was "in love" with Maurice at this point, for I was actually "in love" with every moment of just living. The romantic evenings . . . balmy, soft winds after the daytime heat . . . we sought out places on the deck (or rather Maurice did) after dinner, when the sun had gone down and the stars and moon were the only light. He wasted no time in leading me to the secluded place where he had arranged for us to spend the evening alone. Poor Dora; what a terrible friend I was to leave her to her own devices. But actually I thought it was good for us to be separated, for then she would be compelled to "meet people" on her own, instead of my always making the "contacts" for us. I'll admit it was I who took the leadership on most occasions, and she was only too happy to leave everything possible to me. She explained that, after all, I lived and had a big job in New York, so I was supposed to know more about "doing things on my own," for I lived away from home." In her view, that made me much more knowledgeable about life. Had she only realized my own naiveté!

This "romance" was actually my first. All the others were just longings and daydreaming.

The setting was just like in novels I had read, and I had never before been thus singled out with such constant attention showered upon me. Our daily conversations were so interesting. I learned so much about Egypt and the life there; I was satisfied. I threw away all my "guilt feelings" and gave myself up completely to the thrill and enjoyment that the hours offered. I was always apologetic when, at an early hour in the morning, I slunk into our cabin as quietly as possible, where Dora feigned sleep.

Who could ever forget a detail of our arrival in Alexandria! Without Maurice, we would no doubt have been scared to death. It was late evening, and the boat pulled right up to the dock, which was brilliantly lighted. It was covered with masses of people, all yelling at the same time. All were dressed alike in turbans or felt fezzes, long robes, mostly white, and bare feet. Everyone seemed to be running around like crazy.

All I could think of was a scene from a movie. Maurice caught up with us on deck and told us to get off the ship and to watch everything we possessed, as there was much stealing. He also told us to go to our station under the letter of our names to claim luggage and that he would come over from time to time to see that we cleared customs. He then put us on the right train to Cairo.

I never heard so much yelling! Maurice yelled at all the porters in Arabic and told us to watch our purses and not even open them, as he would take care of all expenses. I realized later that we never could have managed by ourselves. What were we thinking of, to arrive in such a strange place near midnight! Maurice, wherever you are in heaven, remember my gratitude and the love I bore you from that moment on. I was so relieved and grateful. His father looked on from a distance. I thought he was so angry, he was so ugly looking. But perhaps his sickness made him that way. Of course, I never thought of him as a "prospective father-in-law."

We were in a compartment alone on the train speeding toward Cairo. We were so sleepy. Maurice booked us to be alone for he feared other passengers might not be the company he would have desired, and he did not want us in a compartment alone with men passengers. He kept coming to the compartment several times, leaving his father, and always hurrying back. I suspect "papa" was not so pleased and did not think much of us or our families who permitted us to travel unchaperoned! Why, I had not been chaperoned since I left the portals of Simmons College dormitories, where we could not move, even on a date, without a chaperone. I'd had enough of that.

When we got off the train, there was my Maurice, my faithful cavalier, to see that our luggage was taken off. He put us in a cab with loud and strict instructions to the cab driver to take us to the National Hotel, where he would meet us later. What he said to that driver to put the fear of God into him, I'll never know, but he was so kind and gentle and drove his horses right to our hotel. Maurice had already telephoned, so we were expected. Imagine our arrival without reservations; our Swiss travel agent had not made any arrangements. Perhaps in those days there was not the communication system that followed many years later. Perhaps there was not the time to make connections. Anyhow, we were safe in our hotel.

All the servants were so kind and attentive. Our room was huge. There were two large beds, with mosquito nets over each, drawn aside. The beds had spotless white linens turned down and instructions in English warning us never, never to sleep except under nets, and a whole series of instructions on how to tuck them in, etc. It showed huge pictures of malaria mosquitoes and explained in English why we must take every precaution.

Suddenly, while we were in the midst of studying the instructions and feeling not only tired but very woozy, there was a gentle knock on the door. We looked at each other. After all the warnings from Maurice, we were not about to open it. But the voice was gentle, and so persistent that I finally got brave, and, with Dora ready to let out wild screams and yells, I timidly opened the door just a crack. It was the very kind clerk who had taken us to our rooms, with strict instructions from Maurice to "do every service we required." In quiet tones and much motioning, he persuaded me to follow him to the phone on our floor. In those days there was no such thing as a phone in each room.

It was Maurice! What relief to hear his voice! I must have sounded relieved, for he laughed at my concerns and assured me that he wanted to hear from me that all was well before he went to bed himself. Also, at some length he cautioned about using the mosquito nets, no matter how hot it was, for I complained that the heat was so terrible I could not imagine how we could ever get to sleep. He blew me kisses over the phone and said he'd call in the morning and would plan our stay in Cairo.

I returned to our room jubilant and related every detail to Dora. No sooner had our heads touched our respective pillows than we went out like a light. It had been one of the most exciting days of my entire life so far.

When Dora and I planned to visit Cairo, it was to be for just three days. The visit lasted three weeks. We began to think that it would never end. I myself felt it could go on forever. Maurice was so much in love with me that it frightened me. He had his young cousin Albert join us so that he would be Dora's date all the time, so he and I could be alone. Only a pal as good-natured and cooperative as Dora would have put up with it.

Maurice selected our ten-day guide, whom he engaged without consulting us about the length of our stay. His cousin told me Maurice intended to marry me! While it was all so romantic, the very idea frightened me. That was in 1924. Had I not been feeling so far away from home and, I might add, "civilization," perhaps I would have jumped at the chance.

Maurice came to our hotel every afternoon at 5 p.m. to go to Groppi's (I wonder if it still exists). It was the swankiest cafe in the city, where Cairo's elite went for coffee every single afternoon before going home after business. I suppose other drinks were served, but until this time in our lives, we had never had a drink. (I look back and marvel at this, for I lived in New York. The biggest "vice" was smoking!) We saw his father at a distance watching us, but we behaved so to his standards that I thought he began to really believe that we were "respectable" girls.

Usually Maurice stayed and had dinner with us, and afterward we went for a ride in horse-drawn carriages all over Cairo and he told me how much he loved me. Under those star-studded skies and the incomparably bright moon, I gave myself up to the joy of the moment. My head was in the clouds. I'll never forget the picnics he arranged along the Nile when it overflowed its banks.

Every morning our guide came to the hotel to take us to the places Maurice had chosen. Maurice was there every single day to give him instructions. He seemed to threaten him in Arabic, for his voice would rise and I'd inquire what it was all about. I learned that it was only to insure our safety. He impressed this upon the very kindly guide, who only wanted us to have a good time. The guide was thrilled at a steady daily job. I presume the pay was good, for we were never allowed to cash one traveller's check.

Every day there were flowers left in my room, from Maurice's garden. He lived not far from the hotel. One day he told me that he wanted me to visit his garden, by myself. It was a very hot, beautiful, late afternoon when he called for me. We walked to his home, where there was a very high black wrought-iron fence surrounding a huge garden. On a long bench just outside the entrance gate sat about a dozen young Arabs. As we approached, they all rose and bowed. Maurice seemed to have a pleasant word for them, and one came forward with a huge key and unlocked the gate. I could not imagine what was happening. Once inside the gate, I began to understand why there were fresh flowers at my hotel every morning.

Maurice led me around the garden, often looking up at the windows of the mansion. At first I did not understand what was happening, but suddenly it dawned on me that someone was watching. He had told me that his mother and sister were away in Turkey, where his mother came from, during his father's absence, but that they had just returned. I'm sure he must have told his mother all about these American girls, and she must have expressed a desire to see them. But how? Surely the father would not permit it! The pictures Maurice showed me were of two very pretty women. His mother, like his father, was very fat. It was at this time that I began to realize the wealth of this family. Later I learned that the business they owned was in silk goods. In fact, Cousin Albert told me, "they were the silk kings of Egypt." Maurice plucked a few white jasmine from a bush and tucked them in my hair, laughing. He seemed so happy. Why was everything so secret, I wondered? Why did they not invite us to their home for tea or a meal, as we would have done in America? I never knew.

One day Maurice informed me that only we two were invited to tea at the home of a very dear friend. We went. He led me up to an apartment, where a handsome and kindly gentleman opened the door in response to the ringing. Of course, I trusted Maurice implicitly. Nobody else was there. The servant brought in a very elaborate tea service. I enjoyed the "goodies," which were generally sweet. Maurice and his friend spoke in Arabic so, of course, I could not understand a word. If they had conversed in French, which was usually the language that educated people spoke in Cairo, I could have hauled out my high school French and joined in. It was not until much later that I found out that this man was an important employee of his father's, and lovesick Maurice counted on him to meet me and help his cause along with his disapproving father. I thought I made an impression on him, for he was so gentle and exquisitely mannered; a sympathetic soul. I began to realize that Maurice was having a hard time with his father. We were both 28 at the time, I think, and his father thought it time he was married. Until he met me, he had never found anyone who interested him. He sought companionship in his books, for there was not a book I could mention that he had not read. This attracted me.

One day the guide told us about the buried tombs in the desert. He told us he had taken Englishmen tourists on this wonderful adventure and was willing to take us. It would take an entire day; we'd have to leave very early in the morning before the heat began. We would first go to the Sphinx and the great pyramids, where we had already been. From there he would have a young Arab boy to help him. He would have a camel for us to ride in turns. He would have a donkey and cart; the Arab boy knew how to tell fortunes and would entertain us as we rode through the desert. We would visit at least five buried tombs that had been perfectly preserved. I bought us books to look over to see that he was telling the truth. At the end of the trip in the desert, we would all take the train from Memphis back to Cairo and be deposited safely in our hotel. He told us the cost. He would have to hire the camels, the donkey cart and donkey, and the boy.

No one could ever imagine my excitement at the prospect of such an excursion! Dora hesitated, and I assured her that I would just as soon go alone with our guide, for he had proved to be so reliable. When Maurice came that evening, I told him of this plan. He was shocked and said he'd never let us go across the desert alone with an Arab. I said I trusted our guide. He had been faithful and reliable in the ten days he had been with us all day every day. As there was no limit to my enthusiasm and determination, and as all of them saw there was nothing they could do to dissuade me, Maurice decided that he would go with us. I knew he was interested, and so my troubles were over. I made all arrangements with the guide for Sunday, when I knew it was not a working day for Maurice.

The night before, Maurice was in a dreadfully despondent mood. He told me he could not accompany us, as his father suddenly had important business matters for him to attend to. However, his cousin Albert had agreed to accompany us in his place, for he dared not let us go alone for a whole day in the desert with an Arab, no matter how important it was to me. I just knew it was a made-up story and that he was having trouble with his father on account of me.

At the crack of dawn, Dora and I had breakfast and waited impatiently on the veranda of our hotel. Albert was very late, and I was furious. Suddenly, a Ford car drove up and in it was Albert and his cousin from Alexandria, who had arrived the night before in his new car. They were like two kids with a toy. Albert told me it was foolish to try to stay on the desert for an entire day. We would be burned to crisps. Besides, he had "no intention of doing a thing like that." Also, his cousin would take us all for a tour in his car, which would be far more pleasant for all of us. I was furious, and my dark eyes must have flashed angrily. "You promised Maurice in my presence that you would take us." I was ready to cry. He softened and agreed to accompany us.

I should tell you that we never left our traveller's checks behind in the hotel. In those days it was not even considered safe to leave them in the hotel safe deposit box, for theft was the name of the game. I brightened and handed Albert all my wad of checks, and we were on our way to Giza and the pyramids and the Sphinx. It was a clear bright morning, so early that the heat had not yet started. I did not like Albert's cousin at all. I was scared of his irresponsible driving and felt relieved when we saw our guide. All the way out, both boys tried to dissuade us from going through with the trip.

The moment we arrived, Albert went up to the guide and addressed him in Arabic. They had such an awful argument that I finally interfered to find out what was wrong. Albert now insisted that he would not go! The guide was in tears, for he had hired all the animals and he would now be "ruined." It was then that I took matters into my own hands. I yelled at Albert to give me back my traveller's checks. I said to the guide, "I trust you. Mr. Maurice trusts you. We have been happy with you for ten days. We will go on this wonderful trip you told us about alone with you. Mr. Maurice knows you well and expects you to bring us back safely to our hotel. I don't care about these two boys. Let us get started."

He was all smiles and like his own kindly protective self. I yelled at Albert to get along and hoped they would have a fine ride wherever they went, and to call Maurice so he'd know where we were. With that, I handed our guide the wad of traveller's checks, for we did not carry large purses in those days and had the money on our persons. It was too hot to be bothered with them. The guide took them to conceal in his voluminous robes.

It was a long day's journey until we took the train to Cairo.

The tombs were specially preserved and buried in the sand. Only the guide knew where the entrances were. He had taken many English archaeologists to the locations. The colors of the Egyptian tombs were clear and bright and perfectly preserved. We were amazed at the preservation of the paintings; it was such a privilege to see them.

How I trusted the Arab with the light into the dark tomb with paintings on the walls in brilliant colors! The only light in the tomb was that carried by the guide. We entered four tombs as the guide had promised us.

Maurice was waiting nervously on the hotel veranda when we returned. He was the color of the Arabs after being on the desert. His scolding did not interest me because I had had the time of my life.

Dora and I decided that the three weeks were up and we would have to leave and go to Palestine. We went by the Red Sea. Maurice came to see us off. He made sure that we had a compartment to ourselves on the train. It was a long hot trip.

For years after this, my friends who went to Palestine went by way of Egypt, where Maurice would entertain them.

We arrived in Palestine and Jerusalem and went to the American Express office on the Jaffa road, where they assigned an Arab boy to take us to the home of my classmate who had married an Englishman.

The Arab boy took us to the charming residence of Mr. Lowy, which was situated in a big garden surrounded by a high iron fence. Fortunately, the gate that led to the house was open and there was a big knocker on the door. I knocked loudly and heard my classmate's voice, saying "Who is there?" I shouted, "Open the door and you will see." She was excited to see her classmate and friend coming to visit.

We visited for several weeks and had a wonderful time. Albert Lowy had arranged for us to have transportation, and we travelled and saw what was possible to see of the Jewish colonies. We met Henrietta Szold, the organizer of Hadassah.

When she heard that I was a Home Economist/Nutritionist, she begged me to stay there. I told her I was on leave of absence from my job in New York. Now that I had seen what there was to do in Palestine, I promised to return. Little did I realize that I would be back a few years later and spend a year making a dietetic survey of the foods being raised and imported for the purposes of a wholesome diet.

Chapter 22
HOUSE OF GOOD SAMARITAN AND
ROCHESTER UNIVERSITY

My mother and father moved to Boston from Plymouth, and I decided to leave New York and return to Boston. Frances Stern was now head of the Nutrition Clinic of the New England Hospital. Because I was her former protégé', she recommended me for a research job at the hospital named the "House of the Good Samaritan"; its head was the famous Dr. T. Duckett Jones, whose reputation as an expert on rheumatic heart disease in children extended from coast to coast. After a few interviews he engaged me as a research assistant on his staff to develop a diet for children suffering from rheumatic heart disease. For a year I worked under his supervision to improve the diet of the sick children.

At the end of the year of this research, during which I kept careful records, Dr. Jones informed me that he would invite doctors who were interested and hold a meeting at which I would present my work. He was pleased with my efforts and said he would arrange to have an article under my name in the prestigious *New England Journal of Medicine*. He was generous to a fault.

After this experience I was interested in training at a medical school. I had never intended to practice medicine, but it was important to have an M.D. after my name so that doctors would regard me as a professional colleague. This would give respect to my efforts as a nutritionist and get the cooperation of doctors for the education of the immigrant parents to help overcome malnutrition among their children.

My father was very pleased with my decision and agreed to help me financially at the medical school of my choice, i.e., the Rochester University School of Medicine in Rochester, New York. I enrolled at Columbia University, New York City, to finish the requirements for entering medical school. I was living at International House near Columbia University. At first I was pleased with the student body, sitting together at meals and walking to classes together. Then I discovered prejudice against Blacks and Jews in certain groups of students, who, not knowing that I was Jewish, let their prejudices be known. There had been outbursts between Black students and students from our southern states. At meal time I expressed my horror at such behavior among students who were presumably educated and above such behavior. The discussion went on and suddenly turned to Jews and the fact that Columbia and New York itself was overrun with Jews. I suddenly picked up my tray and moved to another table. My friends, who always held my place with them, were horrified. I simply looked at them all, holding my tray, and said calmly, "I couldn't deceive you but I am a Jew from Boston, the same brand as a New York Jew."

In 1928 I was admitted to the Rochester University School of Medicine, the school of my choice—there was one other woman medical student in the class. We often studied together. My pre-med work had prepared me for the need for concentration, and I was enjoying the courses and friendship with my fellow students. I particularly enjoyed the sessions led by doctors who unexpectedly called upon students. The young students accepted me and often discussed their ambitions for the time when they would finish their internships and open their own offices. I was shocked to learn that many were most interested in making money and chose being surgeons as the most lucrative of the professions.

As serious students we studied far into the night, particularly at exam time. I was especially interested in learning about the human body through the dissection of cadavers in the course on anatomy, at which I became quite skilled.

Then suddenly, as if a bomb had dropped in our midst, tuition was due, and my father wrote that he had been caught in the stock market crash and could no longer support me.

I packed up and headed for New York to get a job to support myself. I had held a good position with one of the agencies and had good credentials. I could return to medical school at any time.

Chapter 23
THE GREAT DEPRESSION

The Great Depression began with the stock market crash during Herbert Hoover's presidency in 1929 and was not over until World War II ended in 1945. When I returned to New York in 1929 to find a job, I was well-known for my work as Director of Home Economics and Nutrition in 1921-24 with the United Hebrew Charities in Boston. Friends offered me hospitality, so at least I had a place to sleep. It was humiliating to have to share the simplest food with the family. One remark sticks in my memory, "I didn't realize there were so many ways to cook beans," which appeared for supper every night. My wardrobe was unusually fashionable and was hardly suitable to wear in the long lines of job seekers. Some people in those long lines lived in fashionable areas of New York. These people as well as those accustomed to poverty were suddenly without funds. The poor were accustomed to "going without," and a man was arrested as he grabbed a bottle of milk the milkman had just delivered at the door in a fashionable neighborhood. His excuse was that his baby cried incessantly from hunger, and he could not resist the temptation.

The Puerto Ricans came to New York legally by the thousands, seeking shelter and food and creating tremendous overcrowding in the slum areas. There were fights with landlords who sought payment of rent. The mounting problem of this non-English-speaking population created situations that even trained social workers were not able to cope with.

The five boroughs of New York all suffered alike. Landlords knew of the futility of collecting rent, and often there were evictions and streets were littered with broken-down furniture left out in the snow or rain. On Fifth Avenue and in the better neighborhoods, men were hovering over crates of apples, hoping that individuals on their way to work would purchase an apple for 10 cents, and men in tailor-made overcoats and worn shoes would self-consciously approach a pedestrian with the expression, "Madame, can you spare a dime?"

How to meet this emergency? All the social workers who could be spared from existing social agencies were loaned to the hastily established Emergency Relief Bureau. Police precinct offices were loaned as office space for staff interviewing the long lines of people applying for relief. From these lines were selected some men and women applying for relief themselves; they became the 10,000-member staff of investigators who were given superficial training and whose job it was to deliver food vouchers to the families in their case load. The investigators were required to be eligible for relief themselves. They were paid $15.00 a week and assigned 100 families in their case load, to be visited once a week and to be given their relief orders for food only, which could be cashed at any neighborhood grocery store.

Corruption? Could an investigator feed his family on $15.00 a week? It was reported that investigators carrying a case load of 100 families would make an arrangement with the owner of the grocery store in the neighborhood for a certain number of his clients to cash their relief orders in the store designated. The grocery order was filled with the poorest quality goods and rarely of the selection of the family. The investigator would keep a record of the total value of the family food orders and then, by arrangement with the grocer, collect an amount that represented a percentage of the total amount of relief orders. That was how he managed to get his own family expenses met by literally stealing from his clients.

My first job with the Emergency Relief Bureau was to investigate this practice of assigned investigators. My title was Special Investigator, and for this disagreeable task I was paid $1,300 a year. I had an assignment of 100 families, delivered their food orders, told them I would be their permanent investigator, and told them they could shop in any stores they preferred and could choose their food supplies. I made arrangements with the grocers to be sure I was on the "corruption" trail. Instructions were left with my office to firmly refuse any bribes of boxes of expensive chocolates or any "gifts" that anybody would leave for me. My fellow investigators had no idea what my assignment was. They only knew that I was a trained nutrition specialist, and my very special wardrobe belied my work status.

One day my supervisor, who had worked in the same agency before I left to attend medical school, called me into her office. She said "I hate to give you this special assignment, Sue, but you are the only one who can carry it out." Among the investigators was a "diplomat," so-called because he had been in the diplomatic service abroad and had been forced to return to New York for lack of funds. The "crash" found him in Europe, where he was enjoying himself living off income from stocks that no longer existed. He was well-dressed, carried a cane, and wore a derby hat and pince-nez glasses. He was earning $15.00 a week like the other investigators. It was reported that he had no family and was living in a good neighborhood with his two sisters. It was a fine neighborhood, and responding to the bell I pressed one Saturday morning was a dignified lady; peering over her shoulder I saw that the floors were bare and the curtains were in shreds. The sisters were on relief, and together with the brother they were able to manage by selling what possessions they had. She did not invite me to come in. As I was standing conversing with her, the investigator "diplomat" suddenly arrived. Instinctively he knew the purpose of my visit: someone had reported them, and he knew he was out of a job, and they would be investigated. My supervisor, to whom I gave my written report, cried with me when I said I could never handle a case like that again.

I devised a method whereby all the grocery stores cashing relief vouchers would now operate under a centralized system that each store would be required to follow. The customer could choose her purchases and no longer receive only the items the grocer selected. All the grocery stores in the five boroughs would have to adhere strictly to the rules in order to be paid. Conspicuously posted in their store windows was a big sign I myself designed, which said they were authorized to cash relief checks. In order to get the sign they had to sign an authorization that they would obey the rules of treating the relief clients like customers. After investigation of the first complaint, they would lose their card and consequently the business of cashing relief vouchers.

I spent most of my evenings far into the night acting upon any complaint made about a grocery store. Withholding payment of relief vouchers was my method of dealing with corruption. The grocer could not be paid unless my signature was on the receipt.

Social workers in all the relief agencies fought the battle against vouchers and won cash relief to families based on the number of members in the family. True, the cash was only for food, but at least it ended corruption.

The central office was at midtown in the Borough of Manhattan. We had received notice that on a Saturday morning relief clients would take to the streets with their demand for rent, fuel, and clothing. Mounted police were already in position. Families had brought their children, as well as long hat pins to stick into the horses, which they knew would cause accidents.

We, the staff, were prisoners behind locked doors in our offices, with only the clients' representatives allowed in to plead their case. We knew the Emergency Welfare Budget could not possibly meet the demands. The result of this demonstration was the ruling that landlords could no longer evict families who could not pay their rent and had no place to go.

We lived through trying times, and although Franklin Delano Roosevelt was the new President, with cheering promises to the nation through his fireside chats ("We have nothing to fear but fear itself"), the suffering from loss of jobs and income went on. Special programs were developed, and experts gave their time without pay.

The Works Progress Administration (W.P.A.) was a program established to meet the emergency. The cash relief covered a number of programs throughout the country. Writers, painters, and sculptors were given jobs, and some of their work can be seen today on public buildings. The program of greatest influence on our youth was the Civilian Conservation Corps (C.C.C.) program, under which young men who had never been out of cities had the opportunity to travel across the country, work at outdoor jobs, and be fed and properly clothed. The outdoor work often restored them to health.

It was now 1933. The Emergency Relief Bureau was no longer in existence, as funds were now made available to the New York City Department of Welfare. I was appointed Director of Home Economics, Nutrition, Clothing, and Equipment. My salary was $3,000 a year for this momentous task. It was the greatest challenge so far in my career. Realizing that I would require the support of prestigious people in New York City, I established an advisory committee of experts in my field and of prominent women volunteers engaged in welfare work. I chose women in positions of power, with access to the press and radio.

Experience based on previous jobs in Boston and New York in private welfare agencies gave me courage, as did the experience on my many assignments with the Emergency Relief Bureau that required imagination and organization and not only self-confidence but my reputation of successes in dealing with administrators and staff. From previous jobs I knew that further academic and professional training was necessary and important.

For a number of years I enrolled in courses at Teachers College, Columbia University, in New York and in summer courses in nutrition at Cornell University in Ithaca, New York. The New York School of Social Work was the source of years of courses in various fields. Each course was carefully selected to assist me in my professional advancement.

With the needs of people who could not help themselves always before me, there was careful selection of professional friends whose concurrence I always sought before making decisions when I felt I would require their support before presenting my proposals to the Administration.

It was a daring first step, but with careful planning I felt now it could be accomplished. As police precincts in New York in the five boroughs were our relief offices, I realized our department required a trained home economist-nutritionist to handle the special cases in which the social worker would require help with family budgeting, special diets, etc. A staff of 90 home economist-nutritionists would be required to fill this need to handle the existing case load. As hospital dietitians recommended special diets for patients on relief, the nutritionist on the staff would figure the cost and offer consultation to the welfare worker on each case. The specialist on clothing would be required to work with the W.P.A. Clothing Project under my supervision. With no precedent to follow, I wrote a manual for the training of this unique staff in accordance with the unique needs and regulations of the Department of Welfare. From the stack of applications, I personally interviewed and selected each home economist.

Because of the urgency of supplying each precinct with a specialist, I devised a scheme of eliminating the delays the personnel department paper work ordinarily required and personally presented each one whom I considered would fulfill our specialized needs, made an appointment with the personnel director, and requested she be put on the payroll immediately. Thus I did away with the usual red tape, and the specialist was immediately employed and from that moment was in training and on the payroll. This unique method not only saved time but was a great encouragement to the staff member. The 90 nutritionists met at a staff meeting once a month and helped build a working manual.

TIME. There was not a moment to spare. With one secretary and both phones ringing and nutritionists in training, and attendance at meetings, decisions to be made as improvement to relief standards were worked on, and presentation to budget directors, there was no end to the problems that appeared daily.

The great blow came when suddenly the "resident law" was applied to all city departments in New York. This cut our staff, and adjustment had to be made. Adjustments to changes in regulations required steady nerves. This experience with the Department of Welfare 1932-43 was good preparation for the next step: OFRRO and UNRRA.

During the depression years, Washington was overwhelmed with business executives who were invited by the various departments in Government as dollar-a-year-men, to give their expertise and to offer their services as specialists in setting up projects.

One of these projects was the WPA Manufacturing Project for Clothing and Household Items. In order to keep factories running and people employed, they had to have orders, including orders for their yard good materials that came off the looms.

Relief agencies furnished the source of outlets for manufactured yardage that was available to the Government. Harry Hopkins, the social-welfare-experienced member of President Roosevelt's staff, was perhaps the most important advisor to the President.

A clothing manufacturer from New York was on the Washington staff and approached me as head of the Home Economics

Nutrition and Clothing Department. Miss Coleman as clothing assistant received the assignment from me of working out quantities of clothing and household items needed for the case load of the five boroughs and the method of distribution to relief clients.

Washington sent us samples of available materials for our selection. Individuality was the keynote I had in mind for our clients so they would not be identified as families on relief. I insisted that the finished products be of an assortment of materials and styles to have the appearance of those on the racks of New York department stores. I devised a plan for an appointment with the executive of authority to discuss our needs, which were samples of children's dresses for school age and men's and boys' clothing. They understood my concern at once, so the clothing manufactured by the WPA for distribution to relief clients had enough individuality so that children would not be identified as being on relief.

Washington also offered us the WPA Manufacturing Project, from which we could order sheets and pillow cases, women's and children's cotton dresses, men's and boys' cotton shirts, etc. With one million people on relief in New York, estimates for each item were needed. It was our job to work out estimates of sizes and household needs required for the case load. From this experience we learned population needs and were labelled experts. The samples of clothing were eventually sold to our poorly paid staff members, who were delighted with the bargains.

My experience in the clothing part of the job stemmed from working in our store in Plymouth, Massachusetts. I was exposed to details of the buying and selling of clothing from my early teens. All through college I gained precious experience working in the store during the busiest seasons of serving people and developing special skills in buying and selling. Skill in dealing with staff and in my presentations to executives at meetings I attribute to my early training in our store. The confidence leading to success in these early years led to the establishment of methods in later relief projects, clothing populations in future job assignments.

The method I devised in my theory of "you can't do it alone," establishing advisory committees of persons prestigious in the community with expertise in influencing administrators and especially budget administrators, has served me well throughout my professional career.

World War II began for the U.S.A. on December 7, 1941. Washington was humming with departments to assist in the war effort. Governor Herbert H. Lehman was instructed by President Roosevelt to set up a department in the State Department to deal with problems of civilians. It was named OFRRO (Office of Foreign Relief and Rehabilitation Organization). Governor Lehman invited William Hodson to work with OFRRO. He was Commissioner of the Department of Welfare of the City of New York. The staff was proud and excited and gave a party, but Mrs. Hodson was very nervous and concerned for his safety.

Of course, Bill Hodson, the first to be invited to this awesome assignment, was thrilled and honored. Preparation began for the work for which he gave his life. He was hurrying to Algeria by air as Director of Relief in North Africa of OFRRO, America's first great effort of this war to bring organized relief and economic assistance to people freed from the Axis orbit: fifteen million men, women, and children in North Africa. From Washington, we bade him farewell in mid-January, and two days later his mission came to its tragic conclusion in the equatorial forests of Surinam. He gave his life for his country.

Chapter 24
ENCOUNTER WITH MAYOR FIORELLO LaGUARDIA

I was successful at landing a job in New York during the depression when Fiorello LaGuardia was mayor. He was sworn in on the promise that he would set things right in New York City, ending the fires that were constantly plaguing tenements and endangering the lives of the poorest strata of society. He promised to control crime through his newly appointed Attorney General Thomas Dewey. He promised allowances for the million on relief to provide them with at least sufficient funds for maintenance until he had a chance to get well acquainted with conditions in the city. He hoped to bring things back to normal and make the city the shining example of what a great city should be.

Immediately after being sworn in he set out to keep his promises. I remember him best as a member of the fire department. Almost every night he would answer fire alarms and jump on fire fighting equipment, whizzing off to fires that plagued the city frequently. He was determined to find out for himself the cause of these fires that endangered so many poor families. He made a comical appearance, dressed up in ankle-length yellow waterproof coat with wide-brimmed hat. He was very short of stature, not much over five feet tall, round and roly-poly, probably from a generous diet of spaghetti and other Italian foods. Night after night, according to the newspaper accounts, LaGuardia was a member of the fire-fighting crew until he determined the origin of the fires and was able to put a stop to them.

On almost every corner of the principal streets were beggars of every description dressed in rags, to awaken pity in passersby who dropped coins in their tin cups if they were blind, or in their outstretched hands, which were red and chapped from the cold. All were shabbily dressed, as if their dirty, unkempt garments were a product of years of wear without replacement.

Shanty towns sprang up on the corners of Riverside Drive and the adjacent streets, where singles and evicted families made a makeshift resident area for themselves. They built shelters out of whatever scraps they could gather together, such as heavy cardboard and corrugated tin. Many times they used boxes to sleep in.

It was a dismal sight. The mayor promised to do away with these slums of desperate people. Who would ever believe that the great and prosperous city of New York would sink to such a level? This was the Borough of Manhattan. What about the other four boroughs? It was the same story everywhere ... Brooklyn, Queens, Staten Island, and the Bronx.

Mayor LaGuardia was often described as "The Little Napoleon." He was outspoken, dictatorial, and enjoyed his powerful position. He stood for no nonsense among his employees or from anyone else who tried to cross him or influence him for personal benefit. He was "all for the people." From my knowledge and experience of personal encounters with him, he never deviated in favor of those who were trying to influence him. He could be harsh and "scare the liver and lights" out of anyone. Yet he could come near to tears when he heard stories about hungry children, desperate parents, and the suffering and injustice surrounding him and his administration. The City Hall steps were almost always covered with people who were down and out, trying to see him and tell him their troubles. He was mayor during one of the most difficult periods in the history of New York.

While I was working for the City of New York as Director of Home Economics and Nutrition in the Department of Welfare, I was suddenly called to his office at City Hall. I was frightened because I did not have any idea why I was summoned. My faithful secretary reassured me that the mayor had heard such wonderful things about me that he had singled me out as one of the staff with whom to become acquainted. I hoped she was correct, but nevertheless I felt I should not go to his office empty-handed. I instructed her to gather together a folder filled with our mimeographed educational material that was designed to help families on relief with the products we distributed. These products were canned soups, beans, and many food items that the federal government had in storage for allocation to relief agencies all over the U.S.A.

After I had waited outside the mayor's office for over an hour, his secretary finally answered his ring and ushered me into his office. She did not leave but stood at a short distance from his desk. He sat at his huge desk, which was covered with folders and mail to be signed. He was a black-haired, dark-skinned, heavy-jowled, heavy-set man. His glittering black eyes fixed on me. Sitting in a barrel-shaped chair was a man with white hair. His back was to me as he faced the mayor. He obviously had concluded a conversation but was remaining. It occurred to me that this must be the mayor's bodyguard. I remained standing in front of the desk, not knowing what to do. Suddenly, in a thunderous, menacing voice (his eyes surveyed me from head to foot), he bellowed, "Sit down." Tremblingly, I obeyed. The secretary, still standing a short distance away, looked at me pityingly but did not move.

After what seemed to me a long time, he held up a can with the label removed. He bellowed at me, "What's in this can?" By this time I had recovered my self-confidence. I replied, imitating his tone of voice, "How should I know? It does not have a label." "By this time I thought you'd know what was in each can. You've been distributing them long enough, haven't you?"

"Yes, we have been distributing them for quite some time, but still I wouldn't have the remotest notion what was in the can if it had the label off. And also I wouldn't expect our families to know what is in a can with the label off, either."

"What do you do about helping these people use the cans they get?"

"We test all the food from the federal supply and make up recipes for the best use of it."

"What recipes? Do you take into consideration that these people have their own way of cooking?"

"Yes, of course. Anyone who has worked with different ethnic groups as I have all my professional life should know that recipes have to follow what people are familiar with. For your information, I have nutritionists from different groups on my staff. They try to find how to prepare those foods so they will be acceptable." Much to my amazement, he listened.

"Would you like to see some of these recipes?" I asked now with more confidence.

"No, don't bother."

"I have them right in this folder for you. I can leave them for you when you have time to look them over. I thought you might be interested."

"Well," motioning to his secretary, "take them and tell me what you think of them." To me, "You say you have a staff. What kind of staff and what do they do?"

"They are all nutritionists with a degree in nutrition. As they become a member of my staff, I train them individually because they have not been in social work as I have and need to have training in how to help these families."

"How many do you have? Where are their offices? I want you to come down here tomorrow morning with all their personnel folders so I can see what they are like. Remember, tomorrow at 9 o'clock I want you right in this office with all those folders. . . . Nutritionists," he said sarcastically, "how practical are they?" Looking sharply at me, he said, "You say you test all these recipes? Where do you do this?"

"We have all become beggars, Mayor LaGuardia. When we do not have facilities and we need to get work done, we look around to see what facilities other professionals have, then we beg them to help us. That is how I get my work done, by begging other nutritionists with facilities to cooperate with me."

"Well," said he, softening, "what facilities do you need to do your own testing?"

"Oh," said I, brightening at the prospect of having our own testing kitchen, "there is a huge room right in the building where we have all the welfare offices. It would be ideal for a testing kitchen and for classes to teach families."

"Tonight draw up a plan for such a kitchen, make a list of equipment you'll need, and make an estimate about what it will cost for each operation. Then we'll see about getting the money to accomplish it. And also have all this here at 9 a.m.," he ordered.

To my amazement he stood up. In a less belligerent tone, uncharacteristic of the rest of the interview, he said, "All right now. Go home and do all these assignments and we'll see how we can help you. . . ." His secretary beckoned me to follow her. As we parted she said, "You impressed the mayor. You did just right to get angry and differ with him. He hates people who soft-soap him and agree with him. He likes spunk, and you sure showed that you knew what you were doing. I'm sure he'll help you with your program."

With wings on my shoes I managed to get into the subway and get home. It was 7 p.m. My roommate had been wondering where I was. Our maid had dinner waiting. As soon as I was refreshed and had related what had happened, we both had a good laugh at my spunkiness with Mayor LaGuardia. He was one person whom nobody dared to differ with. I got on the phone and reported to my secretary what had happened, as I knew she was concerned. I also reached the personnel director and told her I needed the personnel folders of every nutritionist, which was a big job as at that time I had 90 nutritionists on my staff. I told her I'd meet her at the office at 8 a.m., as it would take time to assemble them and I had to be at the mayor's at 9 a.m. Then I called my assistant and told her she would have to come to my apartment that very evening and help me design a kitchen to test recipes for federal food supplies and to hold classes. We had often spoken about the possibilities of having a testing kitchen in the building. Now, this was our chance! Far into the night we worked, drawing up plans, making measurements, making lists of equipment that would be needed. In the end, we estimated costs to be about $1,000.

"A thousand dollars!" I cried. "Where in heaven's name are we going to get $1,000? But that is _his_ problem. We have done what he asked," I told myself.

Exhausted but stimulated at the possibilities of my department getting fully deserved recognition, I could hardly wait for morning to come. Promptly at 8:00 a.m. I was at the personnel office. My director was not so enthusiastic about my encounter with the mayor because it netted nothing for her. I gathered all the folders and was off for City Hall.

At 9 a.m., as I was sitting waiting for my appointment, Mayor LaGuardia walked in. He did indeed resemble a "Little Napoleon" as he was often described. He led a long entourage of aides, who followed close at his heels. He was dressed in a dark suit with a black felt wide-brimmed hat, the fashion of the period. I sat quietly for about an hour waiting to be called into his office. I was seated finally on a bench in his office where I could observe him at his desk. A young man was hanging over him earnestly, begging for a request on behalf of a Mr. Polk. Apparently the mayor refused to bestow any favors with which he did not agree or for someone he did not know.

"Who is this Mr. Polk that you want me to recommend for a job? I don't know any Mr. Polk."

"Why, his uncle was the President of the United States in . . ." said the young man. "Well, we'll test if what you say is true." In a voice filled with friendly concern, Mayor LaGuardia called out to me, "Come over here, young lady, and sit down beside me. Have you ever heard of anyone by the name of Polk?" I admitted that I had not.

"See, young man, this lady is an educated college graduate, holding a big position in the Department of Welfare. She has never heard of anyone of prominence in the U.S.A. by the name of Polk. Get some more facts about your friend and come back another time."

"Come over here, young lady," he said in the friendliest manner and tone possible. Let me see what you have brought today." I was flabbergasted by the change in attitude and tone. Now he was so conciliatory and so friendly, even on the borderline of affection as if he had sympathetic feelings for me.

We went over the folders of my staff. As he checked off names and inquired where they were working, he came upon the name of Euphemia. "And this Euphemia, who is she and where does she work?" I told him about this nutritionist and her hard job at the Men's Shelters, where hundreds were housed overnight and given meals that she supervised. I added, "This indeed is a trying job, and it's heartbreaking for these unemployed men, the same ones who have contributed so much professionally in the past. Now they are often found in the gutter, half-starved, with their breath smelling of cheap liquor. How can we save them? How can we rehabilitate them?"

The conversation turned to the experimental test kitchen and the plans that had kept me up half the night but that he hardly looked at.

"I remember that I promised you this kitchen so that you would no longer have to go begging for help. I don't intend that any of my employees have to go asking for help from other agencies. I have

$1,000 in a special fund that I'm passing on to you for your kitchen. I'll tell your commissioner about it so there'll not be any question."

I was breathless. Our commissioner, whose name was Charlotte Carr, had come to us on the recommendation of influential friends, but the mayor took a dig at her on every possible occasion. She had told me she had difficulty in trying to see him to discuss problems in the department.

Then came the most exciting offer. "Do you know how many Puerto Ricans there are on relief? They are the saddest part of our relief population. They are American citizens and are entitled to everything like every other citizen. They are starving in Puerto Rico. When they heard about relief in New York, they began arriving here in large numbers and living under the worst possible conditions. Several families live together in one apartment in the most crowded conditions. They are unfamiliar with American foods and are so poor that the young people are turning to crime. The small children of these big families are not fed properly, and there is lots of sickness among them. I'm very worried about them. They keep on coming, and nothing we can do can stop them. Perhaps it would be a good idea for you to go to Puerto Rico and study the conditions there and learn about what is best for them here in New York."

"Mayor LaGuardia," I said plaintively, "I am so overburdened with work now that I do not have the time to go anywhere or even to go on a vacation. Every day there are new problems and new requests we must honor. Every night I go home with a briefcase full of work and hardly ever have a free weekend to myself. But I agree with your idea, and perhaps later I could go to Puerto Rico and see what I could do. I'll try to get acquainted with any organization here in New York to learn more about their needs and habits and see if we can cooperate. But now it is out of the question for me to leave. My nutritionist who is in charge of the area where the Puerto Ricans live will look into the situation and see what more we can do to help them. I won't forget that you'd like me to go to Puerto Rico, though. Meanwhile I'll do everything I possibly can right here."

The mayor heard me out, paying close attention to what I was saying. I could feel that he knew I was sincere, as this morning he was so friendly and sympathetic, much different from last night when he pounded on the desk while he was criticizing me and I answered by pounding on it in turn to make my point. Anger had suddenly taken the place of fear. Now I thought he was enjoying my visit because I was among those who was not there to ask him for anything, unlike most of the people who came to his office.

Suddenly he stood up, wriggling himself out of his chair. I noticed that the man whom I had thought was his bodyguard was not there. He held out his hand and said, "If you have any problems, just call me. Tell your commissioner that I'll arrange about the funds for your experimental kitchen."

I left City Hall feeling triumphant. I could hardly wait to return to my office. As soon as I arrived, my secretary related what had happened. Miss Carr, the commissioner, came up to my office, inquiring where I was. My secretary explained what had happened the night before.

"The moment Miss Sadow returns, have her come right down to my office." With no further ado, I hurried down to her office, where a meeting was taking place. Generally she scheduled a meeting with a group of social workers who were heads of their departments in the social agencies. Before the depression, they were in charge of all social work in the variety of agencies in New York. They met regularly together with the recently organized public agency to help maintain standards for the welfare families, make recommendations, and consider problems the commissioner brought to their attention. They were all seated around the long table in the commissioner's office. It was not necessary to introduce me, as I had contact with each of them. There was an atmosphere of tension as they all looked up from the files and fixed their gaze on me.

Suddenly the commissioner said in the most sarcastic tone, "Well, I suppose all of you know Miss Sadow was called to the mayor's office suddenly last night. The mayor does not have time to see me on important problems, but he has time to see my nutritionist both last night and all this morning."

"Tell us, Miss Sadow, what happened during those two long interviews?" I related briefly what happened. I told about the experimental kitchen. I told about his interest in nutrition and particularly the Puerto Ricans. I was careful not to mention my loss of temper and how I pounded on his desk just as he had. I did say, however, that he wanted me to go to Puerto Rico to study the problems of families on the spot. I said that I would not be taking the time right now, though.

There were raised eyebrows. I suppose everybody thought I was crazy to have turned down an offer to take that trip.

With the mayor's money we established the experimental kitchen to test the foods. We had several Puerto Rican housewives come to help us prepare dishes according to their tastes so the food would not be wasted. We established a special committee of these women, who proved very helpful to us in the future.

News about my encounter with Mayor LaGuardia spread among the staff. Suddenly the Nutrition Department developed an atmosphere of prestige. The nutritionists' offices in all five boroughs were suddenly considered as those of important specialists and won the praise and respect of the administrators and all the staff.

But, more than this, all my friends called upon me whenever we were at dinner parties, at luncheons, everywhere to tell about my encounter with Mayor LaGuardia. Long to be remembered was the telephone call to me from a very important member of the Advisory Committee to the Commissioner. I had heard about this recently established committee, which was appointed by the mayor himself. Among other duties, they were to inform the mayor about what was going on in the Department of Welfare. After my first meeting with the mayor, I had a call the next day from the chairman of the committee! I did not know who he was. I had only heard vaguely about this important committee since we, the staff, had no dealings with them.

He introduced himself over the phone. He told me he was the man who was seated with his back to me the evening the mayor called me to his office. He heard the whole thing. He was not the bodyguard to the mayor as I had thought: he was the chairman of the recently appointed Advisory Committee to our Commissioner!

He praised me and told me how impressed the mayor was with me and my behavior. Needless to say, I was embarrassed and yet pleased that I had made a good impression.

The story of the encounter with Mayor LaGuardia furnished conversation for several different groups in New York with which I was then socially and professionally in touch. I'll always treasure the memory of it. It increased my appreciation of one of the greatest characters in America, who rose from such modest and unhappy situations in his childhood to become one of the most appreciated men serving the people, thoughtful of their welfare, and determined to destroy corruption no matter what the cost to himself might be.

"The Little Flower," as he was often referred to, had a hard life without too much joy, except success in his work, which was accomplished always at such hardships to himself. He is a good example of how, in our country, one can rise to almost any heights set for oneself, with desire to follow one's principles. One can say of Fiorello LaGuardia that he didn't allow temptations to stain his reputation. With all the idiosyncrasies of his character, he remained the true hero and champion of unfortunate and helpless people.

I've always felt grateful for this personal encounter with Mayor LaGuardia. I felt that it enriched my life and gave me courage to speak up against injustice. His empathy for the underdog and for those who suffered injustices make him a source of admiration and inspiration especially for young people getting started and wishing to establish careers of usefulness.

Following the example of heroes who had only themselves to depend upon, those who believed in honesty in conducting their own lives, has led many to the road to success. The mayor had no use for laziness or making self-indulgence a priority. He had respect for promises and did not make them unless he intended to carry them out.

Chapter 25
VISITING WITH ELEANOR ROOSEVELT

Eleanor Roosevelt was often the main speaker at our meetings of the New York Home Economics and New York Dietetic Associations during the years of the Great Depression. We all needed the inspiration, and she was a master at getting to the core of problems, analyzing the difficulties, and encouraging the members (who literally "ate up" each word of her speeches); she seemed to know of our work and the difficulties we encountered during those awesome days. She spoke openly about the various programs the federal government under her husband, President Franklin Roosevelt with his wonderful team of advisors, had devised and the importance of the cooperation of professional groups such as ours in order to contribute to their success.

She spoke especially of the WPA (Works Progress Administration), in which most of the members of relief agencies were involved. She talked first about the Emergency Relief Bureau of New York City, which later was included in various agencies of the City of New York Department of Welfare.

Her influence on so many of the agencies established to help populations was immense, and everyone who heard her common sense speeches was inspired to improve and update agencies with which they were associated.

We all came out of those meetings not only inspired but no longer frantic about work loads, insufficient funds for carrying out our programs, worries about our clients' needs that we could not begin to fulfill even with our top estimates of funds required to meet the needs of family relief budgets. Eleanor Roosevelt never underestimated the gravity of the problems we were facing; rather she looked always into the future with hope and the temporariness of the depression situation. The result was we went back to our desks with renewed vigor and courage to carry out what was on the books.

But after meeting her personally over lunch, I was even more impressed with Eleanor Roosevelt. During the depression, about

1935, a middle-aged woman was employed as a typist on my staff; she was a college graduate, a history major with particular knowledge about New York's Hudson River and the development of use of its waterways.

Later I learned she was born in the city of New York and loved the stories about the Hudson River. The depression reduced her and her family (as was the case with so many) to the poverty level. The only job she could find was being a typist in the Department of Welfare. I never knew her age. I worried about her having enough to eat. Her clothes had the styling and quality of clothes tailor- made from the most prestigious New York shops. She lived around the corner from the office in a one-room apartment several flights up on a street where the buildings were neglected and where the trash accumulated from week to week until the city department had employees to remove it. The furnishings of that one room revealed "better days": what she was able to keep after selling the most precious antiques for cash to meet urgent expenses.

One evening before I left the office, when all the rest of the staff had gone, she came to me and asked if it would be all right if she stayed a few evenings and used the typewriter, as she had an important letter she had to "get off." "Of course," I said, "if you want this in writing, I'd gladly give it to you anytime." She seemed reassured and no longer embarrassed. Then she said, "Sometime I'll tell you about this project I've been working on for long months, and I'll take you into my confidence."

I replied, "Whenever you wish to do so. But don't feel you have to reveal anything of a personal nature just because I give you permission to use the typewriter." "No, that's not it. I'll probably need to consult you before I mail the letter, for I'll need your opinion on whether I'm doing the right thing," she answered.

"Whenever you wish," I said, "You need not reveal anything to anybody unless it is helpful to you, and you don't need to satisfy anyone's curiosity. Just use the typewriter for anything that will be helpful to you. If you wish to keep it confidential, even from me, please do so."

She blushed, seemed uncertain and embarrassed, and thanked me. I left the office hoping that she had some ideas of securing another job with better pay that would utilize her talents. I hated to see a woman in advanced years with her college degree reduced to being a very poorly paid typist, having to watch every penny. I did not know very much about her except that she was born in New York and had lived in a private house with her family in one of the most prestigious areas of New York.

After some months, she came to me again after all the staff had left. She said "You'll never believe who this letter is for." She held it up with a trembling hand. "Probably I should not mail it." She looked so troubled and uncertain that I said, "Now that you've written the letter, what has made you so uncertain? Why are you so hesitant about putting it in the mail box?"

"It is to Eleanor Roosevelt. I'm asking her to come to my apartment and view the screen I've worked on all these months for President Roosevelt's study. Perhaps she will think it is presumptuous on my part." Quickly I put on my hat and coat, took her arm, and said, "Let's leave together. That letter must be put in the mail box, and I want to be sure that you put it in right now before my very eyes."

Secretly I hoped that this would be a turning point in my typist's life and that she would derive some monetary benefit from it. She then invited me to her apartment. I climbed the many flights of stairs after her, waiting until she put on the lights that would show off the screen to the best advantage. Surprise? I was overwhelmed. She said I was the first one to view her painting. I did not know that she was an experienced painter.

It seems she had studied painting under several masters in several European countries for many years. She had lived in Paris for many years in her youth. She had never married and was the only daughter of an aristocratic wealthy family in New York. She had spent months at the New York Public Library researching the history of the development of the Hudson River, which she knew President Roosevelt loved. She made copies of the various illustrations in the books, so precious that one had to get special permission to study them in a secluded room in the library under the surveillance of the official in charge of the section. She made sketches and then had done paintings in oil for the six-sectioned screen to be placed at the entrance to President Roosevelt's private library at Hyde Park, the family home. She wanted Mrs. Roosevelt to see it only after it was finished, to see if they would like it and if it could have a place in Hyde Park.

The letter's contents were an invitation to Mrs. Roosevelt to view the screen.

Days passed and I wondered if she would ever hear from Mrs. Roosevelt, for I knew that her secretary had to screen her mail. Both of us threw knowing looks at each other every morning! One day she burst into my office saying, "It came! It came! She would love to see the screen."

Days later Eleanor Roosevelt climbed those many flights of stairs to see the screen and to meet my typist...or I should say to meet the artist. Imagine the excitement on that street when she was recognized as the limousine drew up in front of that rundown apartment building!

Mrs. Roosevelt spent some time studying the screen. She said she knew that Franklin would just love it. She would give it to him as a great big surprise. She would let my typist know when the Hyde Park van would be ready to pick it up. After she presented it to Franklin, she would invite her to lunch at Hyde Park so that she could see the screen in its place. She was so grateful that she would have this wonderful birthday surprise to give her husband. My typist friend was so excited. She was afraid to accompany her guest to her official car lest it be known where Eleanor visited and lest some harm come to the screen. She could hardly wait for the Hyde Park van to arrive.

That day came, and there was much excitement on the street as the van was recognized. With great care the screen was brought down those stairs by the four men sent to carry it to the van, which ordinarily was used to transport the saddle horses from Hyde Park to Washington. My friend did not dare to accompany the men to see how her precious screen was handled for fear of being mobbed! She was so relieved that it was out of her apartment with the minimum of publicity.

One day she came into my office all smiles. "How would you like to go to Hyde Park to have lunch this Saturday with Eleanor Roosevelt?" she asked.

"Are you kidding?"

"No, I mean it. We are both invited."

"Why am I invited?" She showed me the note: "Please come to lunch on Saturday. You and a favorite friend are invited, and you will be able to see the placement of the screen. Franklin was so excited and he wants to meet you and thank you for all your effort. With appreciation, Eleanor Roosevelt. The chauffeur will be at the station to meet you to take you to our house."

She was amused at the expression of disbelief on my face. "I could not believe it myself," she said, "I've read the letter over a dozen times."

On the following Saturday we were met at the station by the chauffeur, who drove us to the residence at Hyde Park. I thought I was dreaming. On the porch, waiting to greet us, stood Mrs. Roosevelt and her great and intimate friend, Mrs. Morgenthau, whose husband, Henry, was President Roosevelt's friend and financial advisor.

The informality on the part of both these women put us at our ease immediately. When we were seated at the dining room table, Eleanor pointed out how everything in the decor and even the food was in tones of yellow to greet the spring. Indeed it was a beautiful spring day.

Who can ever forget such an experience? We were in the company of the highest official family in the U.S.A. We were just two workers from the City of New York Department of Welfare, where we toiled in behalf of New York's poorest. Yet here we were sitting at the table of the most important family in all America. How easily we were put at our ease, as if we were old friends who were so welcome. I kept thinking, "In no other country in the world could all this have happened."

When my typist friend saw where the screen had been placed, and that her work graced the home of the President of the United States, she had difficulty in controlling her tears and so did I!

After lunch, the chauffeur drove us back to the station in time to catch our late afternoon train back to New York from Hyde Park. Our tongues did not stop wagging all the way back. Who would believe us? Should we disclose that we had had lunch at Hyde Park? We decided that she should frame the letter of invitation. But what tangible proof would I have of this famous lunch?

In the following days and weeks, I never saw such a change in anyone. My little typist seemed to have grown taller and younger. The troubled lines seemed to have disappeared from her face. I never knew the financial arrangements Mrs. Roosevelt made with her. All I know is this event changed her life and made those last years the happiest for her. As for me, I can no longer recall this typist's name. But it was a turning point in my whole career. I felt like a close friend of Mrs. Roosevelt's with an invisible bond between us. I felt she understood the sufferings of all the unfortunate people with whom we were working.

WHAT A WOMAN! WHAT A HUMAN BEING! Many years later it was my privilege to see her at a meeting in Geneva of the United Nations Human Rights Commission, of which she was the chairperson.

President Roosevelt decided that the many nations involved in World War II should be part of one united body, so he called the nations together in Atlantic City, New Jersey, in 1943 and thus UNRRA (United Nations Relief & Rehabilitation Administration) was born and OFRRO (Office of Foreign Relief and Rehabilitation Organization) was disbanded. We of OFRRO had all been told we would receive a letter announcing which of us would be going overseas almost the next week to assume our duties in North Africa, where we were assigned.

Several of us were on the plane bound for Morocco. A group of OFRRO/UNRRA staff members who had been in headquarters in Algiers had already been transferred to Casablanca, were billeted there, and were hard at work going over many applications for admittance to refugee camps.

Other than names and ages of members of families, so that we knew how many children or elderly persons there were in the group of 37 nationalities, we had no information. We were informed that refugees would arrive via Algiers and we would be given more information later.

The story of one particular group and how they were saved and finally placed at the North African Refugee Center has never been told, as all arrangements and plans were made under the most secret of conditions. Communications took place between President Roosevelt and Churchill and Franco, the Spanish dictator. The Spanish Civil War, fought during the 1930s, left Spain reeling under a new type of government. Since a considerable number of refugees in the concentration camps were from Salonika, Greece, where they had lived since the Spanish Inquisition, when Jews were expelled from Spain in 1492 (still retaining their Spanish nationality), Franco was persuaded to accept them as Spanish "citizens" as a goodwill gesture, which would win him approval and prestige in the allied countries. Spain was neutral during World War II. This secret agreement had been reached sometime in 1943.

A contingent of the U.S. Army was stationed in Casablanca. UNRRA personnel joined their officers at meal times, and British UNRRA personnel had already arrived, been billeted, given titles, and assigned jobs. Joining American UNRRA personnel were Morris Feinman, head social worker; Trevor Pearce, his assistant; one British doctor whose wife was a nurse; and five personnel who had been transferred from Algiers as former OFRRO personnel, two secretaries and I.

Moe Beckelman, Project Director, had been assigned to organize and run the camp. I was billeted with a French family in a five-flight walk-up.

It had been decided to call our camp the North African Refugee Center in order to dispel any remembrances of past experience the refugees might have that could disturb them further.

Next morning we met for breakfast in the officers' mess, introduced ourselves, and were presented with a sheet of refugee applications to which were attached family photographs so we soon became acquainted with camp residents.

Assigned to us were three Chevrolet cars for transportation. Announcements came that Governor Lehman would be visiting our office, coming from Algiers to meet the staff, and Joint Distribution personnel from New York whose assignments were relief of Jews living in North Africa, whose existence had never been known before World War II. They were all more or less poverty stricken and were now being supported by the American Jewish Joint Distribution Committee.

The arrival of Governor Lehman was welcome, and he not only met staff members but visited the refugee camp situated in Fedela, a distance of seven miles from Casablanca.

Governor Lehman returned from his visit to the refugee camp very depressed to find it was a desert surrounded by a high wire fence. He felt it was like a Nazi concentration camp and would remind our future refugees of their escape from such camps in Germany. It had originally been planned as a rest camp for American soldiers, and there was a very large social recreation hall built by the American Red Cross. There were a number of brick buildings and a tent colony of Italian prisoners of war (POWs).

The governor hoped the staff would soon live on the premises and make the refugees welcome and comfortable. The American officers, with offices established in Casablanca, had a huge supply dump nearby, from which UNRRA personnel could requisition food, equipment, and everything needed for the convenience and comfort of the refugees.

The following week the Project Director, Moe Beckelman, moved the staff out to the camp, and our real work of establishing a facility began. A French restaurant was established nearby for feeding the staff, and the brick and wooden buildings served as our housing. We had to become accustomed to the desert sands and being protected by the POWs.

We had meetings to plan for the reception of the refugees whenever we had word of their arrival. At these meetings I learned from the staff that had formerly been assigned to OFRRO in Algiers about the thousands of yards of unbleached cloth for making sheets, pillow cases, and towels. What a find!

I learned from the French social worker, Mlle. Chancerelle, with whom I had brushed up on my French, that she would employ the women to do the sewing project so that it would be ready when the refugees arrived. The U.S. Army would furnish cots, blankets, and palliases (cotton body bags that would be used as mattresses when they were stuffed with dry grass that had been sterilized). Not only food and equipment were my responsibility but also the furnishings.

My colleagues did not give me any ideas or support for the planned treatment of the refugees upon arrival. It was one of my CAN DO accomplishments derived from other large-scale feedings.

The food supplies that would be made available were in Casablanca, all in the huge army supply dump. In addition to food, there were all kinds of supplies, including the equipment I would be required to use for food preparation, warehousing of all supplies, serving equipment, and cleaning and sterilization. I congratulated myself that, when I was in training in Washington, I had had the foresight to visit nearby army camps to learn how a mess was organized and administered. Moe Beckelman, our director, arranged for me to meet the American army colonel in charge of the entire American installation, who was in control of everything that embraced American-based forces in Morocco and Algeria.

The appointment was made for the interview. I was ushered

into his office, and he stood up to acknowledge the introduction. He looked me over from head to foot piercingly I thought, and ordered me to sit down. He was rather young, in his early forties, with a dark complexion, snapping dark brown eyes, a smart thin moustache, and a dapper appearance; he impressed me as a "no nonsense" type. My heart palpitated as I sat in his august presence, feeling somehow that I had done something wrong. He began to fire questions at me. What had I come out here for in the first place? I had learned early, in Washington, that the overseas military were solidly against any woman being shipped overseas. What did I think I was going to do with all these thousands of refugees? On and on he bellowed at me! Didn't I know that subsistence was the worst headache that the army had to contend with? What was a nice young lady like me thinking about, to come out to all this devastation when I could stay comfortably at home? Trembling at this unexpected outburst, I said as firmly as I could "If I had been a man, I long ago would have had a gun on my shoulder to do my country's bidding. But since I am a woman, I want to do what I can for my country to help in any capacity to which I am assigned. I'm a nutritionist by profession, so I know what you mean by subsistence, and I think I know by now what I'm in for. I know it won't be easy. But I'll do my best . . . " His expression softened, and he was silent for what seemed to me an interminable period; I suppose it was minutes or less. Then he said, "Young lady, you are here now. You have a big job on your hands. I think you are a fine woman, so you can count on me to help you all I can. If you are ever in trouble, all you have to do is come directly to me, and I'll do everything to help you." Little did I realize at that moment how important those words would be to me!

Suddenly I felt elated and secure. The colonel then took me out to the dump, which was in charge of a sergeant. He introduced me: "This woman is going to need a lot of help. Give her anything she needs. She'll fill out her own requisitions. You sign and accept them. You do not need my signature for her requirements." Then he turned and left, wishing me good luck!

That was my first triumph. The sergeant was a fine young man who had been overseas for some time. We became good friends on the spot. He was so happy to be able to talk freely with a woman from home. He took me on a tour of the dump, so that I could familiarize myself with the warehousing of all supplies. From that moment on I knew that all my future dealings would be with the sergeants of the army rather than with the top brass, for it was the sergeants who knew where all the supplies were and how it was possible to procure them without going through all the red tape that caused interminable delays.

I returned to the office in a jubilant mood. I was full of courage. Fear had left me. Now I was on the track of knowing what to do. Daily I tackled all the records and made out requisitions.

At our center, we received word that our contingent of refugees, whose arrival we had anticipated for all those weeks, would arrive in three days, and each of us was to make ready, according to plans we had gone over again and again at staff meetings.

My warehouse was filled with food rations and equipment according to the requisitions I had submitted to the U.S. Army. My heart sank. How to get the mess halls and kitchens ready? I appealed to our director. His reply to me was "That is your problem, Sue." Since there were so many Italians on the premises who were no longer considered prisoners of war but allies, I suggested that a number be assigned to me, to get the mess halls and the cooking and serving equipment ready so that when the group arrived food would be available. The director's assistant had been working in the camps established for Japanese-American citizens in the USA (as if they were enemies, instead of citizens of the USA) and seemed to me to be entirely lacking in compassion. He suggested that we follow the system of the Japanese camps: "Just pile sliced bread on tables, have canned meats in another pile, let the refugees form a line, slap the sliced meat on the bread, and continue that way until they've got food." I protested vociferously, insisting that after such a long journey of families with young children and so many old people (one woman in the group was 91) "they should be given a hot meal of as much food as they wanted . . ." I can't forget the anguish I suffered at this meeting. If ever I was scared to death in my life, this was the time! Not one of the staff offered any help to me in my dilemma! I was shocked.

I went to the warehouse to see the equipment I would be compelled to use . . . huge iron kettles! All were new, never having been used before, and they were covered with grease at least one inch thick to prevent rusting. I looked at the oil stoves and the rows and rows of kerosene cans. I looked at the thousands of army mess kits, which would be the only eating equipment supplied. I had diligently studied the army manuals on how to run a mess kitchen and practically memorized every order that army personnel running a mess had to follow.

Sanitation worried me almost more than anything else because I feared epidemics of gastric problems. This center had to be conducted with the strictest emphasis on sanitation because the only medical help available was the one doctor in our group. I knew of the terrible conditions in the French hospitals that would be available to us in the event anyone had to be hospitalized. I also was aware of the prejudices of the French toward the refugees, and that all of them would be subjected to French scrutiny.

I was keenly aware that it was up to UNRRA to give them all possible protection.

I sought out the Italian major who was in charge of the Italians and requested that he assign a number of the soldiers to work on getting the kitchens ready for preparing the food for the expected refugees. He told me frankly that he had no authority to assign them without U.S. Army approval. I ran to the director, thinking he had authority, but he insisted he did not. Why was he Project Director if he did not have authority? He insisted he did not know. I was beside myself. I felt licked, deserted, with no one to help me. I estimated that if I had 25 men assigned to me, it would take at least three days to get those mess halls cleaned (with all of that grease) and the Italians taught how to prepare the meals from our rations for families.

I thought of one strategy: the colonel had told me if I was ever in need, I could come directly to him and he would get me the necessary help. I ran through thick sand to my quarters and dressed as rapidly as possible in civilian clothes. Then I ran to the director and demanded that one of the Chevrolets and a driver be assigned to me at once for I was going to headquarters to demand the use of the Italians to help me. There was no other way. I was livid . . . determined. I threatened to cable Mr. Lehman unless I got his cooperation! The seven-mile trip to Casablanca seemed endless. Finally, I was at the office of the colonel and told the chauffeur to wait because I might be a long time.

I was allowed to enter the building, as I persisted in my request to see the colonel. I had no written credentials to admit me! The sergeant who finally received me informed me that the colonel was "up in Algiers on army business and that he would not be back for several days."

"Then I must see who is next in command." Nobody seemed to know how I could get permission for the Italian major to assign his men to me to get the mess ready for the incoming refugees.

From one to the other I appealed for help. Nobody seemed to know what to do. They were sympathetic about the jam I was in. After two hours of going from office to office and being told no one could help me, I just sat down in desperation and got hysterical. Nothing could stop my flow of tears! I cried and cried and would not leave. I guess our young sergeants did not know what to make of this outburst. Finally, a young officer appeared and came and sat beside me, trying to calm me down. I told him I absolutely would not leave unless I had a note to the major granting him permission to assign his Italians to me so that I could set up the mess halls.

Minutes later, the young officer appeared with an official letter to the major, instructing him to assign as many of his men as Sue Sadow required and for as long as she required, and they were all to be under her complete jurisdiction and would take orders from her exclusively until she was ready to release them. Through swollen eyes I read the directive. For once, army regulations were circumvented. It took a desperate woman's hysteria and tears to accomplish it. The sergeants were all smiles as I departed (either out of satisfaction that I had accomplished what I had set out to do or that I had "busted" army regulations)! I did not stop except to express my appreciation for the cooperation I had received and to request that they inform the colonel, upon his return, of my gratitude.

Back to camp! I sought out the major. In no uncertain terms, I commanded him to have 25 of his soldiers lined up for me at once in front of the warehouse, with several jeeps to transfer the equipment to the mess halls. I dashed to my quarters, got into working clothes, and met the Italians at the entrance to my warehouse in fifteen minutes. I was jubilant. I felt as if I could conquer anything! My planning was coming to fruition. Everyone had better keep out of my way because I had work to do for the rest of the day and all night! Those who approached me to find out how I accomplished this feat were pushed away. I had not time to speak to anyone except my former POWs.

Suddenly, the atmosphere at the North African Refugee Center changed! The Italian former POWs, from the lethargy that had come from having nothing to do, leaped into activity as if they had been released from captivity. Everyone dashed to fill the assignments after listening attentively to my orders, which I gave half in English (which they hardly understood) and half in Italian (which I remembered from an Italian course during our training in Washington, given by Guido Nadzo, who was a member of our OFRRO group and whom I met later as a member of UNRRA's Italian Mission)! When I told him about this encounter with the Italian POWs, we laughed about how I used the little Italian I recalled from his lessons. The Italians literally dashed into the desert to scoop up buckets of sand to clean off the grease that had been applied to all the huge cooking vessels to prevent rusting. Everyone seemed to be running to get the mess halls ready to receive the refugees in the two days before arrival.

I stood over each with the army manuals opened to the page of instructions and read orders over and over. I was baffled by the language used, wondering how our soldiers ever understood what they were ordered to do! The young Italians obviously enjoyed themselves and I daresay looked upon me as a "mother image" to be obeyed! The kerosene stoves we would have to use were complicated beyond belief. Among the "boys" (as I grew to consider them), those with mechanical training were assigned exclusively to cleaning the stoves and keeping them operable. Others were organized into "scrubbing teams" to clean the tables and attached benches. The tables were made of removable slats, each of which had to be removed after each meal and scrubbed on both sides to conform with army regulations for sanitation. There were no sinks. As a substitute the army offered us huge ten-gallon cans to boil water in; they were kept on hand all day long to be used for both cooking and cleaning our equipment.

The work needed to get those mess halls ready in time defies all imagination! The area was a beehive of activity all the rest of the day and all night long. Fortunately, there were huge electric lights lighting the camp for safety. It was interesting to me that none of the staff entered into the activity or the spirit that prevailed.

The Italians sang while they worked. Their beautiful voices were filled with sentiment and nostalgia. Their song "Mama" rang throughout the night as they kept on with the work. After a break of a few hours for sleep and a meager breakfast, we resumed work until the mess halls were transformed into sanitary stations for the food preparation.

From our warehouse we transferred supplies for one day's meals to each mess hall. Since I had decided that the most efficient and economical method for serving was to follow the army's method, we had all the individual army mess kits, complete with knife, fork, and spoon attached to aluminum containers that served as plates. These were washed and sterilized ready for distribution to each person. The kitchens were now set up with the huge pots on the stoves. The cabinets contained the supplies and mess kits, and there were three fifty-gallon cans outside each mess hall in readiness for the boiling water in which each person would dip the mess kits after disposing of any leftover food in the huge garbage can outside the mess hall (which served as the indicator of waste and helped me learn which foods were not acceptable). I felt everything was ready, as I had followed the army manual exactly. I was exhausted physically but also stimulated and free from worry, knowing that a well-prepared meal would be awaiting our guests! I decided to have one kitchen open all day long, with hot food ready for the guests as they checked in after they had deposited their belongings in the tent assigned to them. They could get washed up and walk in a leisurely way to the mess halls to eat their meal with their families. I was in charge of welcoming them and seeing that they got served in the quantities they desired. For this initial meal, I had figured out the rations so there were no restrictions on quantity.

A staff mess hall had been set up in a nearby restaurant, reached only by our Chevrolets. This was a good idea, both from the point of view of getting out of the camp for rest and recreation and also because there was no way to set up a staff mess on the premises. We had no facilities for cooking in small quantities.

I worked out the menu for the first day separately and chose the Italians who would be cooks until the refugees were assigned their duties. The other Italians were assigned to keeping the mess halls absolutely clean. All the equipment was sterilized so that flies and vermin could be controlled. In training these young boys, I emphasized the importance of following instructions in the manuals, which they all saw me studying carefully for each operation. I informed them that we had only one doctor on the staff, so it was important to prevent any illness, especially any upset due to food. They understood and were sympathetic and cooperative and full of compassion for the refugees who had suffered so much.

The April morning of the scheduled arrival was clear and bright. Everything was in readiness. Each staff member arranged his section to receive the refugees. Each was assigned a number of families and knew which were in tent assignments. It was so well organized that, when the people arrived, there was absolutely no confusion. The director had gone to town to receive them. When the gates swung open and the huge trucks came into camp with the families, I confess that a lump came up in my throat. I had to fight to keep the tears from flowing! At last, a home and safety! No fears need worry any of them now.

The atmosphere was friendly, their needs were cared for, and freedom would prevail. I watched from the mess hall steps as the lines moved on, as each family was checked in and sent to their tent. They were a nice-looking group of people. They seemed well-dressed and cheerful. In Barcelona they had had a good taste of city life where there was no fear of war. It must have been difficult for them to give it all up and be taken to the unknown. There were a good number of children of all ages; many promptly began digging in the sand and running about as if they were at the seashore. For the first time we heard the happy voices of children. The young Italian boys stood watching, many with tear-filled eyes. They were so homesick, thinking of their own families and wondering what had happened to their sisters and brothers. I tried to cheer them up.

All day long the refugees came to the mess hall, where I welcomed them in my best French, the language understood by many of them. Each acted as an interpreter to those who could not understand. They were so weary after the long travel experience by boat and by train from Algiers. Some even stretched out on the benches attached to the tables and just plain fell asleep before the food could be served them. Beginning with this first meal, I introduced the system they would be required to follow during their stay at the North African Refugee Center. Each received an individual mess kit, with the admonition that they would be responsible to keep it and it was to be used exclusively for their food. As each finished, I stood at the entrance, not only to welcome them but to demonstrate to them how the garbage cans were to be used. I dipped each mess kit into boiling soapy water and then rinsed it in another can of boiling clear water.

The group was very bright. Even without understanding the language very well, they looked at each other with smiles of approval and followed instructions. We had only one menu for the entire day, as it took many hours to get them all through the lines and settled. They all had permission to return to the mess hall as often as they wished or whenever they wished. The meal was a good meat and vegetable stew, white bread (which they took for cake), and canned fruit, and tea for adults.

In each tent were their sheets, pillowcases, and palliases on cots. At the end of the camp was a pile of dried grass or hay. They were instructed to go to this field as soon as possible and fill their "mattresses" with straw and return to their tents and make up their beds. Suddenly there was much activity in the camp. It was a joy to hear their happy voices and laughter.

In the evening, everyone was directed to the social hall for a meeting with the Director. With an interpreter at his side, he welcomed them as a family and introduced each of us, describing our duties. Then he informed them that it would be necessary for each one to be employed in specific jobs, for which they would be paid in accordance with the UNRRA schedule. Full employment was the rule in order for the camp to function, because no workers outside were allowed in the camp. They were told that this facility had been built as a rest camp for U.S. soldiers when it was expected that the enemy would have to be driven from these shores, and that they were the first inhabitants. The high barbed-wire fence and the locked entrance gate were for their safety. Also, the Italians who were there under their commander were appointed by the Americans in charge of the area, to act in the capacity of guards all day and all night for the protection of all of us, which was why they were armed.

As each job was announced, I called for volunteers. I requested at least 75 persons to fill all the jobs I had outlined for the three mess halls, with additional workers in the event I had not completed my estimates. I required an interpreter who could speak several languages. It was long past 11 p.m. when the meeting was over and everyone went to their respective quarters.

It is important to note that, although the staff that had responsibility for allocating the accommodations for each person had put the teenage and adult singles in the dormitory-like barracks (males in one, females in another), the parents would not agree and insisted that families remain intact, housed in one tent, regardless of age and sex, and nothing could persuade them to the contrary. We had to learn that formerly these separations spelled disaster. For, when it occurred in the concentration camps, from which many of them had escaped, they never saw each other again, or knew what happened to their loved ones. With this experience, parents insisted that families stay together. One began to learn that our "camp family" would not accept that here they were safe just because we told them so.

Next morning for breakfast, each appeared in the mess hall to which they had been assigned, mess kits in hand. They lined up to get food and soon learned the system under which the mess halls operated and observed how the food was served. They took their places at the tables of their choice, families sitting together and with friends they had made during the experience of waiting in Barcelona. Nationalities were inclined to separate themselves into groups where language was no problem. Some spread white linen doilies on the table, set out the eating utensils, and placed the filled mess kits on the place setting. Many tried to preserve the atmosphere of home. I could have cried when I observed this pathetic attempt to preserve the customs of the past when they had a home.

I ran from mess hall to mess hall during each meal to make sure that everything was in order, that everyone understood the system and what was expected of them and what they could expect of us. The Italians carried out their duties for over two weeks, faithfully observing everything they had been taught.

René Saporta, a young man of 22, was assigned to me as my interpreter. He was from Salonika, Greece, and was with his parents. He was blond, blue-eyed, good looking, strong, and spoke several languages, including fluent English. He became very attached to me, protective, constantly complaining that I worked too hard, that all the refugees were worried about my health, were concerned about what would happen to them if I should "break down," for they all felt that I was the one on the staff who understood them and what they had been through, and they appreciated all I was doing on their behalf.

I had been a social worker for years, and my eleven years with the Department of Welfare of the City of New York, all during our Great Depression, was ample preparation for dealing with this group of people, their emotions, sufferings, insecurities, and needs for being understood. As time went on and days became weeks and weeks extended into months, we all became close friends. I spent many hours socially with them, patiently listening to their stories and their worries about relatives who had been separated from them. One evening, as a group of us were sitting on the steps of one of the mess halls, the conversation was devoted to my job and how hard it was. In their various languages they were speaking to each other about me. René later translated it: "If God only loved us as much as we love her, and helped us as much as she helped us, then everything would be good for us." I confess I was deeply touched and on the verge of tears. What had I actually done for any of them except carry out my duties?

Gradually, I replaced each Italian with a refugee who had agreed to accept the assignment, giving each a period of learning on the job. It was a difficult task, for most of these people had been professional and business people and none had worked in any capacity as laborers, which all of the jobs in my department called for. The kerosene stoves caused us the most trouble, getting out of order constantly, and we were entirely dependent upon them as the only means of using the only fuel we had. I organized gangs of the young girls, to scrub the tables and kitchens after each meal, which were the instructions in the army manuals I was following so literally. The young girls, from families where they had been accustomed to servants, came to me in a body to complain . . . "But Miss Sadow, I've never even washed a spoon in my whole life, so how can I scrub those tables and benches?"

My answer was always the same, "In America we do not have servants. Everyone has to do his own work. We are accustomed to it, and nobody complains about work. This is a good place for you to learn, because when you are repatriated after the war is over, you are going to find a big change, and there won't be any servants. Now please get to work and help keep this place sanitary so that no one will get sick." This group gave me the most trouble and often neglected their assignments, either leaving the work undone or making others do it. René often ran after them, yelling at them (he was very good at that) and accusing them of being ungrateful, when it was obvious that Mademoiselle (as they called me) was "killing herself for all of them!" I never could have managed without René. He became my shadow, never leaving my side.

One day, soon after we got organized and the center seemed to be running quite smoothly, there was excitement at the front gate. In marched my colonel and several other top brass officers. They were paying an unexpected visit to see how we were functioning. The noon meal was being served. As usual, I was running from one mess hall to the other to observe and supervise. The army group was observing each step of every activity! I was quaking, fearing that I was not functioning according to "regulations." The colonel, looking very serious, called me over to where they were standing. They looked so serious that I trembled. What was wrong?

"Young lady, how did you accomplish this?"

"Is anything wrong?" I quavered.

"Wrong, wrong," he emphasized, "nothing is wrong. All I want to know is, how have you done this?"

"Oh," I said, almost apologetically, "all I did was follow all the army manuals on subsistence that the sergeants gave me, and I threatened all the refugees that, if we did not do exactly as the U.S. Army Instructions told us, we surely would all get ill, unless we kept the mess areas almost sterile. That is what I'm trying to enforce." Moe Beckelman, our Project Director, accompanied them, of course, and heard this conversation. Was I scared! The officers looked at each other and then burst out laughing. I was embarrassed.

"Young lady, I congratulate you. If any of our messes were kept the way yours is, we'd never have trouble with subsistence. Keep it up." This was my chance to thank him for giving me the Italians to help me. I was so glad that Moe was there, because I'd never forgiven him for not helping me to get the Italians in the beginning. The colonel looked at me sharply, I thought . . . then, smiling, said, "I heard all about that, when I returned from Algiers.

Glad you stuck to your guns! Anytime you need help, just let me know."

Oh, was that my hour of triumph! I thought now I was equipped to conquer any situation that might ever arise during my service with UNRRA. I was so happy that all the refugees who understood English heard this conversation, for there was a stillness among those at the tables; nobody spoke a word all during this inspection, for the sight of uniforms meant authority and conformity. That visit gave a boost to my authority and insistence that it was our duty to follow strictly the instructions in those manuals everyone saw me devouring! I am happy to relate that not once during my stay at the North African Refugee Center did we ever have any problems of illness traceable to the food; if anyone was ill, it was not on account of that.

I tried to improve conditions in my department within the scope of what was possible. I observed that the children either sat on the laps of their parents or that their legs were dangling because the benches were too high for them. That is when I made my pleas to Washington, asking for permission to use nutritional guides rather than guides based on ration scales, particularly for women and children, who needed more milk, eggs, and fresh food than was available in the Casablanca warehouse. To my delight, approval came, and I decided to open a third mess hall, for children only, and to train the cooks to prepare food suitable for children. I had the tables and benches lowered to the size that was comfortable for children to sit at. Then came the problem with parents not wanting their children separated from them even at mealtime. I held meetings. Did they not trust me and my judgment? After all, I was the nutritionist entrusted with the responsibility of serving food that would maintain good nutrition. Children required food for growth in addition to maintenance; I had just received approval from Washington for rations I had asked for, etc. I suggested, since the children's meal hours would be earlier than the adults, that the parents sit with the children and see that they ate their meal, for as long as they wished, until the children got accustomed to eating by themselves. This satisfied the parents. They all came after the meeting and apologized to me and assured me that they would trust me with anything. Again I was jubilant that this was accomplished.

There is one other interesting accomplishment that gave me

great satisfaction, and that was the feeding program I established for the elderly. There were two concrete bunkhouses that were intended as dormitories, and the elderly were housed in them. They were aged up to 91, men and women, very fragile, bedridden. The men were in one building and the women in the other. The refugees built little side tables and placed them at each bedside. On these, each put the only little possessions he or she had managed to preserve; each had a little doily, some even embroidered! On the tables were usually found photographs of loved ones whose whereabouts would never be known, also some little personal effect: a tray, a pin cushion. The visits to these dormitories shook me up more than anything else I experienced. I could weep as I type, remembering the gratitude and the reaching out to grab my hand and kiss it, much to my embarrassment, in expression of gratitude. Of course, among the other refugees were sons and daughters who were content, at last, that bedridden parents and grandparents were given care.

Among the refugees was a tall, beautiful woman whose name was Sophie. She was listed as being Russian. Since hardly anyone knew where all these people who were single came from or how they happened to arrive at our center, nobody thought to ask personal questions. All I ever knew about this beautiful woman, physically strong, kindly of disposition, good natured and smiling, seemingly happy, always wearing a huge straw hat to protect her lovely complexion from the hot sunshine, was that she volunteered for the job of taking care of both buildings for the elderly. Perhaps in Russia she had been a nurse.

During the early days of planning for the needs of my department, I wondered what could be done for food preparation of special diets for those who were unable to eat the food on the rations. This would require family-sized pots and pans. I consulted the sergeant in charge of the dump, for they are the ones in the army who really know what is on hand and available and, more important, how to requisition and obtain it.

He promised to look around and let me know. Shortly after we were established in the center, I was visited by two sergeants. They carried large boxes, and, when we were behind doors in my warehouse, opened them. To my delight there were aluminum pots and pans that had never been used, originally intended for private officers' use, in case they did not eat at the officers' mess. They wanted me to accept them. "No need for a requisition for this small stuff. It is not even on the inventory!" I was torn. I just could not depart from regulations.

"O.K., then, go ahead and make out the requisition, and I'll sign it and keep the whole lot." What they ever did with the requisition, I never knew. I did not question their knowing smile to each other but was satisfied that I was adhering strictly to rules and regulations!

Sophie picked up what was dished out for her elderly charges in these utensils and carried the supplies for each mess to the buildings. Of course we had to use mess kits for serving. Not only did she call for and deliver the food, but she actually dished it out for individuals and even spoon-fed those who were too weak to feed themselves. She also followed regulations for sterilizing the mess kits after each meal. I shall never forget Sophie and her dignified carriage as she walked through the sand back and forth to the kitchen three times a day!

Morris Feinman, a British member of the staff, was in charge of social services. I think Rick Brookbank, of the American staff, was assigned to assist him, as was Trevor Pearce from England. Next to myself, Morris was the busiest person. All day long the refugees consulted with him in his office. Many times I tried to see him during the day but left when I saw the line waiting. Everyone was troubled about their relatives, and, with what information they could supply, it was his responsibility to deal with authorities to help find them. His office, so efficiently run, was the repository of all the sadnesses brought to him by the refugees. He had had considerable experience in England with the refugee problem, but, because he was a man of intense sensitivity, I could see the change in him because of the constant flow all day long and often into the evening. I was concerned about his health, but there was nothing to be done.

One day Morris invited me to his quarters for an evening. He said it would prove to be quite interesting, and he hoped all the staff would come for what he had planned. When we arrived, his large room was filled with all the staff and I don't know how many men. I wondered what was going on. These men were all Russians. I had seen them eating in the mess, but since we knew that the clientele was composed of 37 national origins, I never tried to sort out who was who and why.

We sat all over the floor, on any piece of furniture that would hold a human body. Morris had managed to get a number of bottles of Campari in town, and the drinks flowed freely. All the men were the "husky" type and spoke mostly Russian and some French. Morris had gathered us together for this farewell party.

Utmost secrecy had been observed by Morris and Moe Beckelman, who were the only ones who knew about the imminent departure of this group of men. I think there were about 15 in all. For some weeks, all during the negotiations with the French, there was not the slightest revelation that anything was going on. Now it could be told, as this group had signed up for the French Foreign Legion, which was made up of men such as these who had gotten separated from their army outfits and wanted to continue fighting the enemy. That very day their papers had come and they were accepted. That was the occasion for the party. For entertainment we all sang far into the night. The voices of these men were wonderfully beautiful. They could go on and on. When Morris called upon the American staff, of which we were six, we had the greatest difficulty in remembering songs beyond our national anthem! Why? I've never been able to fathom this unless it was that we had been so absorbed for all these weeks and months that we could not remember our musical heritage. It was most embarrassing. As the Campari disappeared, enjoyed mostly by the Russians, the party got more and more boisterous. Suddenly there was a message brought by one of the Italians guarding the gate. Everyone stood up, the Russians began to shake hands all round, picked up their packs of belongings, and disappeared into the night. The trucks had called for them to take them to Algiers, which was headquarters for the Foreign Legion. The seriousness of men going into battle suddenly struck us. Without a word beyond a mumbling of good night, we literally slunk back to our quarters. This party remains imprinted upon my memory forever, although it took place in 1944, a very long time ago.

All the staff had one day a week off. We would count on the Chevrolets to take us to town and bring us back to camp. There was no other transportation. Some of the staff paired off. Those who wanted to remain overnight in Casablanca could do so, if they could arrange for accommodations. Several had made good contacts at their former billets and would take advantage of this opportunity. It was really necessary to get away from the center for a bit of refreshment and change. There were beautiful beaches nearby. I had made friends with Mme. Benatar, who had introduced Mlle. Chancerelle to me, and she invited me to use her home as my own.

I chose Thursdays as my day off and planned to stay overnight at the apartment of Mme. Benatar. She was affectionate and a wonderful friend. Her two children, Marc, age 10, and Myriam, age 12, were always overjoyed whenever I came. I could send to New York for a cowboy outfit for Marc, for which he had longed all his life. I could use my guest privileges at the officers' mess and take them with me for meals. They were thus assured of a couple of good meals, for as much as they could hold, at least once a week. I could take them to the well-stocked PX and purchase chocolate and other delicacies they had not tasted in years. Mme. Benatar was so grateful. There was so little food in Casablanca that, although she paid the highest prices on the black market, she just could not get enough to nourish those fast-growing children. There was little laughter in them. Only a few years ago their father, age 36, had suddenly died of pneumonia. The shock of this was such that Mme. Benatar had dressed herself in black. She drew all the curtains and vowed that never again would sunlight come into their home. Grief had taken over completely, and she would not permit laughter, music, or anything enjoyable to enter her home. As she was a great help to the American forces upon their arrival in Casablanca, she became great friends with the Army Chaplain, Major Edwards of California, I believe Palo Alto. When I first arrived at her home, the living room was bathed in beautiful warm sunshine. On a chest was a large photo of the Major, autographed, framed in a beautiful antique French metal frame, and beside it a vase containing fresh roses.

I learned later that it was Chaplain Edwards who was the great friend who helped Mme. Benatar in all her sorrow. It was he who drew the curtains so the sunshine would flood the room. It was he who made her realize that the children had to stop grieving and learn to play with others and try to be happy. It was Chaplain Edwards who sent the first large bouquet of roses, although she had sworn that never again would flowers adorn her home, for she and her husband adored flowers and the home was always filled with them. Chaplain Edwards could not persuade her to discontinue her black widow's weeds.

It was work that helped Mme. Benatar the most. She was involved in all kinds of social service among groups of needy people, especially Jews living in squalor in the Mellah and poor French people. My Thursdays were always devoted to helping her with her social service efforts. I visited the kindergartens with her and worked out the necessary foods for the nutrition of those children from the meager supplies available from the rations. When it came time for the children's camp in the mountains that had been one of her pet efforts, I managed to use my influence with the colonel who had helped me so much to get cots and blankets for the camp, as everything had been confiscated during those terrible years. It was not much of a change for me on my days off, except that the problems were different and even more of a challenge than at our center, where everything was organized and going smoothly. Although it was "off limits" for American personnel, I succeeded in persuading Mme. Benatar to take me to the Mellah. She had shown me the maps of the reorganization of the congested Mellah, where a huge population of Jews lived in poverty and squalor beyond imagination. Her husband had been very active in improving conditions there prior to his death. All that remained of his efforts were the maps of the reconstruction, particularly those bringing sanitation into the area. On each street was one faucet. All the inhabitants on that street lined up to draw water into metal pails. This was the only water available for all the uses of the family: cooking, washing, bathing. Fortunately, the American Jewish Joint Distribution Committee was at last alerted to these conditions by Mme. Benatar, who was their volunteer representative.

My duties at the refugee center continued on the same scale. It must have been obvious to everyone but me that there was a great change in my physical appearance. Although there was a staff mess a few miles away, where the staff could get good meals, not army rations, and also a bit of recreation at mealtime, I felt I could not avail myself of this privilege. I insisted that a staff member had to be present at the center at all times. I had observed enough of the high pitch of emotions among the refugees to realize that, unless an authority figure was on hand at all times, one could not be certain of what might happen. Already I had had an experience in one of my kitchens, which my interpreter explained to me. I had come into one of the kitchens right after breakfast, to give instructions to a new refugee who had just been assigned and who had arrived unexpectedly only a few days before. A terrible argument was going on. When I stepped inside, it stopped suddenly, but fear and anger were in the atmosphere. Then René explained what had happened. This new man was recognized by one of the workers as one who had been in the same concentration camp with him in Germany and who, because he had money, was able to bribe the guard to get milk for his children. When the others complained to him that all should be treated alike, he told the guard, and punishment was meted out to the others. Meeting here, in one of my kitchens, they recognized each other, and emotions ran so high that murder could have occurred had I not arrived at that moment! Naturally, I placed the new arrival in another kitchen, and reported it to Moe to be on the look-out, in case of a disturbance.

To satisfy Morris, who had expressed great concern for my health, I did go to the staff mess on Sunday for dinner. All during the meal I confess I was uneasy about leaving the center to the refugees. The staff was relaxing ... it was Sunday after all ... there was no hurry to return, as they were off duty. Suddenly, I insisted that Moe send me back in one of the Chevrolets. Everyone was critical of me, but I hastened back. The moment the car entered the gate and René, who was watching for me, saw it, he came running the full length of the camp, shouting to me to come at once. He was as pale as a ghost. "Mlle., please hurry!" he shouted. "They are fighting with knives. They are bleeding."

I had not run so fast since my college days, when I was on the hockey team. I stood at the entrance of the mess hall where the trouble had started. The other mess halls were deserted, as everyone had fled to their tents for protection, not knowing how far the danger would spread. The place looked deserted. I just stood in the doorway, and suddenly there was not a sound where moments before they were wielding huge kitchen knives. When I appeared, everyone sitting at the tables, not daring to say a word or move, seemed to relax from tension and fear. I shouted "Sammy, put that knife down!" I just stood and glared at the two who were fighting.

After I caught my breath and realized that no one was dangerously hurt, I gave my speech in a voice that quivered with emotion. I could hardly believe that, just because for once I had left the center to eat with the staff for a change of scene, I would return to such commotion. It is true, this was the very first time the center had been left without coverage by a staff member. There was such obvious relief among all, even among those who in anger were ready to kill each other over a mere triviality the moment before! What had happened? It seems that one man in line, one of the quietest and seemingly meekest of souls, not feeling particularly well, had requested the cook to give him less of one of the dishes and more of the other as he held out his mess kit. That anyone would dare to expect him to deviate from the usual practices so infuriated the cook that he lost his temper. There was an exchange of words, and the shouting began, followed by the fight that involved the wielding of knives. One who had dared try to calm them down had received a huge gash in his arm and fled, screaming and dripping blood all over the steps of the mess hall. In a matter of minutes all was calm again. I dismissed those who were sitting at the tables who had finished their dinner, so the clean-up gang could go on with their duties.

What did this take out of me? The calm I managed to assume was followed by worries and fears for what might have been had I not appeared on the scene. Did I have a premonition that made me insist upon leaving the staff mess? Needless to say, from that time on, it became the rule that at least one staff member had to be present at all times. Was it my intuition that had stood me in good stead? Or was it that in my social work experiences, especially during the Great Depression years, I had seen really quiet, law-abiding people get into a frenzy over something ordinarily considered trivial, and then the battle of words lead to a quarrel of such magnitude that they were ready to kill each other? This is what can happen to people who go through so much suffering that the slightest remark can set off the spark that releases pent-up emotions to the heights of complete loss of control. People subjected to these unbelievable pressures need gentle treatment and tolerance and understanding at all times.

A few days later, as I was hurrying toward the mess halls early one morning for the breakfast meal, I saw everyone standing in groups talking together. Frightened children were clinging to their mothers' skirts. Men were holding screaming children. I noticed Moe Beckelman, the Project Director, standing at the entrance of one of the tents. I started running toward him and reached him all out of breath. It is not easy to run through desert sand. What happened? I saw at once that he was as pale as a ghost and so frightened that he could hardly speak. One of the men said in shaking tones, "Mr. S. has been killed."

I was transfixed and could hardly speak. "Killed—who killed him?"

Trying to be as calm as possible, Moe told me what had happened. It was a terrible accident. It seems that during the night Mr. S. did not feel well. He either reached for his flashlight or lit a candle to find his medicine. He was sitting up in bed. His shadow was on the tent as he moved about. One of the Italian guards, mistaking him for a thief who had entered the tent and thinking that the movements were a struggle, fired a shot that pierced the tent and killed Mr. S. immediately. The screams of his wife when the tragedy was discovered brought several to the tent. To think that this family had been through so much, were rescued from concentration camps, and at last after years of struggle were in the one safe place awaiting the end of the war to be repatriated, that such an accident would occur to destroy the last bit of hope. One can never describe the depression that permeated the whole center. As this man was a Jew, arrangements for immediate burial had to be made. That it all happened so quickly was due to the cooperation of the U.S. military, to whom burial was routine. That very morning services were held in the social hall. In all my life I never heard such hysteria expressed. The body was taken away, and our Chevrolets, filled with family and friends and a few staff members, accompanied the body to the place in the cemetery where it was interred. All day long an atmosphere of gloom prevailed. All day long the religious Jews remained in the social hall praying. What sadness!

Sue Sadow, Director of Nutrition for the Office of Foreign Relief and
Rehabilitation Organization (OFRRO), which later became the United
Nations Relief and Rehabilitation Administration.

Chapter 27
UNRRA — ITALY

The experience in Italy was the most useful of all my UNRRA (United Nations Relief & Rehabilitation Administration) years.

The UNRRA Italian Mission was to assist the newly established Italian Government to set up programs for relief of the war-torn population. As chief nutritionist I worked with the Government Ministries of Food and Health in formulating program objectives for overall food and clothing distribution. The first thing was to seek and find my counterpart so that anything I did could be turned over to her. It proved to be Dr. Edvige Fileti, Consultant Dietitian of Italian Hospitals. We made a tour together of many hospitals where she trained dietitians. I had the authority to requisition UNRRA foods to be given to Dr. Fileti. She, in turn, instructed her dietitians to formulate recipes to turn UNRRA foods into palatable dishes acceptable to Italian tastes. As the foods arrived, Dr. Fileti would see to it that the distribution was among pregnant women and nursing mothers and school children. It was the first time we established a school lunch program, which resulted in improvement of the nutrition of school children and of their eating habits.

This resulted in the publication of a School Lunch Manual with recipes prepared by Dr. Fileti's dietitians to appeal to Italian tastes.

I spent most of my time in the field, leaving the office in Rome to my British UNRRA Assistant Marjorie Bailey. I was constantly in touch with the UNRRA Regional Directors to establish preliminary meetings in their districts. These meetings of doctors, nurses, teachers, and housewives were for the purpose of displaying UNRRA goods to the population. I always had paper plates and disposable spoons so that persons attending these meetings could become acquainted with UNRRA foods, and usually they would have ideas themselves about using them in Italian recipes, which differed from region to region all over the country.

Dr. Fileti would often meet me at these meetings and become acquainted with the UNRRA Regional staffs and answer their questions.

The regional conferences I established were of the greatest satisfaction to me for they offered a way of getting professional people together. This made it possible for UNRRA regional professionals to became familiar with universities in the regions for which they were responsible.

A total of 12 Nutritional Conferences were held over a period of one year, which required a lot of preparation. I took Dr. Fileti along during the organizational process, so that she could explain what that process was.

Usually, Dr. Fileti opened the conference. I came next, having written my remarks in English to be translated into Italian by my Italian teacher. I used to stumble over the long Italian words with a great deal of help from the audience, ending up with "Bravo, Signorina." There would be much applause at my attempts, which lent a light touch that my audience appreciated.

The conference usually lasted for five days. The mornings were devoted to speeches on nutrition by university professors. For the first time the professors wrote their speeches, which would later be published in pamphlet form as there were no books on nutrition for the lay public.

The conferences were held at the university's great hall to give them prestige. The speakers were doctors, nurses, teachers, and dietitians. Even the cooks of school lunches attended the morning sessions. The afternoon sessions were held by the dietitians, who displayed UNRRA foods as they were delivered and showed how they should be stored. Then the various cooked UNRRA foods were used for those in attendance to have a tasting party.

Mr. S.M. Keeny, with whom I had worked in Washington, was appointed as chief of the UNRRA Italian Mission. He requested my services in the early spring and sent Abe Hackman, who was on leave of absence from his important job at R.H. Macy's Department Store in New York City, to meet me in Naples, which was in shambles, and drive me up to Rome. The Germans had left their mark on Southern Italy all the way up the coast to Rome. Utter poverty greeted us everywhere.

"What was the hurry to get me to Italy?" I inquired of Hackman.

"When Keeny sends for you, you don't ask questions. You step on it," replied Hackman, who was in charge of transportation.

The country was divided into regions and populations. Under the care of UNRRA, their needs were requisitioned, and truckloads of food were stored in our storage areas.

One day U.S. Army officials sent word to UNRRA that the UNRRA jeeps and trucks were to be taken off the winding hilly roads and would not be allowed to use the roads until further notice. The reason for this was that our Italian drivers had passed the ambulances carrying sick soldiers to army hospitals, causing danger to them on the narrow, winding roads. The Army was furious and would not inform us when UNRRA could use the roads again. A new shipment of UNRRA food supplies had just arrived in Naples by ship. In their eagerness to make deliveries before dark, our drivers had disobeyed army regulations and were sent back to Naples, which was the main storage place for supplies intended for UNRRA officials to use in the feeding programs in their areas.

What to do? The UNRRA regional official was awaiting the shipment for distribution. This was my responsibility. I telephoned army headquarters and explained my predicament about the delivery of food for hungry families. For permission to use the roads I would guarantee that the drivers would lose their jobs unless they obeyed my instructions. I made a quick decision to personally conduct the convoy. I dashed to my hotel in Rome, changed into official UNRRA uniform, rushed to Hackman's office to announce my decision, and ran to the garage where our jeeps were kept. At once I requisitioned a driver and was on my way to Naples, 100 miles from Rome. My destination was the storage headquarters, where I found the loaded trucks and the drivers, who were afraid they would lose their jobs and never be employed by UNRRA again. When they saw me in uniform, they were frightened. Time was of the essence, and daylight and distance were important considerations. Hackman had warned me; he disapproved of my decision. But there was no alternative; too much was at stake.

I quickly lined up the drivers. In my broken Italian I asked them if they wanted their UNRRA jobs. If so, would they agree to follow my harsh instructions? I would take inventory of the contents of each truck. If there was only one bag missing on arrival, the whole group would be fired. There was fire in my eyes as I voiced my authority. They knew that 100 pounds of sugar or flour would fetch a fancy price in the black market. We started. I was in the lead truck; who would volunteer to drive the end truck? We started. They had never seen Signorina Sadow so angry.

We reached the office of the UNRRA official when it was just turning dark. The unloading began, and the count was correct. I sent the trucks back to Naples, warning them that if there was an accident from careless driving, they would all lose their jobs.

I telephoned Hackman. "Mission accomplished." He wanted me to come back to Rome immediately.

"In the dark?" I cried. "Nothing doing!" I yelled, "I'll be back in Rome in the morning," and hung up.

"Why in heck was Hackman ordering me back to Rome in the dark?" I asked the official. "All I want is food, a bath, and a bed. I've had it for today."

Early in the morning I was on my way back to Rome. I cautioned my driver, who was grateful for food, lodging, and sleep before an early drive.

Rome! I was greeted like a heroine.

I discovered that when you are furious with anger, you can accomplish what you set out to do!

Since the city was headquarters for the mission, Rome's hotels were requisitioned for billets for UNRRA staff. Already there were staff from Washington assigned to various departments. The Allied Commission, composed of American and British officers, was appointed to set up the government of vanquished Italy. Elizabeth Fearnsides, who had been a noncommissioned officer in the British Army for five years, was transferred to Abe Hackman's transportation department, and we became good friends.

Having had the experience of organizing the camp for the refugees for the North African Refugee Center, I went about my tasks with assurance. This was, of course, a quite different assignment with quite different responsibilities. I was now dealing with the United States Government and with the war-torn population of Italy, a defeated nation, and a former fascist population who now claimed to be non-fascist. It was a job filled with heartbreaking responsibilities, when populations from infants to the elderly, stripped of all homes and possessions, had been forced to live without shelter under constant shelling. They were shabbily dressed; orphanages did not have sufficient food and clothing for the children, and black markets were everywhere, with prices all out of proportion. Doctors were without transportation because all the vehicles had been requisitioned by the Allied Commission in order to conduct the business of running the country.

A British home economist, Marjorie Bailey, had been assigned to me as an assistant. She was conscientious but without experience in the tasks of feeding and clothing a war-torn population. I found her most helpful during the years we served together. I felt my work was altogether in the field, catering to the needs of our district officers and furnishing them with the UNRRA supplies brought by ship from the U.S. to fill my quarterly requisitions for food, clothing, and equipment for which I had responsibility. They came by ship to feed the population in the British areas supervised by UNRRA personnel, mostly Americans and Canadians, with assistance from Denmark and other countries that had joined UNRRA. She kept the Rome office running while I was in the field. Packages we were allowed to receive from the U.S. were of regulated 5-lb. contents from friends, relatives, and colleagues from all the social work jobs I had held throughout the years. They were not only willing but anxious to help in any way they could. World War II was over; the U.S. prospered. Italy was a defeated nation without supplies.

Upon returning from a field trip, I found my office walls lined from floor to ceiling with 5-pound boxes. I was called to the office of the postmaster to account for receiving so many packages. "Was I thinking of running my own black market?" I was asked. I was overwhelmed and called upon my Italian social worker friend, Josette Lupinacci, to help me. I furnished transportation for all these packages to an Italian orphanage that Josette designated as a "safe" place in the vicinity of Rome where Catholic Sisters could unpack the boxes, organize the contents, and later distribute all of them among the many orphanages in Rome, saving a good portion of the materials for orphanages in other parts of Italy. I wrote countless letters that said "Take a 5-lb. box, go into the 5 & 10, and just go from counter to counter and fill the box. That is how much in need we are over here." The day of the distribution, when all was arranged, Josette invited the staff in my office to see the display of contents of the boxes. Tears streamed down my cheeks as I visualized all those dear Americans fulfilling my requests so generously. All I needed to write was, "There are artists here who are hungry for paint brushes, rolled up canvasses, paints, etc." and presto, boxes would arrive, and the artists were grateful and set to work!

Chapter 28
HEAD START AND THE GREAT SOCIETY

Head Start began with an idea that Sargent Shriver, known as the great idea man, presented early in 1965.

I joined the staff of Head Start on February 19, 1965, as Senior Nutrition Specialist. I was 68 years old at the time and had just recently returned from Sierra Leone, West Africa, where I had served as a Peace Corps volunteer from 1961 to 1963.

My task was to find out where the worst pockets of poverty in the U.S.A. were located in order to set up Head Start classes. I was issued a six-week air ticket with the freedom to travel all over the United States. It was during this time that I learned of the extreme poverty in one of the richest countries in the world.

The conditions in the coal fields of West Virginia shocked me. Never did I expect such things in any part of the United States.

I wrote Sargent Shriver one night when I could not sleep because I was so upset by the poverty and filth. The little children were barefoot and dirty and living in the most unsanitary conditions. They were skinny and undernourished. I reminded him of our Peace Corps "cultural shock," suffered from conditions in Africa that we encountered. I wrote on my tear-stained stationery, "Sarge, I never suffered from 'cultural shock' in Africa, but in my own country I am suffering from one from which I may never recover. Can you do something about it?"

This experience prompted me to take advantage of my six-week plane ticket from east to west, including Alaska and Hawaii. I met nutritionists everywhere I possibly could and got ideas for building up the nutrition component for which I was responsible.

Later, on future visits, I could see that families of Project Head Start were doing their part. The project had been financed, teachers had been trained, and volunteers and fathers and mothers had used colorful paint, window curtains, and homemade tables and chairs to complete kitchens where the food could be prepared, served, and enjoyed. I was overjoyed when I saw what could be done!

For the young starting out, it is my intention to offer encouraging suggestions from an experience extending over 60 years. Many kinds of pioneers came to our shores escaping from religious persecution, famine, unemployment, and other poverty. "Helping the poor get out of poverty" was the theme song that guided me throughout my career. Joining the early idealists and coming under their influence was the foundation for my own ideas. In accomplishing their self-appointed tasks, they sought help from others who are in a position to cooperate. Together, we all made historical advances and gradually, over a period of decades, influenced changes in government for the benefit of the country.

Project Head Start was my final "CAN-DO" project in getting the poor out of poverty. This job as Senior Nutrition Specialist was the perfect job to finish my total professional experience. It seemed as if every single experience I had ever had in all my previous jobs prepared me for this final one. I applied all the "success" experiences to the job of developing my department, which won great success and gave me confidence and praise that inspired me.

President Kennedy cared about the idea of the Peace Corps, and young people responded to the idea of sharing our knowledge and benefits with newly independent nations that demanded freedom from colonialism. In 1963 the whole world was shocked by his assassination in Dallas, Texas.

Vice President Lyndon Baines Johnson was sworn in as President of the United States. The White House was prepared for the occupancy of the new President, Lady Bird, his wife, as she was affectionately known, and their two teenage daughters.

President Johnson immediately put his plans to work. He had conceived the idea of the elimination of poverty in this great nation, the wealthiest of all the nations around the world. He named his program the War on Poverty of the Great Society.

In declaring this War on Poverty, President Johnson got laws passed that were on the agenda left over from the short-lived Kennedy Administration. He got programs established, and he got appropriations sufficient to cover costs. These pointed to the success of his program and resulted in innumerable accomplishments.

In Washington, he set up the big umbrella organization known as the Office of Economic Opportunity (O.E.O.) and appointed Sargent Shriver as the Director.

Sargent Shriver had recently returned from his job as Director of the Peace Corps. He conceived the idea of Project Head Start, reasoning that, to win the War on Poverty, one had to start educating the youngest children from ages 3 to 5, residing in the worst pockets of poverty in the nation of unemployed Black families and the poorest White families. Each lived separate lives in different communities and knew nothing about the other. How to get them together? How about the parents? Many Black and White families had never sat beside each other in the same meeting room, nor had their children played together, nor had the mothers volunteered together.

Shriver sought the help of the medical and dental professions, realizing that many of the children would be undernourished. Some of these children had never had toys or books for a bedtime story. Some had not been properly bathed, or rocked to sleep, or sung a nursery song.

A committee of experts was established to set down the rules to be followed, realizing that children aged 3 to 5 years had something in common though coming from different backgrounds. The chairman, Dr. Robert Cooke, Chief of Pediatrics, Johns Hopkins Hospital, was selected to consider the whole child and his needs. The components this committee considered important in assessing the status of the whole child were:

Educational

Medical

Dental

Nutritional

Psychological, Mental and Emotional

Parent Participation/Volunteerism

Each child was examined and provision made for each component examination. These components composed the Project Head Start Program to serve children, with a specialist responsible for the programs developed by each. Many of the children could not see, smell, or hear well. For some, teeth were rotted clear down to the gums, so the child could not properly chew his food. Many were found to be suffering from emotional problems.

As Goethe wrote, "Whatever you can do, or dream you can, begin it."

President Johnson's War on Poverty was my dream come true. My professional life, from the beginning, when I graduated in 1917 from the Home Economics Department of Simmons College in Boston, Massachusetts, had already been mapped out for me. From education courses required for graduation, I became acquainted with where the newly arrived immigrants lived, often referred to as "slums." The various national origin groups clung together. It was more comfortable hearing your own language spoken, whether Italian, Greek, Yiddish, German, or Spanish. They introduced their own culture to America via familiar foods. They were the immigrants who lived in poverty. I became acquainted with them through the field work attached to my education courses. I was horror struck at what I learned about poverty. This was the cornerstone of my future career; to get the poor out of poverty was my obsession.

A Head Start program was gradually set up in what were considered the worst slum areas. I was so touched and affected by stories of impoverished children, especially one story about a little girl who lived in a shack in the hollers of Kentucky, who had always used the field as the toilet. It is hard to imagine the conditions the people were living in unless you had been there to see it. This little girl would wet her pants at Head Start until she gained enough trust to allow the teacher to take her by the hand to the toilet, where she would sit and use it.

The following describes an encounter that I experienced when I accompanied a social worker on a visit to a home in the hollers of Kentucky, a region of the earth full of calamities:

"I'm right glad you stopped by to see me. There's been so much I ain't know what to do. I been despairin'. It's colder 'n hell up here in this holler this wintah. . . . I tole that perlice officer man . . . no use comin' up 'ere to git Jimmie 'n Rosanna ter school . . . Snow on the ground and neither one of them kids with shoes . . . Both coughin 'n spittin' up, too. Them newspapers you left here last time, been used all up to cover them kids.

Them blankets stink. . . . I cain't carry all them buckets of water up this hill from the bottom of the holler no more, I'm tellin' yer. Even if I could there ain't no wood left to make a fire to heat no water to wash. We been livin' in stink all them weeks. The mines are almost finished . . . nothin' more, the boss sez.

Paw sez, niver in all his life seen a winter like this one. I ain't complainin' mind you, we holler folks niver ferget our respect. We niver took charity. They sez . . . that social security bizness ain't charity, or we'd niver take it, even if we starved. I say, thanks God, it ain't charity.

I been strong all my life, but now, I feels weak all the time. . . cain't do nothin' much. I keep worryin' if I got cancer. They sez it is everywhere, and all them folks dyin' lately got it, an' no doctors, even if they could get into the holler don't know what to do fer it.

Missus Marley . . . up the holler a ways . . . got so skinny you could see her bones. I tried to visit her to cheer her up. The minister came at the end . . . she died since you was here. God, how them kids did scream when they put her in the ground . . .

I keep thinkin' of my kids . . . what they gonna do ef I got cancer, like I worry I got it too . . . so many wimmin in the holler gits all skin 'n bones . . . 'n I'm gittin' like that meself.

You allas been so good ter me . . . what you think . . . what you reckon I better do. All them kids in there . . . the five of them . . . they all got it. I mean that flu they been talkin' about on the radio . . . They keep sayin' as how it gits the kids . . . I ain't even got nightgowns for them to be respectable . . . we allas been respectable people . . . we never took nothin' from nobody . . . we allas been God fearin'. . . . Please, what you think now I better do?"

Perhaps the biggest blot on the escutcheon of this great, rich, proud country of ours is the condition of the people of Appalachia, and the worst thing I ever saw in all my travels around the world . . . are the hollers of Kentucky. I came from Washington on a field trip, and insisted that I wanted to walk through one to see with my own eyes. One can read reports (accounts, articles, books) but only by walking the full length of the four miles, seeing the conditions, listening to the conversations, never daring to utter a word as one would be looked upon as a prying stranger, can one begin to comprehend what these mostly beautiful children are born into and the worn-out women who had lost whatever hope they had managed to preserve in the past. POVERTY in capital letters. The very worst kind of poverty. Hopelessness takes over . . . courage vanishes . . . nothing is left to fight for . . . That walk both ways through that Kentucky holler . . . the stench of human excrement that filled my nostrils, for there are not even outhouses. I had just returned from Africa as a Peace Corps volunteer in one of the least developed countries, but never had I encountered any conditions as degrading as these in the hollers of Kentucky.

To this day, that experience haunts me, and I keep saying, "For shame, America."

Project Head Start was the grande finale. From the very beginning, when Sargent Shriver appointed me as the Senior Nutrition Specialist, I pumped into it all my appropriate work experience.

My job could not be accomplished sitting at my desk in Washington, D.C. Building a staff of volunteer nutritionists who acted as consultants to several programs in the areas was a challenge. Once a year they came to Washington, D.C., where we developed programs for them to follow. These nutritionists brought to the Head Start national program their expertise and experience from their own jobs. Thus we developed enriched programs all over the United States.

Head Start yearly conferences presented booths. Each booth had Head Start posters. As nutrition booklets were developed, these were displayed to attract members of the conference. Booths were manned by nutritionists involved in on-going projects throughout the United States. Distribution of nutrition materials developed from single booklets into kits in sealed envelopes of materials for display. These were interpreted by nutritionists who acted as consultants to Head Start programs in their districts.

A film, "Jenny Is a Good Thing," with Burt Lancaster as narrator, was done with appointed staff members working with me. It focussed on food and nutrition. It was filmed in centers around the country with creative and wide-ranging nutrition-related activities. It reveals some of the excitement and feeling when staff and volunteers care about children and their parents and what happens to them, when the curriculum is imaginative and richly varied, when mealtime and food experiences are skillfully integrated in a program that best serves the Head Start child today and in the future.

This film was shown in Hollywood and was entered for an Oscar. It won an Honorable Mention and was shown in movie houses throughout the U.S.A.

Highlights for the awesome task for building up the nutrition component of Head Start included the parent program. Although it is a successful model now, the parent program started from doubtful beginnings. Parents who had never visited a school before, had never felt welcome, were now to mingle with black and white parents and participate together in evening programs the teacher had devised. To see white and black parents sitting together at tables and finger painting as their children had done a few hours before was an uplifting experience that had never been imagined before. This drew parent interest to make colorful playground experiences and joyous reactions from the children. Parents experienced what could be done on very small budgets and, indeed, from materials that would ordinarily be dumped in the heap of "no use."

Volunteers worked together with mothers and learned from each other what could be done, what could be accomplished, and how love could be spread. It was a happy sight to see a black child on the lap of an "adopted" white grandfather, explaining to him what was included in the drawing accomplished that morning; to see the little boys and girls assigned tasks of setting the tables, serving each other, or clearing the tables for the cook to wash and sterilize the dishes; to realize the success upon hearing about the little 4-year-old who informed his mother "I won't eat sitting on the floor no more," after experiencing the comfort and joy of sitting with other children at the table. He enjoyed not only the nourishing food but the companionship of the teacher sitting at the table with each group and listening to each child tell his story or learn the importance of table manners. He had been taught to wash his hands, take his place at the table, and engage in conversation with other children led by the teacher. At the end of lunch he was taught how to clear the table. The table and chairs were built by the fathers and big brothers at class "in school." Can you imagine what joy I finally experienced on my field trips?!

So, what had happened to Head Start as we assessed it after 25 years? The mothers who were employed at Head Start centers in a variety of jobs and saw their children thriving can tell you: mothers who took advantage of the opportunities offered them at the very beginning and progressed as Head Start grew and developed—mothers who took advantage of the courses offered that steered them into classrooms where they learned of graduation, diplomas, degrees, jobs in teaching where not only their own children benefitted but also the children from other houses of poverty.

Sargent Shriver summarized the success so well in his telegram sent to Denver, Colorado, for the 20th Head Start Birthday Celebration:

"Congratulations to Governor Lamm, Mayor Pena, Sister Rosemary, Sue Sadow and all who are celebrating Head Start's birthday. It is a genuine joy for me to realize how popular and successful Head Start has become. But we should always remember that Head Start is only a beginning in what must continue to be a genuine national effort to help poor Americans get out of poverty. A hand up is always better than a hand out. Head Start exemplifies that philosophy, and we must never forget that Head Start, the Job Corps, Vista, Upward Bound, Legal Services for the Poor, Community Action, Neighborhood Health Centers for the poor, all were inaugurated for the same purpose, namely, to help the poor help themselves out of poverty. Let's pray today that our obsession with military spending will not diminish our commitment to the solution of human problems facing our fellow citizens."

This explains why my years 1965 through 1972 were the most exciting and productive of my career, the grande finale, the frosting on the cake. My part in developing the nutrition component in Project Head Start has completed my dream and obsession to help "get the poor out of poverty."

The Head Start newsletter report (Vol. 6, No. 6, June/July 1972) of my retirement read as follows:

<u>Head Start Senior Nutrition Specialist Retires</u>

Sue Sadow, who has been the senior nutrition specialist of Head Start as well as the "senior" member of the Federal staff, single handedly designed and launched Head Start's famed nutrition program, starting it all at the beginning of the poverty program for preschoolers—February 19, 1965.

She says, "The best way to describe my methods is CHUTZPA. I've never saved up for 'fun' in my golden years. I've had it all the time," she states at the age of 76.

The thousands of staff members who have met her, the parents and staff who have taken her nutrition courses and listened to her sparkling lectures, along with those of us who have worked daily with her at headquarters will miss her greatly—to say nothing of the thousands of people all over the world who have ordered her Nutrition Kits. (Sue, have we sent any to the moon yet?)

So, to Sue we sing:
"You made Jenny a good thing,
You put kits on the map,
You gave Head Start a special zing,
You are the greatest with all your ZAP."

Sue Sadow, Senior Nutrition Specialist for Project Head Start, enjoys a lunch with Head Start children at a day care center in Columbus, Ohio.

PART IV

CRUSADING
IN
LATER
LIFE

WHY THE PEACE CORPS?

Excerpted from *INTO AFRICA WITH THE PEACE CORPS* by Sue Sadow, Beaumont Books, P. O. Box 551, Westminster, CO 80030. Book may be ordered from above address for $7.95 plus $2.00 postage and handling.

"Long distance call for you, Sue," shouted my housemate, Ann Racich, at 7:30 a.m. one morning late in September , 1961. We shared a large old-fashioned apartment in San Francisco. "It's Washington calling."

I was trembling with excitement and fear as I knew it was already 10:30 a.m. Washington time, and I was fervently hoping this was my call to join the Peace Corps group going to Sierra Leone in West Africa.

Earlier I had looked on a map and found Sierra Leone to be a tiny country on the west coast of Africa next to Liberia where we sent our liberated Negroes after the Civil War. In the encyclopedia, I learned it had been a British colony for about a 100 years and had won its independence from England very recently. Its capitol city is Freetown where the natives speak some sort of "pidgin English." The encyclopedia also described it as having "the worst possible climate" and being known as "White Man's Grave."

Despite these discouraging facts about the country, my friends' strong disapproval of my desire to get into the Peace Corps, and the obstacle of my age, I was determined to join the Peace Corps. Why was I so persistent at 65 to volunteer my services to an underdeveloped country?

Every since I heard President Kennedy's announcement about the Peace Corps being organized to spread peace all over the world through volunteer "Ambassadors of Peace," I was determined to be a part of this innovative program.

Early on the job, President Kennedy had stunned the nation by announcing the program of the Peace Corps. He requested that young people volunteer two years of Peace Corps service–without pay-to assist newly-independent, underdeveloped countries with their problems. It was such an innovative proposal, and I was very much intrigued and supportive of the idea. Instead of using enormous sums in preparation for war, he proposed to allocate funds for peace. It seemed to make sense. Kennedy appointed his brother-in-law Sargent Shriver (married to his sister Eunice) as Director of the Peace Corps, charging him with the awesome task of starting up this agency.

It was in the 60's when there was much criticism of our young people throughout the country. When I heard the program being dubbed the "Kiddy Corps," I wished that elderly persons might also be considered for the Peace Corps even though I had great confidence that our youth could be of great help to these developing nations. From my personal encounters with young people, I felt they possessed great idealism, honesty, and sincerity. I felt our elder office-holding citizens had already made their share of mistakes, and I was ready to entrust our youth with new responsibilities.

It was so refreshing to have a young president instill new hope and confidence in our youth. He seemed to surround himself with advisors who were young, brilliant, and knowledgeable, which in turn, filled the American people with new confidence and hope for the future.

Amidst this aura of hope of the 60's, the Peace Corps was born and started attracting great numbers of young people from all over the country. Many were young people who had participated in the Civil Rights Movement to break the poverty cycle and establish justice for the underprivileged.

It was the period when many countries in Africa were gaining their independence from England, France, Portugal, and Spain. After they achieved independence, they appealed to nations to not only recognize their independence but to help them in a variety of ways so that they could govern themselves and compete with other countries. The host countries who accepted Peace Corps Volunteers saw many advantages in having young Americans placed in their countries, who would live in the same manner as their African counterparts and use their training and skills to improve local conditions.

The success of these volunteers can be best measured by the continuous requests of host countries that demanded increasing numbers year after year. Long-standing friendships were established between the people and the volunteers, and in many places the volunteers were welcomed and treated like members of the family. These "ambassadors of good will," who respected the ideals and morals of the people, shared their knowledge and skills and helped the people understand the value of friendships between people of different cultures.

In organizing the Peace Corps, Sargent Shriver felt it was important to visit these newly-independent countries personally. He took key staff persons, like Franklin Williams, with him to discuss specifically with leaders of these countries how the Peace Corps might be able to help. Most host countries were enthusiastic about receiving volunteers and promised to provide simple, native-like housing for them. This was the only expense to the countries, as other expenses were assumed by the Peace Corps, including a small living allowance for the volunteers.

Because I was interested in the Peace Corps, I attended every meeting about it that I found listed in the *San Francisco Chronicle,* always sitting in the front row where the speaker would notice me. After attending a meeting conducted by Franklin Williams following his trip to Africa, I raised the question about older experienced people like myself being included in the Peace Corps. He did not offer me much hope at the time, but instead pointed out that the Peace Corps was strictly for the young because they could stand up under the crude living conditions of the various non-Western countries.

Only days after this meeting I heard President Kennedy's speech in which he announced that now embassies were being set up in these newly-independent countries so we could provide more service to them. He also announced that age restrictions for joining the Peace Corps were being abolished. He said anyone-of any age-willing to contribute two years as a volunteer in any capacity in a host country would be welcomed. After hearing that announcement, I immediately dashed down to the San Francisco office to get applications and information about the Peace Corps. I was convinced that this program–if successful– could mean the end of wars, and I started to plan my next two years as a Peace Corps

Volunteer. I asked people I knew from my previous jobs to write recommendations on my behalf. The one from Senator Herbert H. Lehman was glowing about my four-year UNRRA (United Nations Relief and Rehabilitation Administration) experience. After a few months of such persistency, I knew my file in the Washington Peace Corps office was overflowing with recommendations to Sargent Shriver, the Peace Corps director, but I didn't know if I was seriously being considered for the Peace Corps because of my age.

Later I saw an announcement in the *San Francisco Chronicle* that there would be a meeting in the Crystal Palace featuring three people from Washington Peace Corps staff. Again I sat in the front row. The three staff members were Franklin Williams (who recognized me from the previous meeting), Warren Wiggins, and Bill Moyers, the deputy director of the Peace Corps. They were on a countrywide tour to inform the public about the Peace Corps, but their job was not to recruit.

I gained lots of information from these meetings as I wanted to keep abreast of any changes or new ideas that the public should know about because I was giving talks about the Peace Corps to the public in connection with my lectures on world affairs and experiences in World War II. I also gathered all the printed information I could find for these lectures, and my audiences listened with intense interest when I related information about the Peace Corps as a new path to peace.

After the Peace Corps meeting at the Crystal Palace, I stood in a long line to talk to Bill Moyers. "It is very important for me to know if I'm being considered," I said, my voice shaking.

Bill looked at me sympathetically and said, "If you'll wait right here while I go up to my room and check out because we must leave shortly for the next city on our tour, I'll be back and listen to your problem."

I assured him I would not move from the spot. Shortly he returned smiling and said, "Now I am completely free to listen to you. Tell me what is on your mind."

He was so young, likeable, and direct that I knew why he had been selected for this important assignment. I told him I had to know where my application stood on account of my lecture business. After listening to me, he wrote down all the facts in a little notebook and said, "I promise you that as soon as I get back to Washington in three days, the first thing I'll do is find out about your record. Then I'll either telephone or write you what I find out. Is that all right?"

I was greatly relieved, and I'm sure the lecture I gave that evening was most inspiring. I felt confident that I would soon know where I stood, but I braced myself just in case the news might be disappointing.

Now, at 7:30 in the morning, I knew I was getting my answer. Bill Moyers, deputy director of the Peace Corps, was calling to tell me that I would receive a telegram from Shriver confirming my appointment to Sierra Leone. He said I would start a training program with the Sierra Leone group in two weeks at Columbia University in New York.

The evening I got the telegram (dated October 17, 1961), I perhaps gave my best lecture because I felt so inspired. Everyone in the audience cheered and gave me a standing ovation when I announced this was the last of the series until I returned with more materials and slides after two years in the Peace Corps.

My friends' reactions were mixed with congratulations and admonitions. My friend Bea Goldman congratulated me on getting into the Peace Corps and, at the same time, warned me, "Sue, what about your lectures? You'll ruin your business which you have worked so hard to build." She continued, "How about all these treasures you've collected in your travels around the world? What will you do with them while you're in the Peace Corps? You'll need them again as artifacts to illustrate your lectures–if you ever go back to lecturing. All any of us can say, Sue, is that we've done everything we know of to help you. Write us often and if ever there is anything you need, just let us know, and keep well."

I told Bea, "I don't want you or anyone else to worry about my leaving. I got my wish, and I'll take full responsibility for my possessions so please don't worry. I'll put all valuables in storage, including my precious slides. My friend Alice Gilman has promised to sell my car. What else do I have to worry about?"

I had only two weeks before I left for training, and they flew by. Even the most disapproving of my friends helped me get ready. My housemate, Ann, was of great help as we both had served overseas with UNRRA during World War II and learned to be packed weeks ahead in readiness for assignments.

As I packed, I pondered why I had been so persistent in getting in the Peace Corps. Was it the drive to be a part of this great effort to establish peace in the world? I believed it was because of my intense emotional experiences of World War II when I worked in the refugee camps of North Africa. As chief nutritionist with UNRRA and of the UNRRA Italian Mission, I personally saw that the ravages of war and the memories cannot be wiped out. I relived the Battle of Cassino in Italy graphically when I heard two American GI survivors talk about their step-by-step movement during the terrible battle.

"As we were trying to avoid the constant shelling, we saw our buddies hit and heard them screaming for help," the two soldiers told me when I gave them a lift between Naples and Rome. "They were mowed down like helpless cattle. I'll never forget it. Those d— Germans in that monastery on top of that hill were raining down bombs. What chance did we have? I can't get it out of my head," he said."I don't think I'll ever pass this road again."

It was on this ride that I learned about the cemetery at Anzio where young soldiers who fell in that battle lie buried. On visits to Italy in later years, I always asked myself why it was necessary to torture myself by visiting Anzio. As I stood gazing at the immeasurable rows and rows of those white marble crosses interspersed with white marble stars of David (the six-pointed stars designating where the Jewish youngsters lie buried), I was reminded of those two GIs and I was grateful that at least there were two survivors.

The U.S.A. takes wonderful care of foreign cemeteries where battles have been fought and where the casualties are too many to send the bodies back home, so the foreign cemeteries are really the battlegrounds of American heroes. If we could only establish peace in this world, I reasoned, and we could send the same numbers of our young people–and old–to help people instead of destroying them, what would the result be? How could the Peace Corps fail? The cost would be infinitesimal in comparison.

These thoughts are what spurred me on in my efforts to join the Peace Corps against the reasoning of friends who tried to "protect" me. During the last two weeks, however, they worked diligently to get me ready to leave for what was to prove the most inspirational experience of my life.

When we arrived at Columbia University, I discovered the other young Peace Corps candidates had already received some preparatory physical and survival training in Puerto Rico. I envied the rapport among them, and I felt like an outsider. Several told me that they had heard of me, most likely because, at 65, I was the first and only "senior citizen" candidate.

A number of our lectures were given by Englishmen who had taught school in the British colonies of Ghana and Nigeria, which had already received their independence. Since Columbia offered courses in African studies, their teachers also participated in our training. As we had already been assigned to specific schools as secondary school teachers in former British colonies, we were expected to learn and become familiar with the British way of teaching. In addition to our reading and writing assignments, we had individual and group sessions with African studies teachers, psychologists, and psychiatrists.

I also was required to make tapes of interviews with the university staff to promote understanding of the Peace Corps. As a result of these tapes, I received many letters from former members of my staff, professional colleagues, and even persons unknown to me during my tour of Sierra Leone. They got my address from Washington and wrote me, asking how they could help me.

I studied avidly during the seven weeks of training at Columbia University, taking the work very seriously even though I doubted whether I could use much of it in Sierra Leone. Since I required peace and quiet to concentrate, I spent every weekend at the home of Luise Addiss on Gramercy Park, a dear friend and colleague for over 40 years, who generously offered this hospitality. In the complete privacy of her home, I practiced Mende, the one native language we were taught by a Sierra Leone teacher. I sat by the hour in front of a mirror making faces as I tried to imitate what the teacher had taught us. I tried to shape my lips with sounds from my throat in order to bring forth the words. But it was to no avail. Fortunately I was assigned to a school in the Northern Province of Sierra Leone where Temne was the only language that was spoken, and no one there understood a word of Mende anyway.

The physical aspects of this intensive program only tended to put me into better shape than ever. Photographers appeared from the New York and California newspapers to take pictures of this "remarkable old California lady" taking the Peace Corps training. When it came to "push ups," I could do was well as any of the youngsters in the group. I also kept up with the young people in running around the gym track and as a long-distance swimmer in the Olympic-size pool where the instructor timed us.

Gym was included in our curriculum every day. A British school teacher who had taught in the colonies instructed us in athletic games. As teachers, we would be required to lead and supervise games at our schools. I was selected to join one group for a practice soccer game. The only clothes I had with me to meet the athletic requirements for the game were a pair of shorts, a sweater, socks, and a pair of rubber-soled saddle oxfords. Since it was November, I had to wear my expensive black Persian lamb jacket for protection against the cold New York winter temperature. The coat's fashionable jacket length exposed my knees and bare thighs and looked quite ridiculous with my casual sports attire. The grassy Columbia University field where we were training for our soccer game was near Riverside Drive, and getting to the field meant crossing several wide avenues in uptown Manhattan. As we crossed all those avenues, I hoped and prayed I would not meet anyone I knew. I knew many people in New York, as I had worked for over twelve years as the chief nutritionist for New York City's Department of Welfare.

When we reached the soccer field, I deposited my coat there on bench where I could keep watch over it while we played soccer. We had been warned of many thefts in the area. Murray Stern in our Peace Corps group sensed my lack of familiarity with the English game, and he came over to show me how to kick the ball.

At this time sides were chosen, and I was relieved that my team would be near the bench so I could watch my coat. To my amazement and the wild cheers of my teammates, I kicked the ball correctly and in the right direction. Loud yells of "Atta girl Sue" helped me keep the ball on our side. Others on our side encouraged me shouting, "Get that ball Sue. ... Great work Sue. ... Get it, Sue."

Then suddenly Alan McIvor, a big tall young fellow, was yelling as he thundered down the hill toward me. I suppose since I was assigned to be on his side he was racing toward me to protect my position, but I was sure he would run into me. I panicked and ran the wrong direction toward the bench. Of course our team lost.

Much embarrassed, I rescued my coat and walked off the field. My performance proved to be the end of the game and my popularity. If games were further included in our training, I was never again invited to participate. I could only hope that soccer was not included in the curriculum of the Magburaka Secondary School for Girls. When I tell how I was introduced to soccer, I shout and throw my arms about to "tell it like it was," and I feel like the little old lady who was so popular on a TV commercial yelling, "Where's the beef?"

After the seven weeks of rigorous training were over, I was both exhausted and relieved as we packed to return home for two weeks before the trip to Sierra Leone. Discounting the unfortunate soccer incident, I had proved that a 65-year-old could handle the Peace Corps training as well as the young people.

UNITED STATES OF AMERICA
PEACE CORPS

Hereby commends

Sue E. Sadow

for dedication to her country and service to the people of

Sierra Leone

as a Peace Corps Volunteer

from Oct. 10, 1961 to July 11, 1963

Sargent Shriver
DIRECTOR

A PLEA FOR A PEACE ORGANIZATION
Delivered by Sue Sadow

At a Special Meeting Hosted by The National Council Of Returned Peace Corps Volunteers At The Peace Corps Headquarters, Conn. Ave. and H St., N. W. in Washington D.C., Oct. 29, 1987

Thank you, Loret Miller Ruppe, Timothy Carroll, and your staff, and all of you who have left your offices to come to this meeting, for giving me the opportunity to present my ideas concerning a national organization exclusively devoted to world peace.

I hope what I will say.....what I want to propose....will strike respondent chords within you, and we will find a way to make SHARED DREAMS BECOME REALITIES. What I am going to propose is not new. Dreams of peace have been shared by populations in every country around the world since the beginning of time.

One could say that I have a PASSION FOR PEACE. I was not born with this passion. I developed it after I had learned and observed the pain of war....the distress of war... and the disruption of family life due to war. On the way home after attending the thrilling, stimulating 25th Anniversary Celebration of the Peace Corps, I kept thinking , "What can I do for peace?" I realized then...as I do today... that not many years are left to me. I kept asking myself: "How can I best utilize these years before I leave this planet?"

Then the idea struck me! Why not start an organization of women who formerly served in the Peace Corps to work exclusively to promote an end to war? I have lived through so many wars, and I have seen women, the nurturers of human life, suffer so much due to the destruction of human life in wartime. Women's husbands, sons, brothers, relatives are required to answer the call to war. They go because their government made the decision to go to war. Some never return. Of those that return, many may be scarred, either physically or psychologically, for life. **War really has no winners.**

As a young Simmons College student, I had to study about war in a required freshman history course. The year was 1914, and war was raging in Europe, which seemed so far away at that time. I felt safe but fearful. Then suddenly the United States was drawn into World War I. Colorful posters saying "Enlist" and "Don't Be a Draft Dodger" were appearing everywhere. The mood of our country was such that a young man wearing civilian clothes was regarded with suspicion.

To win the war, we were encouraged to buy Liberty Bonds, to have victory gardens, to grow our own vegetables and to knit scarves and socks for our overseas soldiers. I knitted endless scarves, and my mother knitted socks. Red Cross furnished the khaki colored yarn. I also spent many evenings writing to many male cousins who were overseas fighting in the trenches or lying injured in field hospitals. Many of my cousins never came home, and I saw how their mothers wept.

At last the WAR TO END ALL WARS was over. Democracy had prevailed. People danced in the streets and were at last free to pursue their careers. It was the roarin' twenties. Women were liberated and had their own apartments. Their smoking was a sign of sophistication.

But with the end of the war came a stream of war-torn immigrants into our large cities to find jobs and security in a land "where the streets were paved with gold" —or so they thought. These poor immigrants lived with their malnourished children in overcrowded tenements in the slums of our cities. They needed help. I was one of the pioneers working in the little known science then of nutrition. Through social welfare agencies in New York City and Boston, I established nutrition classes for the children and special food and cooking classes for mothers at the settlement houses.

The festive and comfortable years of the 20's passed, and the Depression of the 30's descended upon us. As I walked to work along Fifth Ave. in New York, I was approached every day by a gentleman who shamefacedly mumbled to me, "Can you spare a dime?" Poverty and fear were rampant. President Roosevelt tried to cheer us with his fireside chats: "You have nothing to fear but fear itself," he insisted. But another large, dark shadow, the shadow of World War II, loomed just over the horizon.

I became involved in global problems when I assisted our family's relatives and friends to relocate from Germany to America. I helped find sponsors for them and met their boats when they arrived in New York. They arrived with worn-out suitcases and their belongings tied in huge bundles. It was wonderful to see the relief in their faces when I stepped forward to explain who I was and to tell them the names of their sponsors. Soon my apartment looked like a refugee center. These people were lucky to leave Germany before Hitler started herding people into concentration camps and committing one of the greatest atrocities of all time: inhumanely putting millions to death in the gas chambers—all in the name of War.

Then came Pearl Harbor. The United States was now involved in World War II. I was appointed as chief nutritionist for the recently organized UNRRA (United Nations Relief and Rehabilitation Administration). During these long war years, I distributed food and clothing to refugees in camps in North Africa and Italy. In these war-torn countries, I personally witnessed the ravages of war, and these memories cannot be wiped out.

I've told about some of these experiences in my book, INTO AFRICA WITH THE PEACE CORPS, which I wrote to promote peace. On the fly leaf of my book, I call the book a "symbol of peace" and ask those buying it to display it conspicuously in their homes and to work for world peace, which I believe is everyone's responsibility.

I'll never forget the terrible war-inflicted poverty and suffering of the people of Italy when I worked with UNRRA after this country became eligible for UNRRA relief when it joined with the allies late in World War II. I suffered from shock over and over. Women were dressed in rags, walking barefoot in the deep snow with no protection against the blistering wind. My duties were to clothe and feed the defeated.

A group of officers, who were our allies, offered to take us from

Naples to Rome since our means of transportation were limited. During a stop in the woods where we were eating our brown bag lunches, I saw a little boy of about eight or nine years old, barefoot and dressed in shabby garments which just barely covered his naked body. He stood his distance, afraid of the uniformed officers while he hungrily watched us eat. As I started to offer him my sack lunch, one of the allied officers grabbed my arm and prevented me from moving toward him. He said, "Nothing doing. The nasty little beast of an Italian is begging." He yelled at the child, and the child quickly disappeared back into the woods. I was speechless. I couldn't understand what made the victorious so heartless. To this day, I cannot get the picture of this little boy, this innocent starving victim of war, out of my guilt-ridden memory.

On another assignment, when I was working on a feeding and clothing project for an orphanage, I can still see a little boy dressed only in a woolen coat which had no buttons—only safety pins to keep out the cold air and to cover his naked body. Some American who had donated the coat to an overseas clothing drive had thoughtlessly ripped off the buttons, saving them for future use. The coat extended almost to his ankles, and he wore shoes which were much too large for him. As he came near me, I reached in my pocket and found only a package of Lifesavers. I gave them to him and he tried to roll a Lifesaver on the pavement. He thought Lifesavers were a toy.

These guilt-ridden memories, which never go away, are what spurred me on in my effort to join the Peace Corps. These are the thoughts that are contributing to my passion for peace today and my desire to start an organization of women who formerly served in the Peace Corps to work exclusively to promote an end to war.

The technologies of war today are so powerful....and could be so evil— if they were used to kill billions of people. The time has arrived when the women of the world must unite and take this problem into their hands. They must be prepared to tell their governments "No" to war.

Am I dreaming? If this is a dream, then let it happen. It is a dream of the future. It will take perhaps 100 years to accomplish,

but as Eleanor Roosevelt so aptly said many times, "WHAT HAS
TO BE DONE USUALLY CAN BE DONE."

Other organizations are devoting their efforts to promote
peace. But the women of the Peace Corps, the women who have
worked with victims of wars, must unite to build a better world,
a world without war. These women who have returned from the
Peace Corps are the first of their kind....the first group of American
women to experience our global society and see the ravages of war
firsthand. These former Peace Corps women can build an effective
and powerful organization for peace— just as women uniting for
other causes have built influential and prestigious women's organizations in the past.

I am still dreaming and I cannot get this dream to pass from me.
Because I am physically unable to actively pursue this dream, I can
do nothing more than tell you about my dream at this meeting. Now
I place my idea...my dream...into your "think tank" to deal with as
you see fit.

Thank you for listening to my dream. What you do with it is
now up to you. If my dream becomes a reality, it will be because
of you. As George Bernard Shaw said, "Life is no brief candle to
me. It is a sort of splendid torch, which I have got hold of for the
moment, and I want to make it burn as brightly as possible before
handing it to future generations."

Parts of this speech are excerpted from *INTO AFRICA WITH
THE PEACE CORPS* by Sue Sadow, Beaumont Books, P. O. Box
551, Westminster, CO 80030. Books may be ordered from above
address for $7.95 plus $2.00 postage and handling.

SIMMONS COLLEGE
Fiftieth Reunion, 1917-1967
RECIPE FOR FIVE DECADES OF SERVICE
by
Sue Sadow
Class of 1917

Well, here we are, Class of 1917, at our Golden Anniversary Reunion! The gazes of wonder of the members here of all the other classes who have many years to look forward to before reaching this septuagenarian state do not surprise us of 1917 in the least. We recall our own reactions when we were once like you—as indeed you must realize we once were! To look forward to a half century seems like an eternity. To look back upon, it is as if we were never any different from those of you of all the youngest classes, who are assembled here this evening to hear what one graduate of the class of 1917 has been up to for 50 years!

I have been asked, as one of the septuagenarians of this gathering, to share some of my professional experiences with you. The limitation of time that has been imposed upon me denies you the chance to hear a lot of what has to be left out. At this time of life we prefer to be heard—to have time to speak out—to be free in making the decisions of what to select. Also it would have afforded a marvelous opportunity to test the attention span of you young people!

As the time schedule of this Reunion Week is based upon Rush! Rush! Rush! for all activities planned, and there is no escape—even here—I invite you to join me on the breathtaking LEAP—from decade to decade—for the 30 minutes the schedule allows—and I hope to land you on your feet at the end. Let us begin!

As certain events of each decade since 1917 have had a distinct influence on our society—and hence upon my professional career—I present this story to you by decades.

Actually, for me it all began during my junior year in 1916. As a student I had resisted courses in education because I feared, once graduated and qualified, I'd have to teach, a field I did not want to enter. But I did want that degree, so I took the one course in education that would get me by. This was the course that launched me on the career I have pursued for a half century! The "field work" assignment of the course was to assist a senior in teaching a cooking class of little children at the Lincoln Settlement House in the South End of Boston. What did I know of poverty? What did I know of slums? What did I know of illiteracy? The historic town of Plymouth, Massachusetts, where I was brought up, did not specialize in anything like this. If such existed at all, and it must have to a degree, it was not evident to those of us who spent our time walking along the unpaved, hard dirt roads of Main Street, lined with beautiful old trees that we used to watch burst into leaf in the spring and take on colors of red and gold in the fall, where summers were spent at the beach or in the woods picnicking or canoeing, and winters with plenty of ice and snow provided skating and sliding down the long hills or sleigh riding to the jingling of the sleigh bells! We surely thought everyone went to school, but that only the "smart" ones would go to college.

As a teenager, this experience of coming into contact with the immigrant poor of Boston aroused all the missionary spirit I could command. I informed anyone who would listen "that something had to be done to correct such injustices as poverty, filthy homes, no money to buy food or clothing for little children; about fathers who stopped at the saloons that lined Dover Street and drank up the week's wages before reaching home, so there was nothing left for family needs!" This was a traumatic experience for a naive teen-aged country girl, and I must admit that to this very day I can recall my anger and unhappiness after each experience. In the dormitory I used to give vivid accounts of what happened during my forays into the slums. The more wide-eyed and attentive my listeners, the more eloquent I became, and my stories, undoubtedly fortified with a good dose of imagination, held my audiences spellbound.

commercial companies, and a variety of other individuals came to Simmons to interview the soon-to-be-graduated and undoubtedly ensnare these young hopefuls into the worlds of industry, science, education. We were made to feel that we were professionals, and our own estimation was that we, about to reach the age of 21, were thoroughly trained, knowledgeable, and eager to get out into the world to put into practice the four years of hard work behind us! Supporting us, too, was the admonition of our professors of "upholding the honor of Simmons wherever we went, as our banner to carry throughout life." We were indeed ready to go out and "show 'em." There was nothing that came up from the long list of possibilities that appealed to me. One day, however, I was called in and told that a woman was coming to interview those who were interested in going to Coney Island to work for the summer at a place called Health Home, a vacation home for tired immigrant mothers from the East Side slums of New York, who would be coming for a vacation with their children. I accepted the job on the spot. It was just what I wanted. In the first place it was far away from home and a chance to learn about the world I yearned to know. Then it was to help the poor and neglected who suffered so many injustices! I dashed home for the weekend to share my wonderful news with my parents. The enthusiasm, I must admit, was all on my side. My father, being a business man, asked "What are they going to pay you for this work?" Of course it had never occurred to me to discuss this unimportant issue. Well, it paid $16.00 a month; you met all your expenses, but you did get your keep. A bargain! Anyhow it was charity. It was with the Children's Aid Society of New York.

On April 4, 1917, the United States entered World War I. We could hardly believe it. We had concluded all our history courses, which seemed to me anyhow only about wars. It was frightening. . . . it was now happening to us! Headlines proclaimed "MAKE THE WORLD SAFE FOR DEMOCRACY, PROMOTE ULTIMATE PEACE IN THE WORLD." Who thinks up all these slogans for every single war, anyhow?

In June 1917 we graduated and received our sheepskins.

In June 1917 we graduated and received our sheepskins. Simmons was noted for preparing its students to go right out into the world of reality—get a job—earn a living—and get acquainted with life. I was ready!

The Coney Island job was an eye opener. Naturally, since I was to be so far away from home, my mother accompanied me to see what the situation was. She left satisfied that I would be properly taken care of and chaperoned, and was herself inspired that I was to have this opportunity to "do good." My dedication was without limits. There were not enough hours of work in the day to absorb the boundless energy I felt committed to contribute to my duties! This included dashing after the mothers and small children all day long to keep them fully occupied and "happy" on their vacation. I look back: if only I had let the poor souls alone who had come for a rest and peace and to relax and gossip and follow their own inclinations, with preferably no one to bother them and tell them what to do. But we were there to help them, to "learn 'em."

<u>DECADE . . . 1917-1927</u>
<u>THIS WAS THE DECADE OF THE ROARIN' TWENTIES!</u>

Let me hurry through the significant events that influenced subsequent decades.

November 1918—Germany sued for Peace. Our boys started coming home. They'd seen GAY PAREE and felt quite worldly but glad to get home.

1920—Women were given suffrage and allowed to vote! How many suffragette marches I had participated in with my college classmates down Tremont Street to the booing of crowds of bystanders!

1920—The League of Nations was formed . . . its purpose was peace keeping. The United States refused to participate.

1922—Russia became the first Communist State in the world, the USSR.

1923—Mussolini rose to power and established Fascism.

1927—Charles A. Lindbergh flew solo across the Atlantic in the "Spirit of St. Louis," opening the way to transatlantic flying.

1927—Talkie movies were born with Al Jolson in "The Jazz Singer."

Radio was developed during the 1920s, which established rapid communication.

During these years of the ROARIN' TWENTIES, our country enjoyed unprecedented prosperity. It was a period of frenzy, and youth took off in all directions.

Fashions changed drastically and daringly. Skirts went up above the knees, long locks succumbed to the barber's cruel scissors, and with one stroke off came the tresses we had boasted about being so long we could sit on them; it was called the Dutch Cut. Girls smoked openly; lipstick and rouge and powder, previously limited to the domain of the stage and the "ladies" who nightly frequented Howard Street (now since disappeared), became a daily part of the toilette. Youth was asserting itself, proclaiming its independence, leaving home to have its own apartments; hitchhiking was introduced and was the sport of boys and girls. Jobs took over with a bang, and more than anything else we wanted to leave our comfortable homes and live our own lives without supervision or suggestion.

The BIG CITY of New York was the lure. The job I persuaded a welfare director of a large agency there to give me was to give "expert" consultation to the social workers on how they should teach their clients to spend their paltry relief allowances to get the most food for the money, indeed how to try to "squeeze blood out of a stone." I was inspired (if not too certain) and under the influence of those sincere and dedicated women who were pioneers in family budgeting.

This was the decade when <u>travel abroad</u> was the rage. It was new; economy ships made travel for middle-class people possible. If you have read Cornelia Otis Skinner's book, <u>Our Hearts Were Young and Gay,</u> you will know in detail the story of my first trip abroad in 1924 for six months. It was my aim to learn about the people in all the countries! My classmate, Adele Shohan, was then living in Jerusalem, Palestine, with her English husband and baby daughter, and I decided to visit her and learn about the people in this far-flung corner of the world. Adele had been on assignment with a team of Americans sent there to help this underdeveloped country.

During the six weeks of my stay, I visited the co-operative colonies established by idealists from many countries—schools, institutions, and homes—as well as all the religious and historical sights. Jobs were offered me to fill the great need in my field. I promised to return.

Two years later, 1926, the highlight for me was the return to Palestine for one year to organize and conduct a Dietetic Survey of the country. Palestine was then under the British Mandate.

Upon my return to Boston, I had the great privilege of spending a year in research at the House of the Good Samaritan, at that time under the world-renowned Dr. T. Duckett Jones, expert in rheumatic heart disease in children.

DECADE . . . 1927-1937

1929—The start of the Great Depression of the United States, which closed 5,000 banks and left 16 million unemployed.

1933—Adolph Hitler and his Nazi Party launched their program of extermination of the Jews and succeeded in killing off 6 million in concentration camps and gas chambers.

1935—Italy invaded Ethiopia, and Emperor Hailie Selassie escaped to live for years abroad pleading for the return of his country.

1936—The Spanish Civil War, which gave rise to the dictatorship of Franco.

All of these events had an impact upon my personal career as chief nutritionist with the New York City Department of Welfare for 11 years from 1932 to 1943. One million persons were on relief in New York City. One out of every seven persons in this great city was penniless. It was the era of apple selling on the street corners—of begging—of "Brother, can you spare a dime?"—of President Roosevelt's morale-lifting fireside chats, "You have nothing to fear but fear itself"—and the program to fight his war on poverty.

I learned a great deal during those years about people's attitudes toward one another, and often, during the long hours of heartbreaking, overwhelming responsibility, I used to say, "If I can survive this, I could even survive a war." Little did I dream I'd soon be called upon to participate in a war—World War II.

DECADE . . . 1937-1947

This was the WORLD WAR II DECADE. On December 7, 1941, the Japanese attacked the Pacific Fleet in Pearl Harbor, thus catapulting us into wars on two fronts.

In 1943 I was called out of my job in New York City to join the staff in Washington of what soon became the first United Nations agency UNRRA, the United Nations Relief and Rehabilitation Administration. Shortly thereafter I was sent overseas to serve in North Africa for a year as chief nutritionist, to organize and administer feeding programs in refugee camps for thousands who were saved from Nazi concentration camps and those who had fled ahead of oncoming armies.

ITALY, already defeated and now co-belligerent, was to be rehabilitated by UNRRA, and I was sent there next as Chief Nutritionist in charge of all feeding operations. In North Africa it was dealing with the military for supplies, teaching refugees to cook using U.S. field army equipment, and showing them how to observe sanitary regulations to avoid disease and epidemics. In Italy it was dealing with the government the Allied Commission was trying to set up, to organize a feeding program for 16 million mothers and children. When fighting ceased, we could reach remote bombed-out areas travelling by jeep over all the war-torn roads of Italy. I usually sat in a jeep for twelve hours a day. No one who has not experienced living in a vanquished country can imagine the ravages of war, the demoralization of the people, and horrible effects of the black market. My work took me to every bombed-out area where inhabitants still lived . . . to schools, hospitals, institutions. Hardest to face were the children . . . hungry . . . troubled . . . frightened. I'll never forget how once I reached into my pocket and found a package of Life Savers and distributed them one by one to the children surrounding me. They looked at them curiously, and finally one little boy tried to make it roll down the road. They did not even know what it was. Anything round like that must have reminded them of something that could be rolled. The little children crippled and blinded by the ravages of war are memories that still haunt me.

May 1945 . . . We got word that the Hitler government had collapsed and Germany had surrendered.

1945 . . . We got word in Rome of the CREATION OF THE UNITED NATIONS on June 26 in San Francisco, whose purpose was to achieve lasting PEACE and stability! Noble idea. We had our doubts. The Japanese War also ended, August 14, and at last we could look forward, at least, to no more fighting and destruction.

DECADE . . . 1947-1957

The return from overseas after four years of conflict abroad and the ravages of war to our own country, where prosperity was restored with unprecedented strides, left one feeling completely out on a limb and lonely. I decided to be an interior decorator to get away from the ugly problems of poverty. I enrolled in classes and went into business. I was not happy with the change and later decided to try California, at the invitation and insistence of friends who had settled there. The life there of semi-leisure, free-lancing, attending UCLA, proved to be unsatisfactory, and I welcomed the chance to take a trip to Europe. This started out as only a brief pleasure trip but developed into my FOUR-YEAR ODYSSEY AROUND THE WORLD, years of incomparable self-enrichment. A four-year independent, uninterrupted journey around the world, learning about the people . . . their life, their desires, ideas, hopes, frustrations, and principally trying to fathom why there was such hatred against the people of the U.S.A.

The years of my journey, 1953-57, were the years of greatest unpopularity of the U.S.A. except perhaps for today. I arrived at the conviction then that the people of all the countries needed to know and understand each other—to try to understand what the officials of our governments operating at such high levels could not convey to the people at the grass roots level, since they had no contact with them.

In each of the 27 countries visited, where I travelled alone by means of whatever transportation was available, trains, planes, donkey carts, elephant, camel, and buses and spent whatever time seemed beneficial to my purpose, I took extraordinary color photos of people at all economic levels, in their natural surroundings. I visited schools, hospitals, clinics, and homes of the poor and the rich. I conferred with professors and doctors. I visited reformatories and juvenile courts. I tried to get a real cross-section of life in cities and villages, of people at home, at work in factories, at play in parks and pleasure haunts and luxury resorts. I visited famous historical landmarks, tourist delights. I wrote, carrying a small typewriter. I painted in oil pictures to remind me of certain places and, with my easel set up in the streets, was surrounded by children offering advice and comments. Once an old man, stopping to watch, said in French, "It is enough. Stop. Don't spoil it." I lived with families whenever possible in order to absorb the flavor of life wherever I was.

Some get around the world in 80 days, and I hardly have more than 80 seconds to make you aware of this journey, or even highlight its implications for me.

Upon returning to the U.S.A. in 1957, material and pictures were put in order and a lecture series was worked out. I launched myself on a new career as a lecturer in world affairs, naming the series "GETTING TO KNOW THE PEOPLE AROUND THE WORLD." I was determined that our people should know about the people in all the places I had been and spent so much time, to try to develop understanding. I was hopeful that through my commentary describing events during the period of my visits, with up-to-date supplementation from constant reading in World Affairs libraries, supported by my pictures of related scenes, I could instill interest and understanding. But our people seem to remain very far away from what does not immediately affect them, and it seemed to me that even with all the intense effort, the achievement was hardly worth the physical and emotional expenditure, in spite

of generous fees. This activity engaged my time and energy for
nearly three years, when I abandoned it to join the Peace Corps as
a volunteer.

PEACE CORPS

September 22, 1961: President Kennedy announced the
establishment of the Peace Corps. It was concerned with "objectives of promoting understanding . . . friendship . . . good will . . .
prosperity." What could have fitted better into my own beliefs and
convictions!? I was inspired and determined to be a Volunteer, to
be a part of a great movement instead of trying to do it myself.

The Peace Corps had lived up to these objectives. President
Johnson, speaking recently to a group of Peace Corps Volunteers,
said, "I wish we had as many of you in your outfit as we have in the
armed forces. If we had more of you we'd need less of them."
There are about 15,000 Peace Corps Volunteers around the world.

As soon as President Kennedy announced that anyone of any
age could apply to be a Volunteer, I lost no time in filling out an
application and taking the examinations. This program completely
met with what I had been lecturing about, i.e., that we must know
the people at the grass roots level and share our knowledge with
them if we were ever going to build understanding and friendship
with other nations, as the basis for establishing PEACE in this
world.

Finally the call came: "Would I be willing to go to Sierra
Leone to teach in a Government Secondary School for Girls?"
Would I!

Our six-weeks training course was at Columbia University in
New York. As this was right at the beginning and we were the first
group, newspaper interviews began and never seemed to end. I was
news because I was at that time the oldest Volunteer in the Peace
Corps. Our physical training was compulsory every day and was
strenuous. I could do pushups more easily than many of the young
people. This resulted in more publicity and photos! I did not feel
any different from the age I had adopted for years (unashamedly I

knocked off 10 or 20 years or whatever I could get away with), but the Peace Corps was famous for publishing ages so the truth was out!

Letters came from all over, especially from San Francisco, where I had been given generous publicity by the newspapers in connection with my lecture series of Getting to Know the People Around the World, asking about the mistake! I never could fathom why a woman's age was an item of importance.

The departure day finally arrived! The 36 of us who had survived the training were selected and left New York in a chartered plane for Sierra Leone, loaded with musical instruments, books, typewriters, cameras, tape recorders, all sorts of educational materials and luggage. We were to be assigned to schools all over the country. Before leaving, one of my friends, a lecturer on world affairs in San Francisco, telephoned me to read from an encyclopedia that Sierra Leone was described as the White Man's Grave because of the unsupportable climate. It had been a British Colony. It was not too late to change my mind. "Why take such a risk?"

A Ministry of Education truck carried eight of us to our respective destinations. One by one we dropped our colleagues at their assigned schools. As we sped on through the overwhelming heat and matching humidity and merciless red laterite dust until we reached the last stop, MAGBURAKA, I began to understand the quotation! Still, nothing could dampen our spirits or our missionary zeal for what we expected to accomplish in two years!

My roommate and I were last: Magburaka was 126 miles from Freetown, the capital, or ten hours of travel. Our house, a prefab manufactured up country, was situated on a barren plot on the outskirts of the campus of the Boys' Secondary School, where my roommate was assigned. In appearance it resembled the TV sets of Westerns: a porch across the front supported by square poles, a corrugated tin roof, cement floors, a living room and dining area, two bedrooms (sheer luxury), inside toilet facilities (for which we were grateful), and running water, that is, WHEN it ran. More often than not, it needed coaxing.

We made our little house charming and cozy, using many very inexpensive local African items for decoration, to us so attractive yet things Africans would not dream of using, preferring the more poorly designed Western things! Conveniently accessible, our house became a 'dropping by' place, and months later, when we got a refrigerator, we became famous for the drink the British cherish: lemon or orange squash. Offering these cold drinks (never refused) is considered only natural hospitality. We learned so much from our African friends during these visits. A people-to-people contact creates an atmosphere of understanding and trust.

My school, only in its second year and situated a mile away, was a two-room temporary prefab. We had 2 classes with 26 in each; the ages of the girls were from "13 plus" up. No one ever really knew their exact age, as there had never been any birth registration heretofore. The girls were all from tiny mud-hut villages from all over the Northern Province, the largest in the country. They were mostly of the TEMNE TRIBE. In our training we had been taught the MENDE language. Great help. I was the only non-African in my school. The language was, of course, English, as Sierra Leone was a British Colony before independence in 1960. My principal, a woman from Freetown, also new in the area, assigned subject after subject to me. It all added up to six subjects: Hygiene, Chemistry, French, Home Economics and Nutrition, Arts, Crafts. It was a challenge to say the least: no books, no materials. In this kind of situation, with no precedents, where do ingenuity and improvisation come in? My brother responded immediately to my cable to send me air mail a Gilbert Chemistry Set, which became part of my lab; the French Embassy, Cultural Affairs, mimeographed lessons from the one suitable book they had on hand. I purchased everything I saw in supplies in Freetown, improvised others, and it was exciting to see how the girls took to painting and designing.

Personal recreation? I would not miss the Saturday night dances at the Adams Hotel at the end of the dusty road of the Main Street of Magburaka for anything! We danced 'High Life' until the early morning hours. It was the only relief from typing lessons, planning, and teaching.

During the three weeks of Christmas vacation I took off for Ghana, Nigeria, Ivory Coast, Liberia, to see what these African countries were like. Our Peace Corps Volunteer pals in all these countries could be counted on for hospitality.

The first year was over. I was to be re-assigned and therefore would not be returning to the Magburaka Secondary School for Girls. Sierra Leone has gold mines. I like to say that I am probably among the very few who took gold out of the country legitimately. This lovely gold pin, with the letters *MSSG* (Magburaka Secondary School for Girls), was especially made for me by local master craftsmen and presented to me as a parting gift in appreciation of my services.

As CARE had arrived to launch a school lunch program, this was my second-year assignment. I was now based in Freetown, and spent all my time travelling all over the country: to the most remote villages to give demonstrations to the school cooks on how to prepare CARE foods, supplemented with local foods, to make balanced meals for children. This was the first time the children had had milk since they left their mothers' breasts. They drank the reconstituted dry milk and enjoyed it, and improved in health. We had a program for 60,000 elementary school children. Time precludes telling the many stories of excitement and interest.

My American friends of unprecedented generosity continuously sent me quantities of magazines, books, all kinds of educational materials, of which there was a pathetic dearth, so that I was able to furnish teachers and workers with books and magazines and even distributed them at the nearby leper hospital, one of my several extra-curricular activities, where the illiterate could at least enjoy the experience of personal possession and could look at colorful pictures and ads. One day when I appeared unexpectedly for a visit to bring books to a schoolboy suffering from the disease, one of the men patients, recognizing me, quickly reached under his pillow for his magazine and seemed to be enjoying it so much. What did it matter to me that he was looking at it upside down? He wanted me to see that it was his personal possession—his way of expressing appreciation.

The highlight of the Peace Corps experience was the personal gift to me, a Peace Corps Volunteer, of 30,000 elementary school books, discards of the Los Angeles County School Board, all in perfect condition: hard covers, excellent print, and beautiful colored illustrations. This was sent by friends in Los Angeles who managed the whole thing, including free transportation. Our Navy, under a program called OPERATIONS HANDCLASP, occasionally made goodwill tours to African countries and thus carried the many tons of books to me. Imagine my excitement when the ships dropped anchor in the harbor! Imagine seeing OLD GLORY flying in the breezes over our Navy ships out in the beautiful harbor of Freetown . . . on the most perfect day of clear blue skies and blue, blue sea! I was made to feel like a heroine all day. The books were unloaded and transferred by train to Magburaka, where I had been teaching. I had promised them all to the Northern Province, the largest and poorest and most overlooked. The official ceremony of the transfer of these books by our American Ambassador to the Minister of Education, with the audience of teachers and principals from schools all over the Northern Province who had come to claim their share of the books, and the many visitors and people of Magburaka, is an experience that will remain in my memory forever. The goodwill and friendship and appreciation that was so obviously generated by this gift of books was worth more than can be expressed. There were smiles, tears, frankly expressed affection. For the first time in their lives thousands of little school children were given the opportunity to hold a school book in their hands from which they could learn.

Thus ended the PEACE CORPS TOUR . . . the two years were up . . . July 3, 1963.

TRAVEL BACK TO THE U.S.A.

Two years had vanished. It seemed as though we had only arrived when it was time to pack up and bid our African friends farewell. The friendships that are built up, the sentiments that literally tie you to the life of the country, make partings painful. But July 4, 1963, found me on the 20-minute flight to Conakry, Guinea, to accept the invitation of an AID official to see the country. Guinea was so different, even poorer than Sierra Leone. Guinea, you know, got its independence from France, and its Prime Minister, Sekou Touré, is currently giving asylum to the deposed President of Ghana, KWAME NKRUMA. Who would have predicted that this university graduate who rose to the powerful position of President would become so corrupt and literally leave his newly developing country in bankruptcy?

Africa, with its fast-mounting number of countries declaring independence, continued to fascinate me, and I decided to visit as many countries en route home as possible. There was no time schedule for my return, and it was an opportunity for continuing self-enrichment following the type of schedule as during the Four-Year Odyssey Around the World. The French ship I boarded at Conakry stopped at 13 ports on the journey down the West Coast of Africa. At nearly every port, as it was summer vacation and schools were on holiday, Peace Corps Volunteers embarked. It was like a Roman Holiday: friendships built up rapidly, and at each port we visited everything we could, even hiring cars to take us into the interior to see the villages. There were so much of art and crafts and sculpture in ivory and sandstone and marble that only by penetrating the interior can one realize the skills of the artisans of these small African countries.

Pointe Noire, Congo (formerly French), was the last stop, where we finally disembarked. It seemed strange to be permanently on land once again. Time does not permit the fascinating stories of experiences and exciting adventures that I and a husband and wife team of Peace Corps Volunteers, on holiday from TOGO, enjoyed together for some weeks. They carried a guitar and knew many songs, and at the drop of a hat we gave little impromptu concerts wherever we stopped.

Our playground for the next 5 weeks was both Congos, the Central African Republic, Chad, northern Nigeria. We entertained our embassies everywhere with stories of our experiences in countries of Africa.

With addresses of friends, missionaries, universities, AID, USIS, WHO, UNICEF, FAO functioning in many of the countries, I "had it made." The fantastic opportunity for learning about the people by accompanying these officials on field trips provided experiences and knowledge found neither in books nor reports.

"Time," our common enemy, precludes the possibility of sharing with you the experiences encountered in the 25 African countries on the journey home. The trip on the Congo River sitting in the bottom of a boat scooped out of the trunk of a tree, and poled across to a village where we received hospitality and shelter from pouring rain in a mud hut filled with children who were so friendly and affectionate, as if we were long-lost relatives, and simple, trusting people offering us anything they had. Or the wandering in the fabulous old walled city of KANO in northern Nigeria, where life has remained the same as it was for thousands of years back. Or game parks of South Africa and safaris, or Nyasaland (now Malawi), whose Prime Minister Banda has just concluded his first visit to the White House.

From Malawi I travelled to Dar Es Salaam in Tanganyika and then on to the beautiful, idyllic island of Zanzibar. Many changes of government have taken place since then, and Zanzibar, which won a short-lived independence, was joined to Tanganyika with the current name of TANZANIA under one government.

Besides the unusual and extraordinary beauty of the island itself, its history is fascinating, and the conglomeration of people making up its population is colorful. Sensitive to the atmosphere of unrest everywhere and bitter feelings frankly expressed, one wondered at the outcome of the Independence Celebration for which great preparations were in progress, at which Prince Philip of England was a leading figure and quest.

At 8:30 a.m., November 22, 1963, as I gaily swung along the main shopping street keenly on the lookout for interesting subjects to capture with my camera, I was stopped by the Rhodesian couple with whom I had shared a car the day before for sightseeing. "Have you seen the paper?" I had to confess I had not. "Then prepare yourself for a shocker, and I mean a shocker." At which he held up the newspaper with its six-inch headlines "PRESIDENT KENNEDY SHOT DEAD."

Everything seemed to come to an end. People everywhere stared at me, for few Americans were on Zanzibar. In a shop a young woman said, "As a wife and mother I feel so sorry for Jackie. Our school children are wearing bits of black cloth pinned to their white shirts. We are in mourning for a great friend."

I left for Mombasa, Tanganyika, to mourn with the contingent of Peace Corps Volunteers stationed there.

Ethiopia, where the Italians have left a permanent imprint of language and culture since Mussolini invaded it in 1935, had a large contingent of Peace Corps Volunteers, which made possible visits and field trips to remote areas. Then on to CAIRO . . . JORDAN . . . ISRAEL.

ISRAEL, the country of fantastic development in the short period of statehood since 1948, stands out as an example of how it is possible to fashion a highly civilized, developed modern country from a barren wasteland. It is hard to envisage the destruction caused by the recent war of only yesterday.

After nearly a year of fruitful travel, I returned to Washington to hear that President Johnson had declared the War on Poverty. Poverty? In our native land? Surely poverty belonged exclusively to the underdeveloped countries we had just left, having gone there to help them out of their illiteracy and ignorance and poverty! It is so hard to justify that in this most highly developed country, the most enlightened and the wealthiest in the world, conditions can prevail in so many places in our land that are far worse than what I saw in the most underdeveloped countries. How can we explain it?

HEAD START

Mrs. Lyndon B. Johnson had called together the most prominent women of our country to the White House to launch the HEAD START PROGRAM. As there are millions of children of poverty families who would enter first grade in the fall—children who had never had a story read to them, never held a crayon to draw with, never snuggled a cuddly toy, children who did not even know their rightful names, nor even understand the language, children to whom policemen represented a threat, children who had never seen a doctor or dentist nor had ever been immunized—then let us get together and do something to give these children a chance. These are the children who are the potential drop-outs, the potential delinquents. They get into school; the teachers, trying to cope with 35 or 45 first-grade children, by-pass them because they seem stupid as they just sit and do not react. They understand nothing of what they see or hear. Let us give them a Head Start!

Sargent Shriver, who of course had been the Director of the Peace Corps from the beginning and now is Executive Director of the Office of Economic Opportunity, had earlier called upon a committee of experts to advise him about this most important problem. Their advice was: act quickly and corral these children, give them the experiences ordinary middle-class children have as a matter of course; act swiftly, without delay—offer communities all over the nation the chance to help these little children and their families. Get communities all over the U.S.A. to set up HEAD START CHILD DEVELOPMENT CENTERS; limit the classes to 15 children to one professional teacher, one paid aide, and volunteers, so that these neglected, frightened children might have individual attention so badly needed and learn to trust adults. Children starved for affection could feel free to jump into a lap and feel the security of being enfolded in loving arms. See that they are fed, as we know hungry children cannot learn nor do they have any interest in participating in activities; see that they get medical and dental examinations and treatment; see that a child who does not see well gets glasses without delay; that a child who hobbles around in shoes too small for him is given shoes that fit; put into these classrooms easels and paints and nature corners with fish and birds and turtles and plants from seeds the children have planted, so they can watch their own plants grow; take them on field trips to farms so they will learn that milk does not originate in bottles or cartons in the supermarket; provide "dress up" corners so they can don high heels, hats, gloves, pocketbooks and see themselves in a mirror for the first time; give them blocks to build with, playgrounds to run in, games to participate in. Give them this chance to learn <u>success</u> instead of failure and defeat, security instead of fear, outgoing friendliness instead of overwhelming shyness.

How about the bill? Who would pay? If communities would do this for their little children, the Federal Government would pay 90% of the cost!

So, working day and night, all of us in Washington and all the communities all over the nation succeeded in enrolling 561,000 preschoolage children in the first Head Start program in the summer of 1965! It was worth it.

How many of you have ever visited a Head Start center? How many of you sat quietly by just watching the children and the happenings in a center? I strongly urge each and every one of you, young and old, to go have a personal "look see," for only then will you be able to comprehend this problem and experience the gratification of realizing that something is being done about it and that nothing must ever happen to interfere with the continuous functioning of this program. If you do this, you may even want to <u>treat yourself</u> to the privilege of volunteering in this great and constructive effort in your community. You will begin to understand the "grass roots" level of our population. Only then will you begin to really understand how we can prevent the failures, the dropout, delinquency crimes so prevalent in our teenage community and even our riots. All I could think of as I tortured myself with the reading of Truman Capote's book, <u>In Cold Blood</u>, was, "if only that poor little half-breed child had had a good Head Start, if only he had known love and affection, if only he had had a home, he might never have lived such a tortured personal life that brought such tragedy upon so many innocent victims as well as himself." As responsible people we must devote our thinking to PREVENTION.

Well, I was lucky! Having decided to settle in Washington, I got the one job in the whole wide world that suited me to a "T." As Senior Nutrition Specialist of the national Head Start program, I have been able to put to work all my knowledge and experience of active involvement with the poor, gained over a period of 50 years. Experience gained in welfare agencies on a local, state, national, and international basis has served me well.

My field trips take me far and wide, from the "hollers" of Kentucky to the Indian reservations, to the migrant camps, to the rural areas, to the big and small cities, from the Virgin Islands to Alaska to Hawaii.

I've been heartsick and shocked at the conditions of our poor people in various parts of our great country that I had never visited before. The Peace Corps, during our training and preparation for what we might encounter in the underdeveloped countries of Africa, brought up the subject of cultural shock from which we would surely suffer. At no time during my service as a Volunteer did I ever encounter such an experience. But I found through visiting the "hollers" in the coal-mining areas of Virginia and West Virginia, the terrible shacks our people live in with no facilities, that it is worse than Africa! The dose of American cultural shock still leaves me unrecovered and depressed.

But with HEAD START one is filled with hope. Already, so much has happened that discloses that what we are attempting is having an impact. Recently, on a field trip visiting centers in a remote rural area, one sweet little boy as independent as could be was pointed out to me. His teacher told me the story his mother had recently related to her. Little Jimmy stormed into the shack that served as home, getting off the school bus at the bottom of the lane, and announced to his mother with all the vehemence at his command, "I ain't gonna eat off the floor no more." He had learned to enjoy mealtime at the center, sitting at a table where he was comfortable, which he had helped to set, with good simple food and the teacher and the companionship of his friends. Already he was aware of the difference and communicated it to his mother. The Head Start program involves parents, and we try to work out arrangements so that the home can carry out what is initiated at the center.

Communication is another problem, and often the teacher wonders if the children really understand, if they are really communicating, especially when they read stories to them. This incident happened in a very rural section where the children live in these "hollers." The Head Start center was in a one-room school house with the pot-bellied stove in the center; these old places still exist, you know. The children were seated in a circle. It was story hour. They were very quiet for they loved story hour. They hung on each word. The teacher was relating the story of Little Red Riding Hood. The greater the attention and silence, the more dramatic was the teacher's voice, "and then Little Red Riding Hood said, 'Oh Grandma, what big eyes you have!' 'All the better to see you with!' 'Oh Grandma, what big ears you have!' 'All the better to hear you with!' 'Oh Grandma, what big teeth you have!' 'All the better to eat you with!,' and then the big bad wolf leaped from the bed and ate up poor Little Red Riding Hood." At which point a little boy's voice cried out, "The s——————, what did he want to do that for?"

Thus we learn about our successes of communication!

So, my friends, the work that has absorbed a half century of my lifetime began with the introduction to poverty at the Lincoln Settlement House here in Boston by teaching a class of little girls of recently arrived immigrants how to cook and learn about American foods. This was the beginning of my war on poverty! Now, a half century later, I wind up my career in the proclaimed War on Poverty as Senior Nutrition Specialist of Project Head Start. What greater privilege could one ask than this grande finale in the service of little children!

It is good to be here, appreciating the opportunity and honor that has been bestowed upon me of representing my class of 1917, and sharing with you my personal recipe for service.

Now, I wish to leave with all of you for remembrance a slice of the nearly finished product, which is this: the rewards of personal benefit and self-enrichment overwhelm the contribution.

George Bernard Shaw has expressed it for me: "Life is no brief candle to me. It is a sort of splendid torch which I have got hold of for the moment, and I want to make it burn as brightly as possible before handing it to future generations."

SIMMONS COLLEGE

ALUMNAE ACHIEVEMENT AWARD

To Sue Sadow, of the Class of 1917:

For persistent altruistic concern for the welfare of people of all lands and in all classes through your work as Chief Nutritionist on the Staff of the United Nations Relief And Rehabilitation Association in North Africa, where you organized and administered feeding programs in refugee camps; and as Chief Nutritionist in Italy, where you organized a feeding program for sixteen million mothers and children;

For building understanding and friendship with other nations by helping people at the grass-roots level and sharing knowledge with them through your work in the Peace Corps in Sierra Leone where you taught for one year in the Government Secondary School for Girls, and through another year of travel all over Africa where you gave demonstrations to school cooks on how to prepare CARE foods supplemented with local foods to make balanced meals for children;

And for continuing to help the underprivileged in your position as Senior Nutrition Specialist of Project Head Start:

The Alumnae Achievement Award for 1968 is presented to you.

In honoring you, Sue Sadow, we honor Simmons College.

Harriet Dorsey Archibald
Chairman, Alumnae Achievement Award Committee

Mary Gordon McCrensky
President, Simmons College Alumnae Association

TWO-MINUTE ADDRESS
Given by SUE SADOW,
1917 SIMMONS GRADUATE,
TO CLASS OF 1990 AT BARTOL HALL
APRIL 25, 1990

Dear graduates of Class of 1990, faculty, and other guests,

Once in a lifetime–if we are lucky–we have an opportunity to fulfill a dream. I have been lucky and my dream has been fulfilled tonight.

What is it that is so important to me? I have lived to be present at this very-special-to-me graduation, a graduation representing my lifetime savings in a scholarship, which I set up at Simmons College just four years ago. It is a four-year scholarship of tuition and residence so that the student will have more time to study.

It's been a dream based on a lifetime of savings. This dream has come true for me tonight. I want to share an old-fashioned lesson with you from my immigrant Jewish parents. We learned in my youth–a very long time ago that you can't count on your fingers, for I am nearly 94 years old–that SAVINGS from anything you earned was more important than spending for the satisfaction you might enjoy at some time later in life.

This is the occasion when I am enjoying the time of my life! I am lucky to be alive and to be present at this graduation of the 1990 class of Simmons College.

Tonight the first scholar graduates. She is the first scholar to do me proud. I want to share my happiness with each of you graduates of the class of 1990 by giving you a gift of my book, "INTO AFRICA WITH THE PEACE CORPS."

This book tells the story of the most important work experience of my long professional life. It was in 1961 when I was 65 years old. This book stands for World Peace. Perhaps one day some of you will join the Peace Corps.

The big envelope for each of you contains the certificate of my gift to you. Please send for it. I have autographed each book.

Tonight it is your classmate, Kathleen Bouffard, who is the first scholar of the **Sue Sadow Scholarship Fund**. Congratulations to each of you.

Thanks for sharing this joy with me. I am proud to be a graduate of Simmons College, Class of 1917.

REMINISCING
November 1991

This autobiography was written over a period of years. In it, I have recalled events which seemed to merit inclusion to validate my personal and professional life spanning some nine decades. As I listened to my friend, Margaret Butler, read the entire book to me this month, it was as if the tapestry of my life were unfolded and, vicariously, I lived again the various scenes. In doing so, I experienced the old emotions of pain, awe, sadness, joy, and satisfaction in accomplishments to serve others.

In this tapestry of my life, I am aware of three themes (1) my ability to make the improbable, or even the impossible, come into being–my "CAN DO" spirit; (2) my sensitivity to the needs of people impoverished in life or in spirit; and (3) my commitment to the importance of working for world peace.

As you, my readers, weave your own life tapestries, it is my hope you will be inspired by these three themes. to make them central in your lives. Through you, the work I have begun will be carried on into future generations.

Sue Sadow celebrates her 95th birthday with friends.

SCRAPBOOK
OF
MEMORIES

Just before Sue Sadow (far left) left for her overseas assignment with UNRRA during World War II, the Sadow family gathered for a reunion in May of 1943.

Sue's nephew, Bernard Sadow, congratulates her the night of her retirement from Project Head Start.

Sue Sadow, Director of Nutrition for UNRRA in Italy, stands in front of UNRRA building.

To:- Vue Vadow - with sincere thanks for all your help in the Peace Corps & in the war against poverty - from Sargent Shriver

Reprinted from *INTO AFRICA with the Peace Corps* by Sue Sadow

FOREWORD

I count it an honor to have been invited to write this introduction to Sue Sadow's reminiscences about her Peace Corps experience in Sierra Leone from 1961-63. But after the Peace Corps, Sue didn't stop. She became chief nutritionist for Head Start, the pre-school program I started as part of the "War on Poverty." So I had a chance to see her at work twice after she had become a senior citizen.

From just these two examples of her life, it became obvious to me that Sue was an exceptional person. But to let it go with that description would be shortchanging her. This remarkable woman not only personified some of the finest qualities of compassion and intelligence of Americans of any age–the very persons we are seeking to enlist in our humanitarian enterprises. She also was a driving force, irresistible in her determination. Let me illustrate what I mean.

I heard from my Peace Corps overseas staff that they used to blanch when Sue approached with confident steps and clear voice. "Here she comes again!" they would whisper to each other, "no doubt she has three major projects, and she wants them by tomorrow!" Usually they were right--only sometimes she had five projects, and she wanted them today!

What followed is strange and remarkable. As one of my colleagues said, "When it comes from Sue Sadow, there is always a product involved–something worth having is the end product, her goal. So–unless someone proves that she doesn't know what she is talking about, we had better give her what she wants, no matter what it takes. She is not just talk–she is real." No one ever proved that she didn't know precisely what she was talking about; so she always got what she asked for, and she always got results.

She was the first senior citizen volunteer in the Peace Corps. Now, almost thirty years later, she has, at long last, decided to write about some of her experiences. We are deeply grateful. Firstly, for the things she did for her fellow human beings, and secondly, for setting some of it down so that it won't be forgotten.

Let us read her book and be proud of Sue Sadow. Let young people–and older ones read it and be inspired by her example. For millions of Americans, Sue Sadow is an excellent role model.

Sargent Shriver
Director, Peace Corps 1961-1966
Director, Office of Economic Opportunity, 1964-1968
Ambassador to France, 1968-1970
Democratic Party Nominee for Vice-President
 of the United States, 1972
Partner, Law Firm--Fried, Frank, Harris, Shriver &
 Jacobson, 1971-1986
President, "Special Olympics," 1983 to date

Standing is Governor Herbert H. Lehman, Director General of UNRRA, who was visiting the Italian mission. The picture was taken at the Esperia Hotel in Rome. Sue Sadow is sitting third from the left.

Sue Sadow paints the mountain scenery in Morocco in 1954 during her four-year travel odyssey.

August 22,1961

Dear Miss Sadow,

Thank you very much for your letter
and the attached material.

I have been in touch with Senator
Lehman and have written to Mr. Shriver
of the Peace Corps. I trust you will hear
from him in due course.

With best wishes,

very sincerely yours,

At 65---She's Peace Corps Rookie

Sue Sadow of S. F. Oldest Trainee;
To Serve in Sierra Leone, Africa

San Francisco's amazing one - woman people-to-people mission—Miss Sue Sadow—can't be reached at her 2195 Sacramento st. home today.

She's in New York, deep in a seven weeks' training course for "my final dedication—the Peace Corps."

She's one of three over-50 women bound for West Africa in January—to Sierra Leone, the tiny British protectorate on its way to nationhood.

At 65, Sue Sadow is the oldest candidate in the delegation—and probably the dean of Peace Corps volunteers in both years and experience.

"SIXTY-FIVE . . . wow!" said one San Francisco friend today.

"I'd have guessed she was in her forties, 50 at most."

Sue was doing pushups and pullups with a youngster's pep at Columbia University Teachers College—where the three "oldsters" and 18 youngsters were conditioning to withstand African demands and to fight the image of the "flabby American."

Boston-born, Sue Sadow trained as a social worker and nutritionist

WORKING WITH New York's desperately poor in the bottom of the depression schooled her for a giant job — chief UNRRA nutritionist after World War II, building bodies of millions in North Africa and Italy.

In the early fifties, Sue decided to go back and pick up the trail at the vanished refugee camps.

She learned to take color slides that she first saw four years and thousands of

films later—after travels in Africa, Nepal, Thailand, India, Japan, Israel and elsewhere.

SUE'S COLOR pictures were so exciting that she embarked on a new career —lecturing and writing. She lectured at the YWCA here in the spring of 1960 and last summer.

"My health will hold up better than the kids' will," Miss Sadow told instructors today. "You'll see."

And seasoned companions in the social welfare world —like Dir. Miachale Schapiro of Children's Home Society and publicity gal Betty Nelson of the YW— guarantee her prophecy.

"Sue's tremendous . . . unbelievable," they say. "When you see her in action you'll say she can outwork folks half her age."

Hold your hats, Sierra Leone.

Our Sue is coming. And the Peace Corps.

SUE SANDOW, 65
Slated for Sierra Leone
—News-Call Bulletin Photograph

Reprinted with permission from the San Francisco News-Call Bulletin - November 27, 1961.

HERBERT H. LEHMAN
155 EAST 76TH STREET
NEW YORK 21, N. Y.

SUITE 1-A
YUKON 8-3883

September 7, 1963

Miss Sue Sadow
c/o American Consulate
Johannesburg, South Africa

Dear Sue:

Mrs. Lehman and I greatly appreciate your note of good New
Year wishes, which you were kind enough to send to us.

I have read the account of your travels with much interest.
The average layman of course cannot possibly grasp how much
ground you have been covering. I am sure that your stay in
Johannesburg will be as interesting as your other wanderings.

As you undoubtedly know from the papers, we here are having
some very difficult times in regard to our racial problems.
I believe, however, that we are making real progress, although
it will take some time really to assure equal rights and equal
opportunities for our Negro population. The march on Washington was most impressive. All of us who are interested in the
subject of racial relations feared that there would be some
serious clashes. Fortunately, however, there was absolutely
no violence, and while I do not believe the march will affect
many votes in Congress it was made amply clear that this was
not a means of intimidating or threatening the members of
Congress. On the whole the feeling was good and most of us
breathed a sigh of relief when it was over. In the next
several months there will be clashes here as well as in the
south. There is constant progress, however, and I believe we
can be much encouraged.

Mrs. Lehman joins me in wishing you many happy years of good
health, contentment and useful service.

With kind regards, I remain

                          Yours very sincerely,

Peace Corps Kept Her Young

By BARBARA HANSEN

YOU'RE never too old for adventure.

Vibrant proof of this is Sue Sadow, who at 64 became the oldest volunteer in the Peace Corps.

Now 67 and back from almost three years in Africa, Miss Sadow said, "I signed up the minute President Kennedy made his speech about age being no limit. It was one of the most fascinating experiences of my entire life."

Miss Sadow told her story while visiting friends in Los Angeles. A former resident of both Los Angeles and San Francisco, she was assigned to the first Peace Corps group to go to Sierra Leone in West Africa.

"I had been studying Africa," she said. "And I was interested in the problems of the emerging nations."

As preparation she went through 10 weeks of intensive training at Columbia University in New York. This involved strenuous physical conditioning, including daily gym work and swimming.

Miss Sadow was thus prepared for an equally strenuous mission in Sierra Leone, where the climate is hot, humid and rugged.

★

A nutritionist by profession she was assigned to teach at a rural secondary school for girls. The school was located at Magburaka, a small community 126 miles from Freetown, the capital of Sierra Leone.

"I taught six subjects," Miss Sadow said. "They were hygiene, home economics and nutrition, French, chemistry, art and crafts."

It was a pioneering type of teaching. "There were practically no books and no materials," she said. "Each night I typed out as many copies of the lessons as I could."

She explained that since Sierra Leone was once a British colony, English is the language spoken in the schools and government.

For her chemistry class Miss Sadow improvised a primitive laboratory from a chemistry set sent to her by one of her brothers.

For her French class she sought aid at the French embassy in Freetown and obtained first mimeographed book chapters, then the books themselves.

The small school where Miss Sadow taught included 50 students, a principal, two African teachers and herself. "The students ranged in age from around 12 to 17," she said. "As births were not registered at that time, none of them really knew how old she was."

Miss Sadow's tour of duty lasted two years. The first was spent teaching, the second working with CARE in its school feeding program. "This assignment took me to the most remote parts of the country," she said.

The most memorable experience of the two years was the arrival of a shipload of 30,000 books from Los Angeles.

"These were discarded elementary school books from the Los Angeles County Board of Education,"

—Herald-Examiner Photo
SUE SADOW, PEACE CORPS VOLUNTEER
...her pictures show the children she helped

Miss Sadow said. "They had been gathered in a warehouse by the Agricultural Technical Assistance Foundation, which donated them to us. The Navy arranged transportation through its Operation Handclasp and the Peace Corps handled distribution."

Miss Sadow ended her tour of duty on July 4, 1963. She then set off on a tour of other African countries, returning to the United States last May.

Her adaptability to Peace Corps life may have stemmed from her previous experience abroad. During World War II she was chief nutritionist with the United Nations Relief and Rehabilitation Administration (UNRRA) and served in Algiers, Morocco and Italy.

After the war she took a four-year journey around the world and became a lecturer on world affairs.

Miss Sadow, who will turn 68 on July 28, plans this fall to go to Washington, D. C., where she will work on a nutrition manual for use around the world.

Speaking enthusiastically of the Peace Corps and its achievements, she said, "It's a wonderful organization. I want to do everything I can to help it."

Reprinted with permission from the Los Angeles Herald-Examiner - July 14, 1964

2-020228E205 07/23/76 ICS IPMMTZZ CSP WSHB
 2029659400 MGM TDMT WASHINGTON DC 100 07-23 1012A EST

MRS SUE SADOW
CARE ROSENFIELD
6100 RUDYARD DR
BETHESDA MD 20014

THERE HAS NEVER BEEN ANYONE LIKE YOU AND THERE WILL NEVER BE ANOTHER.
YOU HAVE BEEN AN INSPIRATION TO US ALL. I HOPE YOU WILL LIVE MANY MORE
YEARS TO CONTINUE YOUR YOUTHFUL COURAGEOUS AND FARSIGHTED
CONTRIBUTIONS. ONLY THE FACT THAT I AM IN MONTREAL TODAY WITH MY FAMILY
AT THE OLYMPICS PREVENTS ME FROM JOINING YOU BUT YOU WILL ALWAYS BE A
GOLD MEDAL WINNER TO ME LOVE

SARGENT SHRIVER

10:12 EST

Sue Sadow stands beside her hostess, Gertrude Lotwin Rosenfield, at her 80th surprise birthday party. Surrounded by friends, Sue said, "This is the happiest day of my life."

PEACE CORPS

Washington 25, D. C.

April 23, 1963

Miss Sue Sadow
Peace Corps Volunteer
American Embassy
Freetown, Sierra Leone

Dear Sue:

Many thanks for your letter of April 14th.
I received Mr. King's letter last week with
the pictures of the arrival of the books which
were great. I've been hearing about your
wonderful work in Sierra Leone and your latest
effort seems to have been a tremendous success.
We're certainly proud of you back here. Keep
up the good work.

I'm glad to hear about your forthcoming article
and hope that you can find time in your busy
schedule to get it done. I'd appreciate having
a copy when it's published.

Your return trip should be fascinating, and, I'm
sure, a wonderful way to culminate your Peace
Corps service.

Again, many thanks. Best of luck in the remaining
months.

Sincerely,

Bill Moyers
Deputy Director

Sue Sadow (fourth from left) supervises distribution of nutrition kits at the Head Start booth at the International Congress on Dietetics at the Sheraton Park Hotel in Washington, D.C.

June 24, 1965

Dear Sue:

Mrs. Johnson thought you would like to have this copy of "School Lunch Journal" and hopes that you will keep up the good work on one of the most vital ends of Head Start- nutrition.

Sincerely,

Patsy Derby
Secretary to
Mrs. Johnson

Miss Sue Sadow
Nutrition Consultant
Office of Economic Opportunity
Executive Office of the President
Washington, D.C.

**Onlookers watch the donated books from the
United States being unloaded in Sierra Leone, Africa.**

**Sue Sadow examines a book with Dr. Wurie, Sierra Leone's Minister of
Education, at the unloading of 30,000 school books in Freetown 1963.**

She Has Conducted a Half-Century War on Poverty

Sadow soon went overseas as chief nutritionist for the Agency. Her first assignment was North Africa, where, for a year, she organized and administered feeding programs in refugee camps to teach the refugees how to cook with U.S. Army equipment and how to observe sanitary regulations. She went on to Italy to organize a feeding program for 16 million mothers and children. She traveled by jeep, usually 12 hours a day. to remote, bombed-out areas that were still inhabited. "The images of little children crippled and blinded by the ravages of war still haunt me," Miss Sadow admits.

Completely drained from her experience overseas, she wanted a rest from the ugly problems of poverty. She tried interior decorating. and then a life of semi-leisure in California. free lancing and attending UCLA: but neither fulfilled her. Still restless in 1953, Miss Sadow went to Europe. What started out as a brief pleasure trip, however, developed into what she terms her "four-year odyssey around the world."

"These four years of independent, uninterrupted travel were years of incomparable self-enrichment. I tried to get a real cross-section of life, visiting cities and villages, people at home and at work. learning about people in all economic levels — their desires, ideas, hopes, and frustrations, and trying to fathom why there was such hatred against the people of the USA."

Reprinted from SIMMON'S REVIEW -Summer 1968

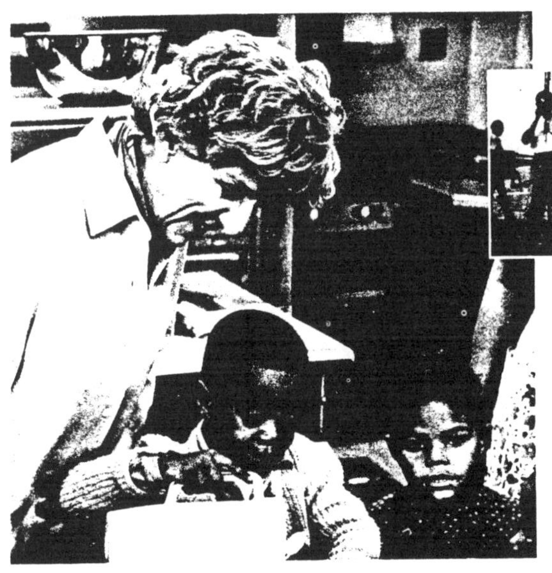

Sue Sadow, now a nutrition specialist with the Head Start program, is shown above with crates of textbooks she arranged to have donated to Sierra Leone schools. With her are the Minister of Education, right, and the director of the Sierra Leone Library.

The Perpetual Career

At 67, after two years with the Peace Corps as a teacher and nutrition expert in Sierra Leone, Sue Sadow could have retired.

Instead she set out to see as much of Africa as possible. A year later, she returned to the U. S., settled in Washington, D. C., and became senior nutrition specialist for the national Head Start program. "The one job in the whole wide world," she said, "which suited me to a T."

Today, at 71, Miss Sadow's field trips take her from the hollows of Kentucky to Indian reservations and migrant camps, and from the Virgin Islands to Alaska and Hawaii.

Miss Sadow had already traveled around the world before she joined the Peace Corps, so she escaped "culture shock" in Sierra Leone. But in Operation Head Start she encountered "a dose of American cultural shock that still leaves me unrecovered and depressed.

"The conditions in the hollows in the coal mining areas of Appalachia, where people live in terrible shacks with no facilities, are worse than in Africa," she said. "But with Head Start one is filled with hope. Already so much has happened that shows what we are attempting is having an impact."

Sue Sadow is one of the few members of Sierra Leone I for whom Peace Corps service did not constitute a real break or realignment in career. Her first job, the summer following graduation from Simmons College, was at a vacation home for immigrant mothers and children from the East Side slums of New York. Then she worked as a consultant in family budgeting in a New York welfare agency, in Palestine organizing and conducting a dietetic survey of the country, at the House of Good Samaritan in Boston and then for 11 years as chief nutritionist with the New York City Department of Welfare.

In 1943 she joined the Washington staff of the United Nations Relief and Rehabilitation Agency. She served in North Africa for a year as chief nutritionist, organizing and administering feeding programs in refugee camps, and then in Italy where she was chief nutritionist in charge of all refugee feeding operations.

In 1953 a brief pleasure trip to Europe developed into a "Four-Year Odyssey," which in turn led to a three-year career as a lecturer.

Then President Kennedy announced establishment of the Peace Corps. "Nothing could have fitted better into my own beliefs and convictions," Miss Sadow said. The first year in Sierra Leone, she taught home economics to high school girls. Then she began traveling to schools throughout the country to demonstrate proper preparation of foods supplied by CARE.

As senior nutrition specialist with Head Start, Miss Sadow is concerned with improving the nutrition of pre-school children from poor families.

"We provide food for the Head Start children as well as nutrition education for their families," she explained. Studies show, she said, that poor nutrition during early childhood not only affects physical growth, but the mental functioning of the child, too.

Sue Sadow says her career of service has brought personal rewards and self-enrichment that far exceed her contributions.

"George Bernard Shaw expressed it for me," she said: "'Life is no brief candle to me. It is a sort of splendid torch which I have got hold of for the moment, and I want to make it burn as brightly as possible before handing it to future generations.'"

Reprinted from "Citizen in a Time of Change: The Returned Peace Corps Volunteer" - March 1965

Alice and Peter Masters congratulate Sue Sadow during her 80th birthday party in Washington D.C.

```
SIA126      WAD186(1543)(1-028657A205)PD 07/23/76 1542
ICS IPMNAWB WSH
  09012 NL GOVT NFWASHINGTON DC 100 07-23 422P EDT
PMS SUE SADOW
CARE MR AND MRS LOUIS ROSENFIELD
6100 RUDYARD DRIVE
BETHESDA MD
DEAR SUE:
     I WANT TO JOIN WITH YOUR MANY FRIENDS IN WISHING YOU
THE BEST AS YOU CELEBRATE YOUR 80TH BIRTHDAY.
     FOR YOUR WORK AS ONE OF THE FINEST PEACE CORPS
VOLUNTEERS IN SIERRA LEONE AND FOR YOUR MANY OTHER ACCOMPLISH-
MENTS, WE ARE ALL SO PROUD OF YOU.
     BEST WISHES.
   SINCERELY,
   SENATOR HUBERT H HUMPHREY
```

BF-1201 (R5-69)

Sue Sadow, 81 (far left) carries a 20-pound pack during a backpacking trip with the Moores at Glacier Lake in Wyoming National Forest. Sue met Ann and Mike Moore (back row) while they were Peace Corps Volunteers in Togo, West Africa (1961-63). Nicole Moore, 8, and Hopi, 11 (front row) also went on the trip.

Richard D. Lamm,
Governor

E X E C U T I V E   O R D E R
PROCLAMATION
SUE SADOW DAY
July 27, 1986

WHEREAS, Sue Sadow has spent her life exemplifying for all of us
what the words ambitious, courageous, dedicated and caring
truly mean; and

WHEREAS, as proof of her commitment to these ideals, Sue Sadow
entered the Peace Corps with the first group of volunteers
going to Sierra Leone in 1961; and

WHEREAS, Sue worked in a secondary school teaching home economics
and nutrition, and she led the effort to open a library in
Magburaka -- steps that provided these village people with
the sustenance they needed to continue their progress
toward a better life; and

WHEREAS, Sue Sadow was the first older American volunteer in the
Peace Corps and has been a driving force behind the
activities of many volunteer programs; and

WHEREAS, for her life long commitment to humanitarian projects and
in recognition of her 90th birthday, the First Family of
Colorado extends best wishes to Sue and thanks her for
serving as an inspiration for volunteers of all ages;

NOW, THEREFORE, I, Richard D. Lamm, Governor of the State of
Colorado, do hereby proclaim July 27, 1986, as

SUE SADOW DAY

in the State of Colorado.

GIVEN under my hand and the
Executive Seal of the State of
Colorado, this nineteenth day of
June, A.D. 1986.

Richard D. Lamm
Governor

Dorothy V. Lamm
First Lady

Ann Moore (left) and Mary Carnaban (right), an administrator of Simmons College, watch while Sue Sadow puffs out the candles on her 90th birthday cake.

Peace Corps veteran, 93, still nurtures dream

Sue Sadow, now 93, was back in Washington this week to pursue her dream of world peace.

She was a young 65 when she joined the Peace Corps and spent two years teaching "almost everything — French, chemistry, arts and crafts" — in Sierra Leone.

After leaving the Peace Corps, she moved to a retirement community near Denver because of her friendship with Mike and Ann Moore, fellow Peace Corps retirees, who lived in Evergreen. She wrote "Into Africa" about her Peace Corps experiences to commemorate the agency's 25th anniversary.

A family wedding brought her here last week, but she also used the time to call on Timothy Carroll, director of the retired Peace Corps volunteers organization, to enlist his aid in her peace project.

"I can't get around as much as I used to," Sadow confided. "I had a bad fall and am dependent on a wheel chair. So Mr. Carroll came down to the car to see me. He said it was the first curbside conference he'd ever attended."

Ann Schmidt

Reprinted with permission from The Denver Post, April 7, 1989

On the 25th anniversary of Headstart, Sue Sadow received this framed poster with the Headstart logo and the following inscription: "To Sue Sadow, who taught me that you can do anything you just put your mind to! With love, Peter Masters."

Sue Sadow, age 95, shows off one of her paintings in her apartment in the Villas at Sunny Acres.

The publisher says about the author:

- Graduate of Simmons College, Boston, MA.; graduate work at Columbia and Cornell Universities, New York School of Social Work, Rochester University School of Medicine and UCLA.
- Director of Home Economics and Nutrition in social welfare agencies in Boston and the New York City Department of Welfare.
- Chief nutritionist with UNRRA (United Nations Relief and Re-habilitation Administration) in Morocco, Algeria and Italy for four of the World War II years.

- Lecturer on world affairs following an odyssey around the world.
- Peace Corps Volunteer in Sierra Leone, West Africa. When she joined the Peace Corps at age 65 in 1961, she was the first senior citizen volunteer.
- Appointed as Senior Nutritionist for Project Head Start upon return from Peace Corps .

Sue Sadow's illustrious 55-year career has been devoted to helping the poor get out of poverty through her work in private and public social agencies. In addition, she completed a four-year odyssey around the world, which prepared her for a lecturing career on world affairs. When President Kennedy announced the Peace Corps program, she became the first senior citizen volunteer. She counts these Peace Corps experiences in Sierra Leone, West Africa (1961-63) as the "most inspirational experience of my life." In 1986, she wrote a book about these two years of her long life called *INTO AFRICA with the Peace Corps*.

Now retired and living in a Denver suburb, the 95-year old author enjoys painting, music, writing, and the theater.

ONE WOMAN'S QUEST FOR PEACE

Sue Sadow, the first senior citizen volunteer who served in Sierra Leone, West Africa, in the 60s, has completed a 144-page paperback.

She embarked on the exciting adventures when she was a mere 65 years old. When the Colorado author celebrated her 90th birthday, the Governor of Colorado proclaimed the day as Sue Sadow Day in her honor.

Order copies now for yourself and friends. You will enjoy reading about the amazing experiences of this role model for all age groups. Only $7.95 plus $2.00 postage and handling.

- -

SEND MY COPY TO:

Name_______________________________

Address_____________________________

City, State,Zip______________________

Enclosed is $9.95 for each copy ordered.

ALSO SEND A COPY TO:

Name_______________________________

Address_____________________________

City, State,Zip______________________

Mail to: BEAUMONT BOOKS
P. O. Box 551 Westminster, CO 80030